The Gentleman Jack Effect

LESSONS IN BREAKING RULES AND LIVING OUT LOUD

JANET LEA

LAUREL HOUSE PRESS

Library of Congress Control Number: 2021914035

Published by Laurel House Press
1431 Seville Road, Santa Fe, New Mexico USA 87505
First paperback edition: September 2021

Illustrations by Vivian Swift
Cover design by Rex Peteet
Interior design by Roxanne Panero

ISBN 978-0-9621837-1-3 (paperback)
ISBN 978-0-9621837-2-0 (e-book)

For Mary Lou

Whether you're part of the LGBTQIA community or not, I think that Anne Lister is trail-blazing. She's uplifting, she's life-affirming, she's courageous, and she believes that everyone has a voice and deserves to be themselves and speak it. And I think in this climate that we need more stories like that.

— SURANNE JONES

THE GENTLEMAN JACK EFFECT

LESSONS IN BREAKING RULES AND LIVING OUT LOUD

CONTRIBUTORS

CONTRIBUTORS

CONTENTS

HOW THIS BOOK CAME TO BE

*I*t never crossed my mind that watching a TV show in 2019 would propel me out of my comfort zone, send me on a transatlantic adventure, and plop me smack dab in the middle of an international community of lesbians, historians, and strong women.

Gentleman Jack upended my life.

The nights I spent in the company of Anne Lister (Suranne Jones) and Ann Walker (Sophie Rundle) were 60 blissful minutes of enlightened storytelling about historical lesbians with high definition closeups of their intimate moments. Thanks to *Gentleman Jack*, I fell in love with a woman who had been buried for nearly two hundred years.

I was stupefied and embarrassed because Anne Lister was, after all, *dead*. But far more mortifying and unexpected was my morphing into a 70-something fangirl. However, when the first season of the series ended on such a high note of epic romance, I assumed what had become my unsettling preoccupation with Anne Lister would end and my infatuation with all things *Gentleman Jack* would surely dissipate.

But no, it didn't. It got worse.

In the weeks following the Season 1 finale, I lost what little was left of my grip on normal, everyday me. I couldn't stop rewatching each episode of the series, again and again. I devoured Anne Choma's official companion book to the series—three times. I searched online for every scrap of *Gentleman Jack* information I could find.

I was obsessed.

It was both a blessing—and a time-consuming curse—when I joined the private *Gentleman Jack* Fans (HBO & BBC TV Show) Facebook group. As a social media virgin, I felt timid about eavesdropping on the tumult of conversations about *Gentleman Jack* in this cyberworld that was so alien to me. But it did give me peace of mind that I wasn't the only one consumed by an insatiable need for details about series creator Sally Wainwright, stars Suranne Jones and Sophie Rundle, and anyone else having anything to do with *Gentleman Jack* or Anne Lister.

The summer of 2019 came and went, and my new addiction showed no signs of abating. *Gentleman Jack* had swallowed my life, and I wanted know who else was in the same boat—and for God's sake, *why*.

I had an idea where I might find the answer.

Three days after my 71st birthday, I found myself sitting in an aisle seat on a London-bound 787. Two days later, I was sipping tea and eating biscuits on a train passing through the green English countryside on the way to Halifax, West Yorkshire, deep in the heart of *Gentleman Jack* territory.

My Anne Lister to-do list was long on people and places, and my time in Halifax was short. Making my way along the Anne Lister Trail, I made stops at Shibden Hall—Anne Lister's home—and paid my respects at Halifax Minster, where she is buried.

If it weren't for historians and authors Helena Whitbread and

Jill Liddington, the Anne Lister that we have come to revere could easily have been lost to history. So my fangirl heart did backflips when Helena and Jill each accepted my invitation for lunch. I listened with fascination as they talked about Anne, their years of work to transcribe and decode her journals, and each woman's genuine surprise at her new celebrity status as a preeminent documentarian of Anne Lister's life, private thoughts, and lesbian love affairs.

Some die-hard fans of *Gentleman Jack* refer to themselves as Lister Sisters, and I was thrilled to meet several of them while in Halifax. They verified what I suspected: the sense of community that this TV show has created will be one of its most important and most lasting achievements.

My five days treading in Anne Lister's footsteps cemented my belief that television has the power to spark individual and societal change. What I had in common with every person I met was our visceral and palpable connection to Anne Lister who, in spite of being, well, *still dead*, seemed very much alive wherever I went and with whomever I spoke.

I came home from my trip to the new lesbian mecca with renewed appreciation for two women in history that I had never heard of before *Gentleman Jack*. I felt different too—more confident, more in tune with myself, more connected to the global community of gay women springing up around me that I was now a part of.

I was as "Listerfied" as ever and excited about what I decided to do next: to fully explore *Gentleman Jack's* effect on the lives of lesbians around the world.

I have no doubt that I am living and witnessing something bigger than anyone could have predicted when *Gentleman Jack* hit the air waves two years ago. Even from her grave, Anne Lister's impact—dormant for almost two centuries—is extensive and far-reaching. This book is *that* story, told through the experiences of dozens of people impacted by a TV show and what it stirred up.

Santa Fe, New Mexico
September 2021

GENTLEMAN JACK 1.0
THE STORY BEHIND THE STORIES

Gentleman Jack, a period drama based on the diaries of Anne Lister, a land-owning lesbian, prolific diarist, world traveler, and businesswoman in northern England in the 1800s, made its debut on HBO in the United States on Monday, April 22, 2019, and on the BBC in the United Kingdom four weeks later during Sunday night prime time. HBO and BBC affiliates worldwide also broadcast the series. The series was created and written by Sally Wainwright, and it stars Suranne Jones as Anne Lister and Sophie Rundle as Ann Walker.

The top hat was Sally Wainwright's idea.

It's a safe bet that very few viewers had ever heard of Anne Lister. That changed in dramatic fashion during the first few minutes of *Gentleman Jack*, when a stagecoach behind a team of four black horses comes barreling down a dusty, cobblestoned street in 19th century Halifax, its driver clad in all black. The driver pulls hard on the reins to bring the coach to a sudden stop and cries, "Whoa!"

That's our reaction too.

*Whoa! Is that a **woman** holding the reins of that stagecoach?*

This clearly is no ordinary female. High hat perched squarely above her brown curls and decked out as richly as any gentleman of the gentry class, this woman bounds down from her perch high atop the coach and goes nose-to-nose with a male passenger who has the audacity to chide her for her recklessness, staring him down until he bows and backs off. She's tough, fearless.

Moments later she looks straight into the camera and directly at us, a sure sign that what we're in for is not our mother's costume drama.

This is our first glimpse of Anne Lister, the title character of *Gentleman Jack*. This Anne Lister is the result of Sally Wainwright's decades-long dream to bring to life on television one of the most fascinating women in 19th century England. While historical Lister isn't known for wearing a top hat, the distinctive headgear is Wainwright's signal to her audience that this character is someone who, brazenly and stylishly, is challenging gender and social norms.

Gentleman Jack takes place in 1832, in the confines of pre-Victorian England where women in Anne Lister's social class are expected to marry well; bear an heir; live quiet and demure lives; and bow to the wishes of their husbands and the men who run the country, own the businesses and most of the property, and make all the rules.

This is not a world that aligns with the sensibilities of Anne Lister.

We are about to get a crash course in the art of rule-breaking.

In the first episode of *Gentleman Jack*, it becomes obvious that Miss Lister is a woman of strong opinions who has no qualms about expressing them. She is a take-charge landowner who doesn't balk at assuming the "man's job" of collecting the annual rents from her tenants when her male estate manager is too ill to do it for her. She has no interest in a traditional marriage, determined instead to spend her life with a woman she loves and who loves her in return.

Her steady confidante is the diary in which she records the details of her daily life. Written in mostly what she calls her *plainhand*, her script switches to the *crypthand* secret code she devised to protect her most private thoughts and tales of her conquests.

As her friend succinctly described her, Miss Lister had "a clever mind and an adventurous spirit." Mother Nature cannot be blamed, the friend also pointed out, if she was "in an odd freak" when she made Anne Lister.

As the remaining seven episodes of *Gentleman Jack's* initial season unfold, Anne's self-described "oddity," her optimism, business acumen, and quest for happiness are running themes. She navigates a man's world with aplomb. She charms the petticoats off Ann Walker, her future wife. She never once falters from living a life true to what she considers her God-given nature.

When Season 1 comes to its romantic happily-ever-after conclusion, I was left awestruck, unhinged, and unable to put aside what I'd just seen. I couldn't understand what was going on with me and the other fans on social media who seemed equally bewildered.

What was driving the binge-watching and the cosplay and the pilgrimages to Halifax? What was motivating the relentless curiosity about every detail in the life of a lesbian in the 1800s who wrote in her diary in secret code, chased skirts, climbed mountains, and broke every rule in the book?

I put my 25 years of experience in research and social marketing to good use in hopes of finding out the extent to which other fans were as dazzled by the series as I, and what effect *Gentleman Jack* might have made in how they see themselves.

I started my investigation with the *Gentleman Jack* HBO/BBC Facebook group and its 10,000 fans of all ages from 100 countries. I narrowed my queries down to a list of 42 questions, and, in mid-September 2019, with permission from the Facebook group's administrators, I posted a survey link and crossed my fingers that I'd get at least 150 responses.

I wasn't prepared for what happened next.

Within two weeks, more than 600 fans from 44 countries had responded to my 15-page questionnaire, many going far beyond simply checking the provided boxes for Yes or No. Hundreds wrote me lengthy, searingly emotional accounts of the impact that *Gentleman Jack*/Anne Lister had had on their lives. In the end, I was swimming in spreadsheets and printouts and confessions that all pointed to the same conclusion: *Gentleman Jack* is a life-changing period drama, and now I had data that clarified and quantified its extraordinary impact.

My initial findings made it clear that *Gentleman Jack* had electrified lesbians worldwide by positively representing us and validating the way we think and feel and whom we love.

We've never seen anyone remotely like Anne Lister on television before, and it both shocked and thrilled masculine-presenting women to see themselves so well-portrayed in prime time. That Anne Lister and Ann Walker are women who actually lived two centuries ago made the *Gentleman Jack* storyline all the more compelling.

As many fans have observed, it's the show we didn't know we needed. When I saw that hundreds of women reported experiencing the motivation to make significant changes in their lives, I knew there was an important story to tell.

What I discovered is that virtually every respondent was experiencing some degree of obsession with *Gentleman Jack*, watching the show again and again with an all-consuming interest in finding out more about the characters in the show and the production team behind it. *Gentleman Jack* got A-pluses for its authentic lesbian storyline, its first-class production quality, and the performances of lead actors Suranne Jones and Sophie Rundle. For many, it ranked first place on their list of the best TV shows they'd ever seen.

Most telling, however, is that 100% of the lesbians in my survey—regardless of age or nationality—expected the impact of *Gentleman Jack* to last. Hundreds said *Gentleman Jack* significantly changed the way they feel about themselves for the better. Gay women reported that the show validated their identity as lesbians and gave them a surge in self-esteem and self-confidence. They said that as a result, they're more willing to take risks, to be more open about who they are and whom they love.

While this overview of fans' reaction to *Gentleman Jack* gave me a better understanding of *what* was happening among its global audience, what I still didn't know was *how Gentleman Jack* was making a difference in people's lives, or *why*. So for 18 months—throughout the coronavirus pandemic in 2020 and early 2021—courtesy of Zoom, I talked to dozens of *Gentleman Jack* fans around the world in search of answers.

There was no algorithm for whom I chose to interview. On Facebook, I asked for volunteers who'd be willing to talk to me about any effect *Gentleman Jack* may have had on them, and often they suggested others. I contacted people whose social media posts caught my attention. I talked to organizers and administrators of popular Facebook *Gentleman Jack* fan groups.

I looked for people involved in the emerging world of All Things Anne Lister. I reached out to those engaged in new Anne Lister and Ann Walker research, as well as enthusiasts transcribing Anne Lister's diaries. I got word of a group of 14 women planning an Anne Lister-inspired mountaineering expedition and I talked to each one of them. I tracked down key people in Halifax whom I believed would have an informed opinion about *Gentleman Jack* and its effect on their work and their community.

This book is about them, the 69 remarkable people from 16 countries, who watched *Gentleman Jack* and told me about what happened next.

I found the answers I was looking for.

COURAGE & CONFIDENCE

IF ANNE LISTER COULD DO IT 200 YEARS AGO, WE CAN DO IT NOW

PATIENCE KAMAU

Nyeri, Kenya & Harrisonburg, Virginia, USA

A FOOT IN TWO CONTINENTS

For thousands of years, her Kikuyu ancestors roamed the sunbaked, equatorial highlands of central Kenya, stalked game in the fertile Great Rift Valley, and made their homes in the shadow of Mount Kenya, the second highest mountain in Africa. Patience Kamau—called Njeri wa Kamau in her native Kikuyu language—belongs to the largest ethnic group in Kenya.

"Tribal affiliation is central to African culture," Patience says. "The advantage is that you always feel you belong—to your tribe and your clan within the tribe—but there are stereotypes and expectations that are very detrimental. I will always love my country, but it is a highly,

highly patriarchal society. Everything is gender-normed. You must do this because you are a man, you must do that because you are a woman. I'm like, 'shoot me dead.' It's a blessing that I left just in time because I believe those expectations would have broken me. And I definitely would not have done well as a gay woman in Kenya."

It's been more than 20 years since Patience moved to the United States for her studies and became a permanent resident. But in the US, then and now, she continues to experience a different and insidious version of limitation: racism.

"Having grown up among black people, it is kind of shocking to realize that almost everywhere I go, people see me first and foremost as black," Patience says. "I have come to realize that's the way this country will always view me, even though that's not the most important part of who I am or how I see myself. I still haven't gotten used to it. I very often will forget that my skin is black because where I grew up, everyone looked like I do. Even so, I thrive here."

Thanks to *Gentleman Jack*, Patience has blossomed in ways she could never have predicted. A short trailer for the show during the final HBO season of *Game of Thrones* kickstarted her transformation.

"I caught a snippet of Anne Lister when she adjusts her top hat with her stick, and I remember thinking, 'What is that? That looks gay.'"

She made a mental note to watch it and then promptly forgot all about it.

Seven weeks went by before Patience, bored and looking for something to watch on television, recalled the character with the crazy curls and top hat, and queued up *Gentleman Jack*.

"It was in the afternoon," she recalls. "I pushed play on Episode 1. I had no intention to keep watching, but I was there for seven hours straight. I had to wait a few days for the last episode to air, and I was just blown away. I sat there thinking, 'Who can I talk to about this?' and that's how I ended up on the HBO/BBC Facebook fan page."

Besides Patience's entry into the world of people as ravenous for information about all things *Gentleman Jack* as she, other developments quickly followed.

First, her "friends with benefits" arrangement with a male acquaintance came to an abrupt end.

"I had fallen into this curiosity streak of wanting to discover the heterosexual side of me, though it wasn't really satisfactory," Patience says. "I think it had something to do with my body's biological drive to reproduce, which was different from my own intentions. And then I watched *Gentleman Jack,* and I recognized I had strayed so far away from who I am. It was like I got lost in the wilderness before this show pulled me back."

Wardrobe changes came next. Something as simple as getting rid of clothes that no longer suited her set Patience on a new path.

"I cleaned out all the feminine shoes in my closet that I never wore that weren't really me, and I started buying what I actually liked," she explains. "Wearing different clothes then caused me to actually show up at my job in ways that I felt more comfortable and more self-assured."

A fierce sense of self-worth was a byproduct of her new confidence, and that, in turn, led Patience to challenge decisions imposed upon her at work. She had what she describes as her "226 pounds, 17 shillings, and 6 pence" moment (reminiscent of Anne Lister's well-reasoned explanation in *Gentleman Jack* as to why she was entitled to this specific amount for her coal lease).

"When the pandemic began, I was very quickly furloughed from my job," Patience says. "I had no problem with being laid off, but the reason given didn't match the reality of the situation. Later when the same rationale was given for eliminating my position, I came back rather ferociously, challenged the system's blind spots, and made my case for what I believed was best for the institution's future, and my role in that. I thought this was the time to shape the position that was needed and that I wanted to have."

Her boss was eventually won over by Patience's arguments, and in the end, Patience not only saved her job, but refashioned it into something new, more challenging, and considerably more rewarding.

"I had to really wrestle and fight, and I know I would not have done that prior to *Gentleman Jack*," she says. "I don't know how I could have."

Patience says all the credit goes to the example set by Anne Lister.

"My mind is blown by the fact that she knew who she was," she says. "She wasn't looking to be validated by other people. She just knew it—in an environment where the culture didn't even have words to describe who she was."

Gentleman Jack has played a pivotal role in Patience's awakening to her true self.

"A show like this helps us live more fully as who we are, and then we present ourselves to the world that way," she says. "It has made a huge difference for me. I feel like I have stepped into a comfortable bodysuit that was made just for me, and I never want to remove it. Now it is part of my skin."

Kenya will always be where her heart resides, but other than extended visits to see her family, Patience has no plans to go back and settle there. Gay rights are virtually nonexistent in Kenya, and laws are still on the books that classify sex between same sex partners as a "gross indecency" punishable by five years in prison.

"It's not that I am hiding any part of who I am," Patience says, "but when I am in Kenya, the side of me that becomes apparent is the side my family is more apt to see and understand, and they don't know anything about gay culture. It's no different when I am with my gay friends here who don't share my African upbringing. For either one, it's like speaking a completely different language that the other person can't understand. It means I sometimes find myself in a place where nobody truly knows the full me, except me."

To her credit, Patience has mastered the ability to coexist in different worlds.

"I feel that I flourish in the United States, but when I go to Kenya, I'm all the other identities that I know myself to be. Both countries are my home. When I am in East Africa, people see me and recognize me as African in a way that no one in the US sees at all. But here I can live the other part of me fully without fear or intimidation."

Patience says any remnants of self-doubt about her identity have disappeared, and her self-confidence has soared.

"I feel like I flew out of some kind of jail that I didn't even realize I was in," she says. "I know I have many sides to me, and I also know being a lesbian is central to who I am. I feel far surer of myself in the ways I interact with people. I have many new friends. The creativity I now bring to my work is different and better. But to this day, I can't quite articulate all that has happened to me because of *Gentleman Jack,* or why. What I do know is those eight hours of television had a profound impact on my life in many ways, and I'll never be the same."

∞

KATE BROWN & DIANE MILLER

Mullica Hill, New Jersey, USA

AGE BECOMES US

*A*s young women, they were polar opposites. Out and outspoken at 17, Kate Brown found comfort and a sense of belonging among a group of lesbians in Baltimore, Maryland during the mid-1970s. Diane Miller was cautious and closeted, a dutiful daughter who fell for a high-level female government employee who had a reputation they were both determined to protect.

By 2005, Diane and Kate each had experienced long-term relationships that came to an end. They met online and maintained a long-distance romance for five years before moving in together and sharing the same home for the past decade. Now in their late 60s, they have more in common than they have differences.

Although Kate has always worn short hair, neither Kate nor Diane feels her own appearance to be particularly masculine or butch. Yet for most of their lives, both have been subjected to a steady stream of misgendering and verbal abuse primarily because of how they look.

"I was very out when I was young," Kate says. "I always got shit, always—name calling, bottles thrown at me. I mean constantly. But I would just say 'fuck you,' or I'd wear a t-shirt that said *Dyke*, or *Matriarchy is the Answer* or *A Woman Without a Man is Like a Fish Without a Bicycle*. And I think now, how could I *do* that?"

Diane can relate.

"When I was younger, I used to think I can't wait until I'm in my 60s and then maybe people will stop making fun of me or looking at me or making snide comments," she says. "And now I'm in my 60s and on occasion there are still people who make rude comments and I'm like, 'Why are you bothering me?' I'm just one woman trying to get through life and this space without being harassed."

When they watched *Gentleman Jack* and were introduced to Anne Lister, everything changed. For the good, they say.

Here was an unconventional woman from the past who also loved women, who had to put up with the same kind of disrespect Kate and Diane had endured for decades, who was brave and strong and kept marching forward, and who, in the end, triumphed and got the girl, too.

"We watched *Gentleman Jack* maybe three times—we loved Episode 3, the hilltop scene, and Anne playing cards in the pub. Oh my God," exclaims Diane. "I'm in love with this woman!"

Kate says, for her, it was seeing the courage that Anne Lister had.

"Seeing that, on TV this late in life and knowing there was a real person who experienced what we've experienced and she did it 200 years ago, was so validating for me," she adds.

Overcome with newfound and life-altering courage, Diane felt compelled to go to Halifax to visit Shibden Hall and feel the presence of Anne Lister in her home and hometown.

"I just had to be there," Diane says, and by October 2019, she was on her way. But to suddenly pick up and travel alone to a country where she had never been before?

"For Diane to go to Halifax when she did is so extraordinary," Kate explains. "This is a woman who does not make decisions in a minute. This is a woman who makes lists, and agonizes, and plans, and accounts for any and all events that could possibly happen. But she just packed up and went because of *Gentleman Jack* and Anne Lister. That she just took off, flew over, and stayed by herself—it was truly remarkable."

Diane agrees.

"I'm so glad I went when I did," she says. "It was just astounding at Shibden Hall—the vibration, the connectivity. I was so happy there. I'm hoping I knew Anne Lister in a past life because that's how strongly I felt to the location and her story. And I can't wait to go back."

A quick transatlantic adventure wasn't the end of *Gentleman Jack's* influence for either woman. Diane and Kate made plans to travel with friends to the Anne Lister Birthday Weekend in Halifax in the spring of 2020. When the global coronavirus pandemic forced its cancellation, they were as heartbroken as the hundreds of other lesbians whose dreams were dashed.

Diane had looked forward to taking a bold step during her second trip to Halifax. For 20 years she had envisioned buzz-cutting her hair, and she had made arrangements with Gentleman Jack Barbers to do the honors at Shibden Hall.

"I came up with every reason not to do it for all of those years. What would my mother or people at work think?" she says. "Now my hair is very gray white, and I just thought I'm going to do this. *Gentleman Jack* is why. It's all about just becoming who I really want to be, really who I have been all along."

Busted plans are hard to swallow. But Diane's courage hadn't waned. So, 31 days after her buzz cut appointment had to be cancelled, she picked up a pair of clippers. Then she cut a swath down the middle of her head from the top of her forehead to the nape of her neck. In a matter of minutes, years of resistance lay piled on the ground.

"Look at my hair!" she exclaimed and stuffed the clippings in a jar like a hard-won trophy.

Gentleman Jack profoundly touched Kate, too.

"Watching *Gentleman Jack* brought up a lot of thoughts I'd had when I first came out, memories of the abuse I experienced and how I handled it," she says. "It gave voice to something really hurtful I had gone through. Anne Lister went through similar experiences hundreds of years ago, and she survived beautifully. I didn't feel as alone as I have sometimes felt, and that did something to me. It made me feel strong and proud again. I'm no longer the in-your-face-fuck-you-if-you-don't-like-it kind of person the way I once was. But I'm not afraid, and I'm certainly not ashamed. Hurtful things aren't as hurtful any more. Anne Lister and *Gentleman Jack* did that for me."

Having withstood painful decades of being mistaken for men, taunts, stares, and the prejudice leveled at generations of lesbians, Diane and Kate have arrived at a place where self-acceptance comes easy.

"If I had known about Anne Lister when I was 25, I would have chosen a totally different path for my life," Diane says. "I think I would have packed up and moved to Halifax, and I would have been interested in doing research, maybe even transcribing her journals."

She can't help but wonder how the lives of so many older gay women would have been different had they had strong lesbian role models.

Friends were—and still are—an important source of support.

"After my 15-year relationship ended," Kate says, "I thought I would never be in another relationship. I decided I would concentrate on making friends. I didn't know any of them, but I heard about a picnic that a lesbian group was having in Buffalo, New York. I was living just outside of Buffalo and I drove up and met five women. From that day, even though we are so different, we just clicked and have stayed close friends for 19 years—and now they love Diane too. In addition to the other things that *Gentleman Jack* has done for us, it has also given us something else we value—a new community of online friends."

Diane looks forward to the day when all of Anne Lister's journals will be transcribed and available to read. She hopes it happens in her lifetime.

"Anne Lister will have a long-term effect on me, one I know I'll carry until I die," she says. "I am just overwhelmed that she existed. She connected me to a different part of myself. She changed my life."

FIONA EVERED

Mytholmroyd, West Yorkshire, England, UK

MY UPSIDE-DOWN LIFE

*D*uring a midlife crisis, a woman might experiment with a drastic new haircut. Maybe she'll paint the kitchen turquoise. She could take up skydiving. She might train for a triathlon, buy a sports car, have an affair. But it's the rare woman who is brave and adventurous enough to change every single thing in her life all at once . . . because of a television show.

"I never saw it coming," Fiona Evered, mother of two young adults, says. "At this time two years ago (May 2019), I had no plans to do anything different. I wasn't going to give up my job. I wasn't going to move houses. I certainly wasn't going to move to Yorkshire. It all happened as a result of *Gentleman Jack*, and it happened really quickly."

Even in retrospect, Fiona can't quite put her finger on why she decided to buy the *Gentleman Jack* DVD boxed set in the first place. When the series first aired in the spring of 2019, she hadn't heard anything about it. Now it was September, and her 19-year-old son had left Gloucestershire in southwest England to go to university. It was just Fiona, alone at home, with no responsibilities for looking after anyone else. With plenty of free time on her hands, she started watching the series. Her reaction was instant.

"I felt like I was going home," Fiona says. "Watching *Gentleman Jack* for the very first time, everything just fell into place for me. Until then, I'd never really noticed I had always been attracted to women. But now looking back, I can see that those feelings were always there. What Anne Lister felt—her feelings about herself and her situation—all resonated with me."

On the heels of watching *Gentleman Jack* came a quick trip to Shibden Hall.

"I loved it," Fiona acknowledges. "There is a sense of Anne Lister there. Whether that's because it's what we would like to feel or whether it actually is there, I don't know and it doesn't matter. It's quite a small, intimate home. I do know it was just pleasant to be there."

Weeks of turmoil promptly followed in October and November.

"That was when I realized I actually am a lesbian and not anything else," Fiona explains. "I knew I had to make big changes. I absolutely did not want in five or ten years to wonder how my life would be different if I didn't act on it. I even got a tattoo on my foot that says "Courage" in Anne's *crypthand*, and honestly, it kept me going."

Six months of what Fiona describes as "madness" came next.

"I've been a dentist for nearly 30 years and I thought, 'I don't want to do this anymore.' I just gave it all up and threw in the towel," she says.

By December 2019 she was in Halifax scouting for a new place to live. The day before the coronavirus pandemic lockdown went into effect in England in March 2020, Fiona moved into her rental property in Mytholmroyd and began her new life—in quarantine.

"I don't know exactly what it was that flipped the switch and made me notice how I feel about women," Fiona muses. "But it does make absolute sense of the last 50 or so years. It is the reason I've given up everything and just moved to Yorkshire with no plans and no prospects, and it's all going really well."

Fiona still marvels that watching *Gentleman Jack* upended her life.

"Now that I know who I am, I think to myself how did I *not* know until now. I really feel lucky that I finally understand myself. Once you know and can do something about it, it's great. My poor children have discovered they've got a completely crazy mother. They've been fine about all of it, completely accepting, no issues at all."

Fiona says she quickly settled into the next and unexpected phase of her life. She took a temporary position working at a care home. She's active on *Gentleman Jack*-related social media. She began making new friends.

"It's the best move, and I'm thrilled I've done it," Fiona says. "I'm here. I have a job. I've come out. I've got a house. I've got some pals I've made. So what more can I ask for really? A girlfriend would just be icing on the cake."

Ever the optimist and expecting only the best, it's no surprise that a delicious relationship materialized for Fiona in the fall of 2020. She met and fell in love with a *Gentleman Jack* Facebook friend, and they're now living together in her tiny mid-19th century millworker's cottage about a 30-minute walk from Hebden Bridge and just five minutes from the beautiful Calderdale Valley countryside. Though she contracted Covid in the spring of 2020, Fiona fully recovered and has no lingering side effects. She left her position at the care home to look after an elderly woman living nearby. She and her new love have plans to explore their new surroundings when the coronavirus lockdown is lifted.

"I came to Yorkshire with no plan at all and just the thought that everything would be ok, and it is," Fiona concludes. "I feel really lucky. I don't have a single regret about any of it, and I couldn't be happier. *Gentleman Jack* changed my life. Coming to terms with who I am and whom I love is such a relief because it makes sense of everything in my life. I wouldn't have it any other way now. Onward and upward."

∞

JENNY CORKETT

Swindon, Wiltshire, England, UK

NOW I AM VISIBLE

*M*any gay women say they knew at a very young age that they were different from other girls. For Jenny Corkett, her realization came at the age of eight. As a child she watched other girls be taunted with hurtful jeers and names, so she learned early on to hide her feelings.

When she joined the Royal Air Force at the age of 18 to begin 23 years of military service, the world was anything but a friendly place for a young gay woman. Keeping her sexual orientation secret was a high priority and a matter of survival; discovery would mean shame and a dishonorable discharge. No matter that Parliament had just passed the Sexual Offences Act of 1967, finally decriminalizing homosexual acts between consenting males who were 21. Same sex relationships, whether male or female, remained socially taboo.

But over time how does someone square who she is with her strong Christian faith? With scriptures that refer to homosexuality as an abomination? With the likelihood of being made to feel unwelcome in her own spiritual home?

Like so many other women, Jenny managed by keeping herself to herself. For more than 50 years, until 2019.

"The year before, I read Vicky Beeching's tell-all book called *Undivided: Coming Out, Becoming Whole, and Living Free From Shame* where she recounted her story of hiding her sexuality as she forged a successful career as a Christian worship leader and songwriter in America," she says.

"So much of her story resonated with me, and it lit my own slow-burning fuse to admit who I am."

And then she saw *Gentleman Jack*. Something clicked. Now a Methodist local preacher, she found herself in the middle of the controversy facing her church: while many in the denomination support gay marriage, others still oppose it. Inspired by the courage of Anne Lister and Ann Walker, she felt she needed to speak up. But it felt terribly risky, and her confidence came—and went.

"If Anne and Ann could be themselves nearly 200 years ago, surely I could do the same in 2019," Jenny says.

She made up her mind. It was time to come out, and she would do so at an evening meeting of church members and other local preachers gathering to weigh the pros and cons of same sex marriage ceremonies in the sanctuaries of Methodist churches.

On that fall day her job as a bus driver took her on her regular route through suburban neighborhoods. But on this day, something was different. Jenny encountered something she had never seen on her route before and hasn't seen since.

A large green and red lorry (moving van) was approaching her bus. She was surprised to see that the name plate on the front said *Yorkshire*. And as the truck passed her, she noticed something completely unexpected in tall, yellow block letters on the side of the truck: *LISTER'S OF HALIFAX*. Could this lorry, which was more than 200 miles (322 km) away from home, be the nudge she needed?

Some might call it a coincidence. But in Jenny's world, there are no coincidences. She calls them *Godincidences*, and she felt the truck was a heaven-sent sign.

Hours later, she heard herself making a simple statement to her peers:

"I think it would be great if the Methodist Church would allow same sex marriage to be held in our churches. Being gay, if I got married, I would want to do that in my own Church, in my own tradition with my own church family and friends there."

She remembers the sound of the applause in the room. Retired ministers and church members came up afterwards with hugs, congratulations, and support for her and the statement she had made. Supportive emails arrived from other local preachers whom she notified a few days after the meeting as a courtesy, wanting this small group also to be aware of her revelation.

Next it was time to make the announcement to her family—in person—and that, too, went well.

"To just be me is liberating," Jenny says. "Nothing is different, and at the same time, everything is different."

At the age of 65, now she feels free to dress the way she always wanted to, and she proudly wears her ever-growing selection of waistcoats. She regularly comments in the safe spaces that the private Facebook fan pages provide. She is available to listen to members of her congregation who may be struggling with or unsure of their sexual orientation. And as she ferries people in town wherever her bus takes them, every day she finds an opportunity to happily repeat a favorite phrase from *Gentleman Jack*: "Must be my driving!"

Jenny made the leap to bravely introduce her true self on October 10, 2019. It wasn't until weeks later that she learned she had made her simple announcement, a revelation that had been decades in the making, one day before the Human Rights Commission's International Coming Out Day.

Another *Godincidence* perhaps?

MICHAELA DRESEL

Wellington, New Zealand

I KNOW MY OWN HEART

*H*er silky brown hair, once so long she could sit on it, is now short and stylish. Dresses and skirts have given way to short-sleeved button-up shirts, sweaters, long pants, and a fashionable suit for special occasions. At 21, Michaela Dresel is a young woman exploring who she is, how she looks, and what she wears.

Her evolving self-realization began when high school friends introduced her to Tumblr and a glimpse at same sex relationships.

"That's a thing you can do?" Michaela wondered, and then discounted because, after all, she had a boyfriend.

A year later at drama school, a question arose that demanded an answer.

"Wait a minute," Michaela found herself thinking. "Why am I more attracted to that random girl I've never talked to than the boy I've been dating?"

By 16, she had come out to her parents. By 17, she was away at college majoring in psychology and involved in her first relationship with a female partner. Now four years later, newly single and beginning her PhD studies in developmental psychology, she's experimenting with new ways of claiming her identity and interested in meeting other gay women for friendship, or more.

"First off, I have really shitty gaydar," she says. "Also, a lot of people in the LGBTQ+ community here are nonbinary or trans or gender fluid.

Wellington has one gay bar, but it's full of guys, which is like, the wrong demographic, and I really don't like to go to bars anyway. Finding gay friends or someone to go out with just isn't that easy."

Then *Gentleman Jack* came along, and with it, a world of possibilities. At first, Michaela had her doubts about this new BBC/HBO drama. Having only glimpsed the trailer, she was sure a show with a storyline having something to do with coal wasn't high on her list of must-see TV.

"Sometime later when I was on Tumblr, the people I followed suddenly were freaking out because Episode 3 had just been released," she recalls. "So that night I sat down and watched all of the first three episodes." (For the *Gentleman Jack*-uninitiated, the third episode features the series' first kissing and lovemaking scenes between Anne Lister and Ann Walker.)

"*Gentleman Jack* was one of the few times I've seen anything that I could so strongly relate to," Michaela says. "Every week I watched the next episode, but I didn't have anyone to talk to about it until I convinced my mom to watch it with me. The fourth wall breaks in the show when Anne Lister looks into the camera and quotes from her diaries got me hooked. The story isn't about some kind of overly dramatic internal conflict Anne Lister was having as a lesbian—she was totally OK with who she was—and that really drew me in too."

Michaela soon immersed herself in the expanding communities of *Gentleman Jack* fans. She discovered the Shibden After Dark podcast and Facebook group, as well as other private *Gentleman Jack* Facebook communities.

"I definitely interact the most with the Shibden After Dark group," Michaela says. "I find it to be such a safe space. Because we all have an understanding about each other and a deep connection that started with

Gentleman Jack, it means we can talk about anything. Especially during lockdown when I moved back in with my parents for seven weeks, it was nice to talk to people that I have so much in common with and can connect with on many levels."

An open Zoom room where people can pop in at any time to chat is another welcome outcome from *Gentleman Jack*. Michaela says her new online friendships from around the world have played an important role in her life.

"This is the first time I've had lesbian role models," Michaela says. "The people I interact with are all at least 10 years older than me. It has prompted me to think about relationships and what I want to get out of one. I've connected with a couple who've been together for about 30 years. Just seeing how they are with each other and the kind of relationship they have helps me see the kinds of things I can achieve in a relationship too. They've helped me see if I'm not getting what I want or need, it's better to end it than dragging things out and trying to beat a dead horse."

Gentleman Jack has delivered on other fronts too.

"There has been a definite change in the way that I dress or express myself in that way," Michaela says. "School uniforms with skirts are what girls wear in a small town in New Zealand. I've never felt comfortable in women's clothing but I wore it because that's what my mother chose for me, and later because it is what I could find to buy. Seeing the way Anne Lister was presented in *Gentleman Jack* gave me confidence and nudged me to say to myself, 'Hang on—why do I feel I can't wear the clothing that I want to?' So now a lot of what I wear comes from the men's section, and no one cares."

Michaela says *Gentleman Jack's* positive representation of two women in love, plus learning about the experiences of other lesbians who she's met online, has boosted her confidence and self-acceptance.

"I am more comfortable with my identity and my more masculine-of-center presentation," Michaela says. "There is no point in trying to fit myself into a box. That doesn't work, just like you can't put a square peg in a round hole. From the community I'm now part of I've learned you can be any age and still change the course of your life. I see that in the characters in *Gentleman Jack* and in the people I am meeting in real life. I hear about people who haven't come out until they're in their 50s, and things are working out for them. Wow, it's so good to know I don't have to freak out if my life isn't together by the time I'm 25."

A tattoo on her upper chest near her right shoulder keeps her grounded.

"I wanted something in Anne Lister's handwriting, but not in her code because I thought sometimes I might not feel like explaining the code," Michaela says.

She opted for the first four words of a longer passage in French that Anne Lister wrote in her diary on August 20, 1823, quoting Swiss philosopher Jean-Jacques Rousseau. *Je sens mon coeur.* It's a simple phrase that succinctly reflects Anne Lister's recognition of her nature, and it resonates with Michaela as well. *I know my own heart.*

"It reminds me if she can do it, then I most certainly can too," Michaela says.

∞

BRANDY HYER

Boston, Massachusetts, USA

FOUR LESBIANS AND A WEDDING

The best way to guarantee that there always will be fireworks on your anniversary is to get married on the 4th of July, a national holiday celebrated in the United States with pyrotechnics and dazzling, fiery bursts of color in the summer night sky.

Brandy Hyer and Krista Hyer chose Independence Day 2020 for a poolside wedding in Brandy's parents' backyard in northern California. In attendance were Brandy's mom and her wife of nearly 40 years, plus a giant peacock and an enormous unicorn, both of the inflatable pool float variety. Seventy-five guests participated virtually, watching the event on Zoom. *Gentleman Jack* was very much there too.

"I always wanted to get married, but that just hadn't been something that anyone I had previously been with was really into," Brandy says, "but it's something Krista and I had seriously talked about early on in our relationship. For our wedding, she dressed a little bit more like Anne Lister in that she wore a white tux jacket and white jeans that were really fun, and I was a little more traditional in a long white dress, a little more like Ann Walker."

It's no surprise that the spirit of the Annes had a lingering presence on Mrs. and Mrs. Hyer's special day, delivering what Brandy says felt like an air of legitimacy to their ceremony.

"Knowing that Anne Lister and Ann Walker married during the time period they did really blew my mind," Brandy says. "It's not the same for us in that no one was objecting, and we weren't fighting against the same kind of odds they faced. Still, it just felt so right for us to be able to legally marry, and it's just what I wanted to do."

Theirs had been a long courtship with assorted distance challenges, family obligations, and career shifts. They were in their 40s when they met in college in Iowa and fell in love at the least convenient time, just as Brandy was about to begin her training, first in Bali and then in California, to complete her qualification as a Transcendental Meditation teacher.

The couple weathered that two-year separation, and then had to cope with the subsequent rigors of Brandy's PhD studies and the demands of moving to a different state to care for Brandy's mother as dementia began to take its toll on her.

And then *Gentleman Jack* hit the airwaves in 2019. Expecting nothing more than a relaxed hour or so of TV entertainment, Brandy was, instead, mesmerized by Anne Lister's bravado from the moment she appeared onscreen, tearing into Halifax in the driver's seat of a speeding stagecoach.

"I had never seen television or women represented like this before," Brandy recalls. "Though I grew up with a lesbian mother and her partner and basically was raised with two moms, I had a very distorted under-standing of lesbians because I only saw the *Leave It to Beaver* version of being gay. My mother was in elementary education so she felt she had to be very careful about how she presented herself to keep her job and custody of me, so things at home in the late 70s and early 80s were quite repressed and closeted. Even though I had seen a lot of gay and lesbian content from TV and film and later from working in media production in Los Angeles, nothing compared to *Gentleman Jack*. It is in a league of its own, and it was transformative."

As the series progressed, Brandy recognized more of herself in Anne Lister. As a child, she also had written letters in secret code. As a young woman, she'd kept a journal to help her come to terms with her sexuality, as she too was figuring things out on her own.

The predictable signs of *Gentleman Jack* obsession began with her binge-watching and urging friends and family to tune in to watch this paradigm-shattering series. She experimented with transcribing pages of Anne's diary. She looked into creating YouTube video mash-ups from clips from various episodes of the series. She joined and became active on *Gentleman Jack* Facebook groups. She selected a picture of Anne Lister for her Peloton profile and began to pick up mannerisms and figures of speech from *Gentleman Jack*.

And then there was the show's existential impact. *Gentleman Jack* blew the lid off the perceptions women often have toward themselves and their assigned place in the world.

"I have this expression that I call APWMO," Brandy says, "which stands for 'Another Privileged White Man's Opinion.' As a woman, if you've been around this planet for a half century like I have, you have just been inured to it, and *Gentleman Jack* has helped me break free from it."

"*Gentleman Jack* gave me a lot more confidence in my profession to speak up for myself," Brandy continues. "I've always been fairly bold in certain ways, but at the same time just seeing Anne Lister not be bullied by men in her time really helped me. I had a hard time asserting myself with certain authority figures and executives I deferred to or was intimidated by, and watching Anne Lister gave me courage to stand up for my opinions and share my thoughts without fear."

She also says Anne's lessons reverberate with her every day, noting Anne's enlightened acceptance of her sexuality without shame, or the approaches she chose for every aspect of her life.

"Like, calling Krista my wife is a huge thing for me," she explains. "I notice I do it all the time, and probably it's really annoying to some people. But I love it, especially in places that are very patriarchal. Krista and I hold hands when we walk, and I do not take for granted what is ok to do today. But even in my lifetime, there were years when I would not have felt comfortable to do things like this in public. I think about Anne Lister and how she was able to craft a life for herself that was true to herself. It inspires me to check in with myself every day and wonder if I am doing the same. I ask myself, 'Am I living an authentic life where I'm true to myself?' I am so grateful that I do get to live my life today in a certain way, and with someone I love."

Brandy's experience as a Transcendental Meditation practitioner and teacher informs her insights as to why *Gentleman Jack* has had such a dramatic impact on her and so many of its millions of viewers.

"Every human shares consciousness of our existence on this planet," she says. "If you think of our human consciousness as an ocean with individual waves rippling out, all of us are connected through our waves and ripples to the deeper ocean of human consciousness. I think *Gentleman Jack* served as the conduit for Anne's voice to first reach our individual consciousness on a deep level and then move through to our collective consciousness. Anne Lister was ahead of her time, and the world was ripe for this show. Her spirit and her message is right in tune with what I think almost every person really needs to hear today. The show just lit a spark that touched and resonated with people everywhere."

In retrospect, Brandy says her wedding day a year ago now feels like a blissful blur, coming in the middle of the coronavirus pandemic and exactly three weeks after she completed her doctorate. Since then, Brandy and Krista have settled into their new life in New England, where Krista is training to be a cabinetmaker and Brandy is continuing her work as a teacher of Transcendental Meditation. *Gentleman Jack* still stirs intense emotions, and a pilgrimage to Halifax is on the couple's bucket list.

"I walk in the world differently now," she says. "Now, 'I rise above it,' and that's not a cliché. I want to draw on the same source and call forth the same quality of spirit Anne Lister had. I want to feel the same unifying connection I felt the first time I watched the show and that I also feel anytime I go to Facebook pages and read other people's responses."

Brandy believes she has an obligation to keep stride with Anne Lister's outsized swagger.

"I don't know why, but I feel a sense of duty and responsibility to carry myself in a certain way in the world and speak my truth and not bend under pressure to male authority as has been taught. I feel like it's upholding Anne's legacy and paying homage to her for what she has taught us. Thank God she lived, and thank God she did what she did."

∞

There are three known portraits of Anne Lister, including an oil painting commissioned by Ann Walker after Anne's death. It was painted by artist Joshua Horner and is on display at Shibden Hall.

INNA CLAWSETTE

United Kingdom

I FOUND MYSELF AT SHIBDEN HALL

*S*he is blonde, soft-spoken, and 71 years old. She is a widow with three grandchildren. She lives in a village where everyone knows everyone else. She wishes she knew what it feels like to kiss a woman. She worries she never will.

Being attracted to women for as long as she can remember is something she knew to keep to herself, convinced at first it was just a girlish thing that would pass. Now she wonders how her life might have been different if a show like *Gentleman Jack* had been on television in the 1970s when she had her whole life in front of her. Would she have better understood the crushes she had on other women and acted on them? Would she still have done the expected and gotten married?

"*Gentleman Jack* has changed my life," she says. "The other side of me has come out."

Watching women loving women was transformative. She admits she longs to experience the passion and emotional intimacy she believes she would find in the arms of a woman. Now she can no longer ignore the powerful emotions she kept tucked away for decades.

Still, her sudden and surprising burst of courage caught her off guard.

She had already begun testing her limits by belonging to several *Gentleman Jack*-related Facebook groups. That's where she first heard about plans for fans to gather in Halifax around Heritage Open Days, England's largest annual countrywide festival celebrating its history and culture. Until *Gentleman Jack*, she had never heard of Anne Lister and Ann Walker and their love story, and now she was obsessed with both of them. She plucked up the nerve to make plane and hotel reservations for a four-day trip to Halifax in September 2019. Then she dug deep for even more courage to post on Facebook that she'd be attending alone, hoping to find that someone from her area might be planning to be there too. Score. Two women responded, and the trio made plans to rendezvous at the event.

"I felt I just had to go to Shibden Hall to see where Anne lived and meet other people touched by *Gentleman Jack* the way I have been," she confesses. "It was amazing for me because I won't step out of the door of my own house. I still can't believe I did it. It was the irresistible pull of *Gentleman Jack* that got me there, and I'm so pleased I went."

For the first time, she found herself in the company of dozens of lesbians.

"They were lovely," she says, "all so friendly, nice, and at ease with themselves."

She met up with the two women from her Facebook connection and they have since maintained a casual friendship. Never had she felt so free to talk about how she really feels.

"For the first time in my life, I could just be myself," she says, "and that changed me."

She went back home to her quiet life in the village, filling her days with walking the dog, doing church work, and watching her *Gentleman Jack* DVD. Her circumstances were the same, but she wasn't.

"Other people don't know I'm different inside now," she says. "We have the internet and all of this technology, so I have a separate life apart from what people see on the outside. I didn't have that before, and that's a shame."

Lately she has turned to retrospection.

"I was in my 20s when I met my husband. I had only known him for a few months when I fell in love with him and we got married," she recounts. "We were happy together for more than 30 years. He gave me a good life. But as I think about it now, it wasn't what I think love should be. I wouldn't want to disrespect my husband, but now I see I wasted precious time on something that should have been more fulfilling, but wasn't."

The intensity she saw in *Gentleman Jack* between Anne Lister and Ann Walker never materialized in her own relationship.

"I don't feel I've lived fully," she says. It prompts her to wonder what would Anne Lister do. "I'm not like Anne Lister," she admits. "I'm more like Ann Walker striving to have Anne's courage."

Gentleman Jack gave her permission to be herself, she says, but her long-held fears hold her back from opening up to family and friends.

"If I came out to people," she worries, "I don't know what they would think or what they would do. But it's more in my own mind, isn't it?"

Gentleman Jack came at exactly the right time for her, she concludes.

"I know if *Gentleman Jack* hadn't happened, my feelings would just have stayed under wraps until I died," she says. "At this stage of my life, I'd like to have communications with other gay ladies of my age and make new friends. I'd even like to find love. I'm so new to it all, and I'm like a baby. But maybe it's not too late for me."

It is tempting to chalk up the resurrection of undeniable attraction toward women as a late-in-life crisis. But the reality is that a TV show unexpectedly became a bridge to late-in-life clarity and budding self-acceptance that guided a shy woman first to Shibden Hall—and finally to herself.

Fear of repercussions for announcing her sexual orientation is real for thousands of women. In respect for this woman's privacy and appreciation for her willingness to share her story, her name has been withheld at her request.

KATHERINA OH

Singapore, Republic of Singapore

MORE CHANGE IS COMING

When 21st century technology broadcast a riveting period drama around the world, a gay Chinese woman from Malaysia living in Singapore was transformed by the story of an audacious 19th century English woman who never set foot in the Orient or even knew the word "lesbian."

Thousands of miles and scores of years removed from Anne Lister, Katherina Oh says the television show *Gentleman Jack* changed her life.

A 30-something clinical researcher, Kat has been living in the city-state of Singapore in Southeast Asia for more than a dozen years. She appreciates the opportunities, quality of life, and blend of diverse cultures in its dynamic, modern city with British colonial roots, although she's well aware of its darker side.

Singapore's LGBTQ+ community is confronted by flagrant housing and employment discrimination, excluded from marriage, banned from adopting children, and governed by antiquated colonial-era laws that still make male homosexuality illegal. It's a "don't ask, don't tell" world that relegates thousands to secret lives in the shadows.

"As a gay woman, I feel fortunate not to have personally faced discrimination of any kind, but I think it's because of a couple of factors," Kat says. "I'm at the privileged place of being Chinese, which is the majority race here, and 'passing' as a straight person, outwardly, also has protected me."

It's no wonder that *Gentleman Jack's* depiction of a courageous historical lesbian couple two centuries ago—a stark departure from the American television sitcoms popular among young Singaporeans— immediately grabbed her attention.

"I think I speak for myself and a lot of lesbians that when there is a lesbian movie or something out in the media with a lesbian in it, we just consume it," Kat says. "Once I watched *Gentleman Jack*, I was, like, I need more, I want more. So I turned to Tumblr, and that led me to the Facebook fan page and Lister Sisters. It was obvious that *Gentleman Jack* was something beyond just a good TV show."

As someone who never watches the same show twice, Kat found herself violating her own rule.

"I actually saw all the episodes of *Gentleman Jack* three times," she says. "I discovered the Shibden After Dark podcast, so after each TV episode, I'd go back and listen to the podcast about it."

Kat was completely enchanted by what she saw.

"For me, it's a beautifully written story with amazing characters," she explains. "I loved when Suranne Jones broke the fourth wall. She is very cheeky when she does the raising of her eyebrows and flirting with the camera. I really enjoy lesbian entertainment, and I totally loved the show."

To her astonishment, Kat noticed *Gentleman Jack's* effect on her almost immediately. Within the first two hours of viewing, she felt an internal shift.

"I don't know where it came from, but I started feeling a lot more confident," she says. "I was definitely inspired by Anne Lister, someone I had never even heard of before. I am a really timid and introverted person, but she inspired me, not so much to be outspoken, but definitely to have a lot more confidence."

Next, Kat noticed she was suddenly more active. Like Anne Lister's gait on screen, her walking pace accelerated. She lost weight. Her new engagement on social media brought new friends and shared interests.

"When I was watching the show, I had been single for three years," Kat explains. "It's hard to be on my own in a country where my family is not here, and sometimes it gets really lonely. I was going through the ups and downs of being single, and the show made me feel a lot better. I started thinking, 'Hey, if this woman in the 1800s can find a girlfriend, why not me too?' So I really put myself out there."

Kat downloaded dating apps and began going out. But this time, her dating approach was different, courtesy of *Gentleman Jack*.

"I used to think that I have a 'type' of person that I date, someone who is more feminine," she says. "But after I watched *Gentleman Jack*, it just changed my thinking, like I shouldn't just confine myself to a certain type. So I went out on a few dates with different people I wouldn't have gone out with before, and then I actually met my current girlfriend on Tinder."

Kat's membership in private Facebook groups changed her opinions about married life too.

"It's not possible to get married here, and it's even more impossible to have children as a lesbian couple, so there is really no example for me here in Singapore," she says. "Meeting married lesbian couples online from the US and the UK for the first time really opened my eyes. So on top of being inspired by Anne Lister, I was also inspired by a lot of fans in the group because they changed my perception about gay relationships. They showed me that it's possible in my lifetime, even in this country, to find a longtime partner to go through life with. It made me even consider starting my own family because I saw so many women with their wives and their beautiful kids."

Eager to share her excitement about *Gentleman Jack* by getting others in her circle of friends to watch it, Kat was surprised when she ran into their resistance.

"I thought other lesbians would be into it as much as I am, but some people just aren't interested," she says. "I'm not sure if it's because we're Asian, and it's about two white women in the UK that is so far away from us and our culture. A show like *Gentleman Jack* just didn't have much traction here."

But for Kat and her Anne Lister-reshaped vision of what her future could entail, she will be part of the vanguard that reshapes the world in which she lives.

"I don't know what might happen in my lifetime, but I feel that the younger generation is a lot more liberal and is exposed to more media from the United States and other countries. Even if it may take a long time, I am an optimistic person, so I do hope things get better here."

Looking back on all that has happened in the two years since she was introduced to Anne Lister, Kat says *Gentleman Jack* is the only TV show that has ever had such a dramatic impact on her.

"I met my girlfriend because of the show," she says. "It's really changed my personal life. I've participated in the Lister Sisters postcard exchange with people I met online, which was fun. I was in a birthday video for Suranne Jones in 2020. That's really insane, and something I wouldn't have ever done before *Gentleman Jack*."

Kat says her personal evolution is just one part of the greater cultural impact of *Gentleman Jack*.

"It's huge that history is being rewritten as the show progresses, right?" she says. "Until now, Anne Lister seems to have existed in the past as a small, minor person, but from now on, she is going to be such a significant person in the LGBTQ+ community and an inspiration for so many women. And it's all because of the power of a TV show."

JEN CARTER

Nagpur, Maharashtra, India

MORE PRIDE, LESS PREJUDICE

*I*ndia is a hostile place for millions of women. Arranged marriages and diminished social status remain their plight, fathers still dictating when and whom their daughters will marry. Once a woman is married, her fate seldom improves since customs allow her husband and her male relatives to continue to hold sway over her. While same sex relationships are no longer illegal in India, disapproval of them remains high, and efforts to secure marriage equality for the Indian LGBTQ+ community are stalled.

Given long-held cultural beliefs and discriminatory practices toward women in her country, the prevalence of homophobic attitudes, and even the threat of rape by men who assault lesbians because of their "abnormal" nature, Jen Carter's coming out story is a testament to her courage.

"Women are the most oppressed here because ours is a patriarchal culture," Jen says. "When you're born in a heteronormative society, there is social conditioning that you're supposed to like and love and marry the opposite sex, and you cannot do that with your own gender. So if you ever have certain feelings, you just try to deny them all of your life and suppress them with the thought that you're weird, or crazy, or there's something wrong with you. That's why so many people here are in the closet or actually unaware that they are gay."

Jen says she has always known she wasn't like other girls.

"When I was younger, I was always told I was different," she recalls. "My mother wanted to dress me in saris, but I preferred trousers and shorts and jeans. I was a total rebel as a teenager, and my parents would say, 'She's uncontrollable and she doesn't listen to us, and she's not like how a girl child is supposed to be.'"

Still, Jen understood what society and her parents expected of her, and she tried to conform.

"I was always taught that you're supposed to make a man fall in love with you," Jen says. "But I did not know how to be coy for a guy, and people would say I was just too bold. I tried going out with men when I was in college, but they would want to kiss me, and it was something I didn't want to do. Later there was someone who was an amazing human being and a really good guy that I thought I wanted to marry, but I didn't want to have sex with him. That wasn't fair to either of us, so we ended it."

No potential relationship had even come close to matching the standard Jen had set for herself. When she was a child, her father had given her Jane Austen novels to read to improve her English, and she was enchanted with the stories of young women in 19th century England.

But unlike the readers who swooned over handsome Mr. Darcy in *Pride and Prejudice*, Jen was more interested in *being* Mr. Darcy. She longed for reciprocal passion in a relationship, and like the novel's female protagonist Elizabeth Bennett, Jen was determined to marry only for love.

Unsure if her idea of love would ever materialize, Jen focused on getting an education and starting a career.

"My father called me and asked, 'When do you want to get married?' and I said I wanted to finish my studies first," Jen says. "I thought about how far can I stretch and postpone this, so I decided 25 sounds fine."

By the time she reached the agreed-upon age for finding a husband, Jen had already begun thinking about how to ease her parents into accepting her intention to remain single. As she approached her late 20s, the unexpected occurred.

"I met this girl I really liked, who really liked me, and we got into a relationship," Jen says. "I told my father I wanted to live with her. He was okay with it actually, and he said I must have financial stability first. He told me 'If you have money and financial independence, if people say something to you, you can live with that because you don't have to depend on anyone.'"

Jen says she was elated that she and her girlfriend were experiencing the romance of Jane Austen novels, and they desperately wanted to spend their lives together. But their happiness was short-lived. The father of Jen's partner had already arranged her marriage and threatened to kill himself if she failed to live up the commitment he had made for her.

"Things didn't work out for us because she could not fight her family," Jen explains. "She felt she had no choice. At that time, I felt all the emotions. I felt anger. I felt sadness. I felt hatred for the whole society. I didn't want to live."

In despair, both women attempted suicide, and both survived.

"We all in India try to kill ourselves," she reflects now. "You know, okay, so lesbian relationship doesn't work. So let's kill ourselves."

The seriousness of the situation forced Jen's hand. At the age of 30, she told her parents she is a lesbian, and in no uncertain terms, she also declared she would never marry a man.

"I was depressed for a very long time," Jen says. "I thought I couldn't live without my girlfriend for even a day. And then I decided that if I'm living without her, I'll make the best of my life. I got back on track with my education and completed my master's degree in business. Then I just worked and made my own money."

Nine years passed. Self-employed, Jen's career blossomed. Her parents never brought up the topic of marriage again. She tried online dating, but abandoned her attempts to meet someone when she discovered the sites were filled with desperate men pretending to be lesbians. Jen assembled a stable of male and female friends, though none is gay. She filled her life with books and movies.

In the spring of 2019, she chanced upon an HBO preview of *Gentleman Jack*.

"I was like, this will have carriages and hats and costumes and be something out of Jane Austen's era, and I'm definitely watching it," she says. "I had a crush on a girl for about a year, and I had finally told her how I felt since she was giving me all these gay vibes, and then she went all homophobic on me. When I saw the first episode of *Gentleman Jack* and Anne's problems with Vere Hobart, I thought to myself, 'Oh my God, I'm watching this—it's my life!'"

That Anne Lister was a historical figure, not a fictional character, was inspirational.

"Wow!" Jen says. "The first thing I felt was, 'What am I doing with my life? What is wrong with me?' Here is a real person from 200 years ago that had so much courage."

Her discovery of the Shibden After Dark Facebook group set the inevitable in motion.

"I wanted to know everything about Anne Lister and to talk about her because I had no one in my life to discuss her or *Gentleman Jack* with," Jen says. "I saw that everybody in the group was so kind and thoughtful, and I wanted to be part of this group."

When the coronavirus pandemic struck, it triggered Jen's realization that life is fragile and it was time to stand up for herself.

"I don't want to live a lie anymore," she decided. "I definitely wanted to come out."

But there was an important conversation to have first.

"I told my father I am going to post something," Jen says. "We had a whole discussion because whatever I do about business decisions and these kinds of things, I ask my father for advice. I told him this is something I am going to do, and I hope he is on board because there will be people who may call and ask questions. He said, 'Well, if they ask me, I'll tell them we have no issues.' He was very cool about it."

I love and only love the fairer sex

Jen's long-delayed moment came on April 3, 2020, Anne Lister's

229th birthday, when she posted her photograph and her story on the Shibden After Dark Facebook group.

"There was so much love and support not just on my post, but on private messages, and everyone was so kind," she says. "I felt like I'm with my own family. I did not feel scared. I felt confident."

Jen didn't stop with an online pronouncement to a supportive community. Next came the revelation about her identity to her circle of friends and various relatives.

"I never felt I was doing anything wrong with my ex-girlfriend," Jen says. "What I admire most about Anne Lister is that she never questioned her orientation. She accepted the fact that she always wanted to be with women and love and cherish them. When she says 'I love and only love the fairer sex,' that touches me the most."

Jen's life is fuller and happier now. She is still active on private *Gentleman Jack*-related Facebook groups. She's made close gay friends for the first time.

"It makes a whole lot of difference when it's lesbian women," she says. "I agree with whoever said that pain connects people. We have all been through being suppressed and being closeted, having our own demons, and fighting internalized homophobia, disapproving families, broken hearts, and so many other things we've faced."

Jen is quick to point out that *Gentleman Jack* has been life-changing.

"It has been a milestone for me," she says. "Without *Gentleman Jack*, I don't know when I would have had the courage to come out. What was stopping me was the fear of someone attacking my parents, or making them feel I am a disgrace to them and having them feel ashamed about it. They tell me they are okay with my decision, and they don't care what people think either. When you have your family's support, it makes a huge difference. I wish I would have come out sooner. I wonder how it would have changed my life if I had had more confidence earlier."

Jen is grateful for the online community she can rely on for information, support, and advice. She's proud to display a rainbow flag on her profile photo. She looks forward to falling in love with a woman again and hopes to be able to marry when that time comes.

"I am bearish that a same sex marriage law will be passed one day in India because I think it will help more people come out, and it will normalize our relationships. When the law supports it, nobody can stop us."

Fear of repercussions for announcing her sexual orientation is real for many women. Out of respect for this woman's ongoing concerns about her safety and professional reputation, her pseudonym has been used at her request.

LOUISE ALEXANDER

USA

A RADICAL AWAKENING

S he doesn't remember where she read that the hilltop scene in *Gentleman Jack* is the greatest moment of lesbian television ever made, but Louise Alexander does remember desperately wanting to see it, never suspecting that a TV show would transform her life.

She devoured the *Gentleman Jack* series and found herself

among the ranks of fans who were galvanized by Anne Lister's story. A clergywoman in a long-term relationship with a woman, Louise had almost forgotten how to celebrate and take joy in her lesbian identity, which had been all-important to her in her youth.

"From the first five minutes of the show, I felt that Anne Lister herself had injected me with an electrifying new love of my lesbian self," she says. "I was dazzled by Anne Lister's energy, self-assurance, and determination to love and be loved by only women."

She says her reaction to *Gentleman Jack* resembled a peak experience, an extraordinary moment of timeless euphoria with heightened, mystical aspects.

"One of the hallmarks of a peak experience is that you can't articulate it. You can't explain it," Louise says. "That seems to be the reaction so many of us have had and why we have such difficulty putting our feelings about *Gentleman Jack* into words."

The explosion of interest in Anne Lister, driven by the international obsession with *Gentleman Jack* and how the show has inspired so many of its fans to make drastic and fulfilling changes in their lives, led her to some powerful insights.

"The *Gentleman Jack* phenomenon has all the hallmarks of a new religion," Louise says. "Many lesbians are understandably allergic to the very word, but I believe it's a very positive thing. The root of the word 'religion' is a word meaning 'to bind together.' Anne Lister's story has bound thousands of lesbians together in this amazing international awakening."

Louise says she see parallels to another, more familiar religion.

"The Holy Spirit, in the Anne Lister story, is the undying spirit and presence of lesbianism in the world—especially muscular, butch lesbianism," Louise explains. "Anne Lister is the prophet who brings this lesbian spirit into the light. Shibden Hall is the birthplace of this religion. It is a sacred shrine to which we make pilgrimages. Other places that feature in the Anne Lister story, such as the York and Halifax Minsters, are also holy sites."

Louise draws a variety of other comparisons.

"Anne's journals take on the role of scriptures, which need transcribing and interpreting," she continues. "That's where the Lister Sisters come in. They're the converts, interpreters, and missionaries. Facebook groups are congregations of the faithful. Many Lister Sisters have described the frustration of encountering lesbians who are not aware of *Gentleman Jack* and the evangelical zeal with which they've pleaded with friends to give it a try."

Louise acknowledges that Anne Lister's story as it unfolds in *Gentleman Jack* has a spiritual and salvation-inducing power.

"As lesbians, we have been made to feel shame about who we are," she says. "We have been made to feel invisible—and unworthy not only of society's respect, but even of our own self-respect and self-love. It's as if our essential, sexual, passionate selves have been hidden under a bank of gray fog. *Gentleman Jack* burns away that dulling, concealing fog like the sun rising on a summer morning. When we see Anne Lister commandeering a stagecoach, jumping over a wall, striding to Ann Walker's house, we feel seen, loved, honored, energized . . . reborn." Louise concedes that for her, *Gentleman Jack* also has been both electrifying and disorienting.

"Life as a minister, even in a very liberal denomination, can be inhibiting," she says. "Over the years I had shut away a huge part of my identity. Seeing the authentic portrayal of Anne Lister and Ann Walker stirred up grief and longing: grief for what I had missed and not allowed myself to feel for a very long time, and longing for the passion and the wholeness that Anne Lister represents."

She reports the upside is that she felt a tremendous jolt of self-confidence inspired by *Gentleman Jack*.

"I started coming into my own in a new way," Louise says. "Whole aspects of myself that I'd put away on a shelf were suddenly at hand and vibrating with potential. It's been intensely exhilarating—and intensely uncomfortable—to begin to come to terms with this powerful identity that I had set aside for so long."

A monthlong stay in Europe gave Louise an opportunity to explore this disconcerting awakening. While in a library in Belgium, Louise found herself writing a fanfiction story based on the personalities in *Gentleman Jack*. Set in 1947, *A Careful Appraisal* imagines that Anne Lister and Ann Walker served in the Women's Royal Naval Service during World War II and rediscovered each other in Halifax two years later. Response to Louise's steamy fanfiction story (published on the *Archive of Our Own* website) was fervent, unexpected, and somewhat disconcerting.

Above all else, Louise says that her reaction to *Gentleman Jack* revived a deep craving for lesbian community. She's now summoning the courage to start writing a novel, and will visit Halifax as soon as is feasible. Louise believes *Gentleman Jack* is about loving the truth of who we are and demanding our right to love as we will.

"Its lesson is to let our old, lusterless selves die away and give birth to our vital, passionate, essential lesbian selves," she adds.

Louise admits her life would be much easier if she had never heard of *Gentleman Jack*.

"It has disrupted and disturbed my tranquility, made me profoundly dissatisfied with my status quo, and set me on a path into the unknown," Louise says thoughtfully. "But that is exactly how spiritual awakenings behave. Out of control, uncomfortable, chaotic, radically transformative—and profoundly life-giving."

Louise Alexander is a pseudonym. Out of respect for this woman's privacy and appreciation for her willingness to share her story, her name has been withheld at her request.

JOHANNA PIHLAJAMÄKI

Hämeenkyrö, Finland

RISING ABOVE THE DARKNESS

Sometimes the pale green and pink lights of the Aurora Borealis dance in the night sky above their little farm 10 miles (16 km) away from the nearest town. The quiet, slow pace of life in the countryside appeals to Johanna Pihlajamäki and her wife in spite of winter's subfreezing temperatures and the daily chore of bringing in wood to warm themselves, their two cats, and their rambunctious Golden Retriever puppy. Johanna says the recent streak of "black winters," so-called because so little snow has fallen, has made it much easier to deal with the usual trappings of the season.

But when her mother died suddenly from breast cancer four years ago, finding comfort in even the smallest pleasures of daily life became a struggle.

"It was a big tragedy in my life when my mom died," Johanna says. "It was really hard because we were so close. She was the one I talked to every day and asked everything."

Her father's poor health and disagreements with her brothers made a sad situation worse. Progress on her master's degree stalled. Her work in a factory was unfulfilling. Things were rocky at home, too.

"Losing my mother caused me to have PTSD, and I didn't have the space for grief," Johanna says.

She started therapy, and afterwards, when least expected, two additional lifelines appeared. *Gentleman Jack*—and a group of strangers—set Johanna on a new course.

Johanna says she was immediately mesmerized by *Gentleman Jack*. Every day for a year she watched elements of the show, absorbing the details of Anne Lister's audacious life story. As surprising as her positive reaction to *Gentleman Jack*—Joanna says she's not a period drama fan— was her discovery of the Lister Sisters private Facebook group.

"I just kept thinking how can there be this kind of group in this world," she says. "I'm in about 30 other groups, and there is something negative going on all the time. And then there's the Lister Sisters with hundreds of people, and no one is aggressive and no one is ever disrespected."

Now a day seldom passes without her checking in with her new online friends. The steady solace and support of their virtual presence have been transformative to her way of thinking.

"Clothing isn't important to me," Johanna says. "I repair our cars, do carpentry, and all kinds of boy things, so my clothes are always messy. I found out from Lister Sisters that some people find that attractive. How did I not know that masculine things like that appeal to some people?"

It wasn't long before Johanna felt a welcome boost in her self-confidence.

"I was like a sponge taking in everything about Anne Lister, her attitude, the way she dressed," Johanna says. "Seeing and hearing 'I rise above it' made me think I could do that too. It made me decide to take risks and start a new life."

Everything began to change. She dropped out of school, walked away from her dead-end factory job, and set out to start a new career.

"Ever since I was in my 20s I wanted to be the one who goes to companies and says, 'This is what you're doing wrong, and here's what you should do to fix it,'" Johanna recounts. "*Gentleman Jack* gave me the confidence to walk into a pet store and ask to talk to the CEO. I offered him my creativity and expertise and asked him for a job, and he hired me! It's my absolute dream job to be able to figure out how our customers feel and come up with new and better ways to make them happy."

Just as important as a new job to Johanna was rebooting her relationship at home. She and her wife, Mirka, met a dozen years ago when they were the leading couple in a children's play, Johanna in the role of Robin Hood and Mirka starring as Marion. The romance continued offstage. They moved in together, and with Mirka's then-11-year-old daughter, became a family of three. Their marriage began to suffer after the death of Johanna's mother, when her prolonged mourning not only took its toll on Johanna but also on her wife.

"There were some difficult years, but we cared about each other so much that the conversation always came to 'Do you love me?' and the answer was always yes," Johanna says. "Divorce or breaking up was never an option. For me, whatever comes to your mind, just talk, talk, talk, talk, talk. So we just worked to get to the good place where we are now."

Recharging their relationship was cause for celebration, so Johanna and Mirka marked their 11th anniversary with a trip to England. In York, they sat and held hands in Holy Trinity Church, Goodramgate, in the same pew where the Annes sat on their wedding day in *Gentleman Jack*. They traced Anne Lister's steps in the Lake District and made their way to Halifax.

"I wish we had had more time at Shibden Hall," Johanna says. "I wanted to just sit there, smelling the walls, feeling the history, breathing the air where Anne lived, and imagine what it was like."

Johanna says the impact of *Gentleman Jack* shows no signs of letting up.

"I've never been so obsessed with anything," she admits. "Anne Lister has come into my life, and she is here to stay. The background on my phone is still from Shibden Hall. It's been well over a year since we were in Halifax, and we still have our pictures as a slide show on our TV. I do things in my life I've never done before. I'm comfortable wearing boy clothes. I'm proud of myself now. I still visit the Lister Sisters Facebook page every day. You know, now that we all feel more confident and we believe in ourselves, something good can happen, and maybe it can change the world. It certainly changed me."

∞

DOREEN GALINDO GOMONIT

Cebu City, Cebu, The Philippines

SWIMMING WITH THE TIDE

or someone who loves beaches and snorkeling, it's hard to imagine a more perfect place to live than a country with the fifth-longest coastline in the world. Dora Gomonit makes her home on Cebu, one of the largest of the 7600+ islands that compose the Philippines. She and her menagerie of six rescue cats and a rescue dog named Indie live in Cebu City, the oldest city in the nation and its former capital.

As far as she knows, Dora is the biggest *Gentleman Jack* fan in town.

It all started when surprising content began showing up on her phone during a trip to visit her family in Australia.

"I was wondering how Facebook knows I'm gay because as soon as I arrived, LGBT ads started popping up," Dora says. "One of them was from HBO for *Gentleman Jack*. I clicked it and I'm like, 'OK, this is good.'"

Unable to find the show on the air Down Under, she was forced to rely on YouTube clips until she got back home and had access to the series on Amazon Prime.

"Now all the episodes are on my phone, my laptop at home, and my work laptop," Dora laughs. "I've probably watched the series about 100 times."

Dora says *Gentleman Jack*—and learning about Anne Lister and Ann Walker—opened her eyes to a new world. First, she was transported to the 1800s and awed by Anne Lister's courage.

"Wow, she had the balls to do all kinds of stuff," Dora says. "That was inspiring and very refreshing. But I guess I'm Team Ann Walker because I feel really protective of Ann because of her mental health issues."

Seeing Ann's emotional plight contributed to Dora's new awareness of the challenges people in her own community face.

"Unlike in Western countries, where you have help and support groups to deal with mental issues, that's not common here," Dora says. "People in the Philippines tend to bottle things up and not talk about them. So, if I have friends who might confide in me or ask for help, I am more open now, and I'd like to be helpful," she says. "That is a very important thing I learned from *Gentleman Jack*."

Dora herself luckily escaped any of the emotional turmoil at home that often comes with being a lesbian.

"For me growing up, I think my family always knew I'm gay," she says. "My brother is gay too. When we were little, I always played with my brother's toys, and he played with my girly stuff. Neither one of us ever came out to our parents—from the time we were young, they already knew the way we are."

However, there are no nationwide protections against LGBTQ+ discrimination on the books in the Philippines, and same sex marriage and same sex unions are still illegal. The country's most active gay community is in Manila, 500 miles (826 km) away from Cebu City, and lesbians in Dora's hometown rely on Facebook and other online platforms to meet one another.

Through social media, Dora has connected with *Gentleman Jack* fans worldwide, and it's given her a welcome opportunity to share her Filipina culture and learn what goes on in other countries too.

"I tend to be a loner," Dora explains. "I'm an introvert and pretty shy, so it really surprised me that I have made lots of friends all over the world through Facebook, Twitter, and Instagram. Normally I don't interact with other fans, but with *Gentleman Jack*, it's totally different. Now I'm on Zoom calls all of the time. I've traded postcards with people in the US, the UK, Indonesia, Singapore, and all over. I never expected this, and to have all of these new friends is really awesome."

Dora hasn't been one to just sit back and savor her global network of new friends. Before *Gentleman Jack*, she would have been reluctant to push beyond her comfort zone. Now, newly emboldened, she dove headfirst into the volatile world of cryptocurrency.

"When it comes to business, just like Anne Lister, I decided to be bold and take some risks," Dora says. "I quit my job for a new one, and now I'm involved with IT and cryptocoins and buying international stocks for the first time. My family thinks I'm crazy making these investments for my retirement, but I believe cryptocurrency is the future. You never know what will happen if you don't take the risk. Anne Lister showed me that."

Thanks to her Anne Lister-inspired confidence, Dora, who can't swim, recently strapped on a life vest and plunged into the Pacific Ocean to paddle alongside whale sharks, the biggest fish in the world. Swimming with these massive aquatic creatures that can weigh 20 tons (18t) and reach lengths of up to 60 feet (18m) doesn't faze her.

"They're actually very gentle, though they are very big," Dora says of snorkeling with sharks that are the size of a school bus.

By comparison it makes her forays with turtles, dolphins, and schools of sardines in the Tañon Strait, a deep superhighway for marine life west of where she lives, sound tame.

Dora says the challenges of a new career, her rewarding online social life, and the joys of spoiling her seven pets don't leave time or energy for much else. But she does have her eye on a stack of books about Anne Lister that are waiting for her to have a free moment, and Ann Walker is in the picture too.

"I'm so excited that Ann Walker's diary recently has been found," Dora says. "I made sure the notification bell is set on Twitter so every time there is a new tweet, I can read it right away."

Because of *Gentleman Jack*, Dora's quiet island life has undergone a sea change. Bolder and braver, post-pandemic she'll be back to kicking her flippers among a shiver of whale sharks and looking forward for whatever new excitement awaits ashore.

MY NAME IS SECRET

USA

NEVER TOO OLD FOR A NEW START

Haven't we all had times in our lives when it feels like the universe is piling on? For Secret, it began with the childhood trauma of being sexually molested by a family member for many years, a devastating experience that she has kept hidden from her family for more than half a century. When she was in her 40s, in the span of two years, Secret's husband died young, and her best friend, her beloved grandmother, and her mother and father also passed away, her parents within months of each other.

Now, at 65, after losing a job she loved as a result of circumstances outside her control and that left her questioning her capabilities, Covid has claimed the lives of two relatives. She holds out hope that her brother who survived the disease won't have any long-term side effects.

"A lot of tough stuff has happened, so I've had my fair share of depression in my life," Secret says.

But never did Secret imagine that a television show about women who lived 200 years ago would be the improbable medicine that would set her on a course to recovery.

"I absolutely loved *Gentleman Jack*," she says. "Like so many women who've watched it, I can't help but admire Anne Lister. But really I identify more with Ann Walker because I've experienced losses like she did, and I understand what it's like to have that kind of depression."

Secret says the TV show and books that detail how Anne Lister and Ann Walker navigated their situations have dramatically changed her outlook on life.

"*Gentleman Jack* has given me courage and confidence I never knew I had in me," Secret says. "Finally feeling good about myself reminds me of when I was a teenager and attended a rally for Bobby Kennedy, President Kennedy's brother. Bobby Kennedy changed my life that day because he made me believe that one person can make a difference."

She credits Senator Kennedy for her lifelong interest in politics, which resulted in a stint as a legislative aide to a state senator, a job as a political campaign manager, and a career in community relations. Making a difference has once again become her goal—in her next job, and as a grandmother.

"Seeing the courage of Anne Lister and Ann Walker has taken me to a different place in my life," she says. "I am letting go of the past, and I find myself looking forward to the future because now I have the courage to face it. I know something good is coming. I know I will never put myself in a box like I've done my whole life and limit myself again."

It's prompted her, she says, to look at jobs she would never have considered before.

"I'm open to whatever is new and whatever is next," Secret says. "After all I've been through, that's not something I've ever done before. Because of *Gentleman Jack*, I also decided that I'm not taking crap from anyone, and it's something I want to teach to my granddaughter."

That's why Secret has begun keeping a journal for this 10-year-old girl who holds such a special place in her heart. She is recording her advice, a lifetime of memories, and experiences she's never told anyone else.

"It's all about legacy," Secret explains. "I want my granddaughter to hear it from me that it's OK to be strong, and I want her to know she can do anything she sets her mind to do. And I especially want to tell her to always stand up for herself and follow her heart."

Secret says her determination to live proudly and authentically is bolstered by what she sees in so many *Gentleman Jack* Facebook groups.

"I want fans to know we straight girls love Anne Lister too," she says. "Just to see what many say about being validated as a result of *Gentleman Jack*—well, there's no price for the value of that. It makes me recognize how fortunate I am that I didn't have to personally face so much of what they have gone through. I know I am very lucky to be surrounded by friends and family who think whom you love doesn't matter."

Moral support, online and otherwise, has special meaning for Secret as she looks forward to the new world of possibilities that *Gentleman Jack* has opened up for her.

"I couldn't live without my women friends and acquaintances because they are the ones I truly trust," she says. "Women power couldn't be more important than it is right now in these crazy times."

The lessons she's learned from *Gentleman Jack* will stay with her for the rest of her life.

"The show has certainly had a wonderful effect on me, and I am so grateful for that," she says. "If I ever saw Sally Wainwright, I would give her a big hug for introducing me to Anne Lister and Ann Walker. Thanks to all of them, there is something better and different about me now that I know will last until the day I die."

Incest remains a difficult and painful subject for many of its victims. Out of respect for this woman's privacy and appreciation for her willingness to share her story, at her request, her name and location have been withheld.

∽

Shibden Hall, Halifax, West Yorkshire

VOICES FROM HALIFAX
INSIDE ANNE LISTER'S HOMETOWN

LAURA JOHANSEN

Halifax, West Yorkshire, England, UK

PUTTING HALIFAX ON THE MAP

*N*ot everyone enjoys growing up in a small town. Anne Lister didn't always like Halifax in the 1800s, and Laura Johansen didn't like it in the 1990s either. As a teenager working her first job in the café at Shibden Hall on Saturdays, Laura had a front row seat to tales about Miss Lister. What she most admired about her then, Laura says, is that Anne Lister managed to escape and get the hell out of West Yorkshire. As soon as she could, Laura followed suit and moved away for college before beginning an international career that took her to Paris, Copenhagen, New York City, Kinshasa, and Hanoi.

Just as Anne Lister boomeranged to her hometown, so did Laura when she was hired in 2017 by Arts Council England and Visit England. Her new job: head up an experimental "cultural destinations" project to entice more people to visit Halifax and the Calderdale borough that encompasses five other towns and dozens of small villages in northern England.

Her timing was impeccable. Something big was underway that soon would catapult Halifax to its new position as the hottest lesbian-friendly tourist destination in the world. Award-winning television writer Sally Wainwright, a native of West Yorkshire and its No. 1 booster, was working on a new TV series about Anne Lister to be filmed at Shibden Hall, Anne Lister's ancestral home, and at mansions, businesses, and other locations in Halifax, Calderdale, and the surrounding area.

"I knew Sally would do a great job with the remarkable story she had to tell, and it would be an absolute gift to us," says Laura. "My job was to tell the best story I could about what tourists would find to see and do here and decide who would listen."

When Season 1 of the series aired worldwide in the spring and early summer of 2019, it unleashed a tsunami of curiosity about everything related to Anne Lister and where she was from. Visitors by the thousands began pouring into Halifax. Laura was prepared for an influx of LGBTQ+ tourists mostly from Great Britain. She had had a two-year head start to collaborate with local cultural sites and organizations to showcase Calderdale's heritage and provide visitors with a memorable travel experience.

"I could feel what was coming down the track, but the response to *Gentleman Jack* is even bigger than any of us expected," Laura says.

Waves of lesbians began arriving not just from Wales, Scotland, and nearby regions in England as anticipated, but from around the world. The number of visitors to Shibden Hall where Anne Lister and her wife, Ann Walker, lived, for example, surged to more than 14,000 in August 2019 alone compared to 2,500 the previous August.

Wherever Miss Lister and Miss Walker had gone, gay tourists went too. They laid flowers in the 900-year-old Minster where Miss Lister was baptized, worshipped, and is buried. At The Piece Hall, one of the most important 18th century buildings in Britain, they visited shops and ate in restaurants refashioned from the stalls where traders sold wool in Anne's day. Many made an unrelated side trip to nearby Hebden Bridge, a quirky and picturesque village recognized as the lesbian capital of the UK.

It was one thing to follow Anne Lister's footsteps throughout Halifax, but *Gentleman-Jack*-fans-turned-tourists also wanted to know more about the real woman who had defied 19th century conventions and loved only women. Laura decided to organize a small festival in the summer of 2019 for visitors hungry for more details about Halifax's now most famous resident. She invited Lister historians Helena Whitbread and Jill Liddington to present a talk about Anne Lister at The Book Corner, a small independent book store.

"Crazy and berserk," Laura says, "is the best way to describe what happened."

When the event sold out in seconds, she moved it to the bigger Town Hall. When that venue also quickly sold out, the next and only remaining option was Halifax Minster, and 250 lucky people from the United States, United Kingdom, Canada, France, Spain, Belgium, and a handful of other countries snagged a ticket to get in.

"It was so magical to be part of that experience," Laura now recalls.

"There was something really special about this gathering of women and the solidarity you could really feel. It was so emotional to look out into the audience and see so many women, many in tears, giving Jill and Helena a standing ovation for their years of work to transcribe Anne Lister's journals."

She thinks their intense reaction was because lesbians and other women have never been represented in a positive way that is so grounded in a true story.

"It just goes to show that women have needed something like this for such a long time," she says.

Anne Lister and her determination to be true to her nature is not only good for the psyche of lesbians, she's good for business too. Cultural tourism pays big dividends. Keeping up with the growing demand for accommodations and other requirements that tourists have may turn out to be a good problem to have for a region unaccustomed to its new volume of visitors.

"We know the majority of lesbian tourists making their way to Halifax are between the ages of 35 and 65 with disposable money to spend on hotels, inns, restaurants, taxis, and in shops, and that's wonderful for the local economy," Laura points out. "I don't see any let-up in the surge of lesbian tourists for the next five to ten years because Anne's is an important story to tell, and no one can tell like we can. I'm not a lesbian but I am a strong ally, and I believe what we can provide here is important for such an underserved audience that has such an aching need to have it."

Halifax's roots as a once grimy industrial center dependent on coal production and the "vulgar" wool trade that Anne Lister found so distasteful have given way to the area's standing as a popular setting for film and television productions, a dynamic contemporary literary scene, and a mecca for women who love women.

While *Gentleman Jack* introduced Anne Lister and Ann Walker to millions who had no idea either woman even existed, Laura's single-minded focus on telling her hometown's unique story has played a big part in putting Halifax on the map for countless lesbians and other fans.

"I love Anne Lister, and I've loved her for a long time," Laura says. "I love her story and what she has done for this region. And I feel so proud that the place I'm from can be such a welcoming place for so many women."

DAVID GLOVER

Halifax, West Yorkshire, England, UK

WELCOME TO ANNE LISTER'S HALIFAX

*I*n the company of historian David Glover, president of the Halifax Antiquarian Society, visitors to Anne Lister's hometown are in for a memorable encounter with living history. What could be better than viewing the places where she lived and studied, walking the streets she walked, and experiencing the 19th century through Anne's eyes?

"My knowledge of Anne Lister came together over a period of time, and I spent several years assembling bits and pieces," David says.

When *Gentleman Jack* became an international phenomenon in 2019, lesbians in droves began flocking to Halifax to see for themselves where and how Anne Lister lived. David assembled his "bits and pieces" to create what can be aptly described as the Anne Lister Trail. He is its chief guide and historical interpreter.

"I've always enjoyed history—ever since I was small when I was at school, even when I was about eight years old," David says. "I always loved stories from history when most of the other boys were interested in sport."

His early interest in British history took on a more local flavor after he moved to West Yorkshire from the London area in the late 1980s. A job in a secondhand bookshop gave him access to books that whetted his curiosity about the people and places in historical Halifax.

"I went through a period of poor health in the 1990s when I had to spend a tremendous amount of time resting," David adds. "This gave me the opportunity to study and read very widely, and gradually I became focused on the history of Halifax."

He says his interest in Halifax took him down many paths, from the exploration of the city's deep industrial roots to the discovery that a sizable number of people from the Halifax area sailed in the wake of the Mayflower to start new lives in America in the 1630s, including several Listers.

Anne Lister first appeared on David's radar about 20 years ago. "I was already somewhat interested in Shibden Hall as a local historic house, but I had not yet read much about Anne," David says. "I wasn't quite sure how Anne Lister fitted with me until I began to study some of what she wrote, and put it in context with the general history of Halifax in the early 19th century."

It was the discovery of the pieces of Anne Lister's tombstone in the Halifax Minster in 2000 that captured David's attention and sparked newfound interest in the woman who has since become Halifax's favorite daughter. In the two decades since her broken grave marker was found beneath the stone floor in the rear the church, David's ongoing research into the history of the centuries-old parish church has uncovered its many connections to Anne Lister.

As did other prominent local families, the Listers long held and maintained private pews in the church, and many Listers are buried there. The family coat of arms is painted on the church's ceiling. Anne herself was baptized here, worshipped here, and its vicar was one of her early teachers. She was so enamored with the unusual double-twisted upright pillars on the communion rail separating the congregation from the church's high altar that she had them replicated and hand-carved, at considerable expense, for her own staircase at Shibden Hall.

Besides Halifax Minster, David leads his guests to the house near North Bridge, where Anne Lister lived as a child—the place she noted in her journal where she broke free at night to wander through the bawdy areas of Halifax. He points out the location of Anne's likely birthplace, though the old Northgate House has long since been torn down. Other stops include where she went to school and where Eliza Raine, her first love, also lived for a time. Some buildings on the trail will be familiar to *Gentleman Jack* fans because of their association with Christopher Rawson. Both Hope Hall, Rawson's home, and Somerset House, his bank, are stops on the trail.

David's knowledge of the historic characters in *Gentleman Jack* extends beyond the Listers and the Rawsons to Ann Walker, of course, so his tours also include Lightcliffe, where Ann lived, and the cemetery where she is buried.

"It seems unfair to compare Ann Walker to Anne Lister, for Anne Lister has to come out on top because we know so much about her from her own words. We have masses of information about Ann Walker, but nearly all from Anne Lister's pen," David explains. "Ann Walker is an emerging figure particularly through additional ongoing research, but we cannot compare the two because one is almost like a Colossus and the other is a bit like the shadow of the Colossus."

Despite his extensive knowledge about Anne Lister, David is a modest historian.

"I'm standing on the shoulders of giants such as Helena Whitbread, Jill Liddington, and Patricia Hughes in particular, along with many others in the antiquarian society who have studied Halifax history," he says.

But no one else has David's unexpected two-degrees-of-separation connection to Anne Lister. Her distant cousin John Lister was the last Lister to inherit and live at Shibden Hall, beginning in 1867, and he is credited with saving Anne's journals from destruction in spite of their perceived scandalous content. John Lister was the first president of the Halifax Antiquarian Society, a position David now holds.

And, as John Lister did more than 100 years ago, David also takes an activist role, giving lectures and adding to the scholarship of Halifax history by authoring articles for local publications.

"If you read through John Lister's papers, they're enormously valuable about the history of Shibden Hall and other aspects of local history," David observes. "But I think that listening to his talks about them must have been quite tedious because some of his accounts were dry as dust."

It's something David says he works hard to avoid. He customizes his half-day and all-day private tours to match the interests of the mostly American women who turn to him to explore where Anne went and what she did.

"I've never yet met a person—and they have been quite different types—in connection with Anne Lister that I didn't like," David says. "So I think that says a lot for the students of Anne Lister."

David shares the views of the many tourists he meets who admire Anne Lister for her boldness and bravery.

"Anne worked out a way to live her own life as she saw it. As a person who has had to try and do the same against considerable odds, I admire that in Anne, 200 years later," he says. "Anne's ability to live her life in a 'fulfilled' way and yet accept and incorporate faith into it is another thing which I find significant, as it is something we share."

The Halifax Antiquarian Society researches, preserves, and records the long and rich history of Halifax. The Society has a membership of over 250 (including several overseas) and continues to develop interest in the study of local history through its varied activities, its library, and its publications. Annual dues are £25 (£30 if outside the UK). Visit halifaxhistory.org.uk for more information.

JANE FINN

Halifax, West Yorkshire, England, UK

FEW LEAVE HALIFAX MINSTER UNCHANGED

*A*s they've done for centuries, pilgrims throughout the world journey to holy or sacred places. In Tibet, Buddhists trek across the country's rugged landscape to reach Lhasa's Jokhang Temple. Christians find their way to the Holy Land in Israel. Jewish pilgrims gather in Jerusalem, Hindus at the River Ganges. Hajj is among the world's largest pilgrimages as millions of Muslims visit the Holy City of Mecca.

Now, as a result of *Gentleman Jack*, thousands of new pilgrims are drawn to an unlikely location: Halifax, West Yorkshire. The significance of Halifax Minster to Anne Lister—the parish church where she was baptized, prayed, and is buried—isn't lost on those who find themselves paying homage at this place of worship that dates to the 12th century.

There to greet them is Reverend Jane Finn, curate and priest at the Minster. A former corporate executive, math teacher, and food bank administrator, Jane was ordained as an Anglican priest in 2018, one of the seven percent of the Church of England's worldwide clergy who is female. She acknowledges that she, too, felt the undeniable pull of Halifax as the place to begin her ministry.

"I find that everyone who is turning up at the Minster is pilgrimaging in one way or another," Jane says.

She has noticed that those who've been ill-treated in their church in the past aren't sure what kind of reception they're going to receive.

"I know for some people just seeing me, a female with a collar around my neck who is clearly welcoming them, comes as a surprise," she says. But it's important to me that people feel safe here at the Minster. Every single person is really important no matter who they are or why they're coming in. We're here for any level of consolation or healing that our visitors need."

The remains of Anne Lister's tombstone were found in 2000 beneath the stone floor in Halifax Minster. The original inscription reads as follows: In memory of Anne Lister of Shibden Hall, who died 22nd Septr 1840 at KOUTAIS in GEORGIA, and was interred here the 29th April 1841, AEt 49

Anne Lister's church has become a touchstone for many women, especially lesbians, because of the important role it played in Anne's life. Many initially come to pay their respects in the church that is her final resting place. Being in a spiritual space that meant so much to Anne Lister—or perhaps sensing her presence there—often has a profound effect, reducing some to tears, Jane has observed.

"Different responses show me that there are still unresolved issues for people, whether it is around their sexual identity or their faith or whether their fear is that God has rejected them just as other people have," Jane explains.

Jane points out that Anne Lister's strong faith and her unwavering self-acceptance is a powerful combination, one that she believes serves to validate women who love women.

"Anne is a brilliant example of the voice that many need to hear at this point in time," Jane says. "Anne is saying, 'I am who I am, I was born like this, I would be going against God's will if I weren't with somebody who's the fairer sex.' I believe God wants each of us to be true and authentic to who we are. And He loves us for whom He made us to be. If we're busy trying to be something else, then surely that's the part that's wrong."

Jane has observed scores of Halifax pilgrims and she's learned that, whether they are aware of it or not, many visitors come to the Minster in search of peace—and even themselves—which they may not find during the short time they spend at the church. That's why she is the driving force behind the creation of a self-guided, day-long pilgrimage-within-a-pilgrimage: *Anne Lister Way of the Setts.*

"Setts are the stones that make up the cobbled paths that you'll follow from Halifax Minster to Shibden Hall and back on this walk of self-discovery," Jane says. "My hope is those who make this simple pilgrimage will see it as a walk of revelation and a way to connect with themselves, with God, and with the spirit of Anne Lister."

The 3½-mile (5+ km) pilgrimage focuses on the most important aspects of Anne's life: her church, her home, and the route she walked that connects the two. It starts at the baptismal font in the Minster, proceeds to a steep path, and then on past Walker Pit (the coal shaft Anne named for her wife Ann Walker), through Cunnery Wood on Anne's estate, to Shibden Hall. The return is along the same path, ending at Anne's broken grave marker in the Minster.

"Along the way, I hope pilgrims will take the time to stop to enjoy the panoramic view of Halifax that Anne would have seen. I encourage them to pause at various marked spots to reflect on where this pilgrimage is taking them—in their hearts—and be aware of what they are discovering about themselves, what they are laying down or picking up, and how God's ever-present love and acceptance feels," Jane explains.

Back at the church, pilgrims can light a candle and record their thoughts in a book that resembles one of Anne's own journals. The ancient rite of making a pilgrimage on foot is made fail-safe by today's ability to download a GPS map that displays the Setts route on a smartphone.

Whether or not visitors to the Minster opt to extend their experience by taking the *Anne Lister Way of the Stetts* pilgrimage walk, Jane believes most do not leave the church unchanged in some way.

"There is a sense of gratitude from people that is above and beyond what you'd normally expect," she observes. "The effect of the Minster is often very unexpected and very deep. Many believe they've already processed how the world treats them and how the church treats them. Maybe they've not been able to go to church or take the sacrament for x-number of years. They seem quite on top of it to start with and before long, actually there is still a lot of raw hurt and rejection that begins to surface. They start to unravel long-buried things they didn't even know were still there. Anne has opened a door for people to tentatively push at and see if they can get any consolation, and any homecoming."

Newfound self-acceptance, confidence, pride, joy: Jane has seen it all among the Minster's visitors.

"There are conversations I've had with people who've come in, and they are changing their lives," Jane says. "And it's not simply about being a lesbian or coming out or owning who they are. It's about recognizing that they've never really fully lived and been the person that God made them to be. Once they've shifted the way they think or feel, it's as if someone has just pressed the fast forward button on everything. They don't want to waste any more time, and they want to get on with living the life they were intended to have."

Recalling her interactions with so many of the women who've made the pilgrimage to Halifax and to the Minster, Jane says it is as if Anne Lister is speaking to us from 200 years ago.

"Anne's voice is the voice that I expect God to have, constantly reminding us to be true to ourselves," Jane says. "Anne encourages us, or calls us, to live our best lives, and to be our authentic selves."

Directions and details about the Anne Lister Way of the Setts pilgrimage can be found at britishpilgrimage.org.

∞

SHIRLEY JONES

Wakefield, West Yorkshire, England, UK

YESTERDAY'S DIARIES, TODAY'S TREASURES

*W*hat if Anne Lister hadn't kept a journal for more than 20 years? What if John Lister hadn't ignored his friend Arthur Burrell's insistence that her journals be burned after they cracked her secret code and discovered the scandalous things she had written in them? What if neglect and the passage of time had rendered the journals unreadable or too fragile to even be touched?

Anne Lister's far-reaching impact—now and for posterity—would have been lost forever.

Instead, we have the last Lister to live at Shibden Hall to thank for putting Anne's journals in a safe place, where they lay undisturbed for more than 40 years. We have Sally Wainwright to thank for underwriting the costs of conserving and digitizing the journals so that they are protected and easily accessible for historians and others interested in Anne Lister and early- to mid-19th century England. And we have Shirley Jones and her team of conservators and the archivists at the West Yorkshire Archive Service to thank for the painstaking care they have taken to preserve Anne Lister's journals and ensure that her life and legacy will have a permanent place in history.

Anne Lister's journals, along with the extensive Shibden Hall collection of hundreds of letters and other documents, are housed in Halifax in an air-conditioned, state-of-the-art strong room within the Calderdale Central Library. Beginning in 2016, it fell to Shirley Jones, the archives' Head of Conservation and a specialist in book conservation, book binding, and paper preservation, to oversee critical repairs to Anne's 24 main journals and 14 travel diaries.

Shirley and her team were delighted to take on this important assignment.

"It's been fun to have the journals, and in fact, I think it's other people's awe and their responses to them that has made the journals rather special for us to work on," Shirley says.

Two hundred years isn't that old in the big picture of historical documents, Shirley explains.

"Anne's main journals are very typical of the early 19th century," she says. "Apart from their uniqueness as they relate to Anne and the content she included in them, the journals are pretty standard in terms of format. What is unusual is the extent of the standardization. They do spread over quite a long period of time and they are all the same size and very much the same style. It made me wonder if that is something Anne actively maintained."

Most, if not all, of Anne's journals were probably purchased at Whitley and Booth Stationers on Crown Street in Halifax, her favorite bookstore.

Viewers of the first season of *Gentleman Jack* may remember an early scene in Episode 1 when Anne takes her journal out of a trunk. With its gray and white mottled cloth cover with a reddish-orange vellum spine and corner protectors, this television prop is a replica of the real thing. Shirley says each journal is slightly wider in size than an iPad and contains roughly 200 pages of thick, good quality handmade paper. Anne wrote on both sides with good quality black ink, and her straight handwriting on every page is likely the result of her following the very faint horizontal "laid" lines transferred onto the paper by a wire frame generally used in the 19th century papermaking process. Anne included dates, indices, and contents at the beginning and end of her journals.

"Anne was obviously very careful with her diaries because the text blocks were in fairly immaculate condition," Shirley concluded after her initial assessment. "The only problems were relating to the binding and damp damage on two of them."

The challenge facing the conservators was to repair the damaged bindings using most of the same techniques that would have been used in the early 1800s to construct the blank journals. Originally the pages were folded into folios and grouped into sections that were handsewn together, the threads wrapping around the outside of the spine. Animal glue was applied to the spine to help hold the page sections in place, and vellum (calf skin) then would have been glued to the spine to complete the binding.

Shirley notes that as often happens, both the animal glue and the vellum on the spine became brittle and flaky over the years, and the spines had actually cracked on many of Anne's journals. This, in turn, caused the sewing thread holding the pages in place to split. Without replacing the bindings, the pages would no longer be secure and some of the journals were in danger of falling apart.

The four conservators working on the project set out to restore the journals to their original condition and protect thousands of affected pages. As it happens, the broken bindings turned out to be advantageous when it came time to scan the journals to create a digital archive.

"We didn't repair any of the bindings before the digitization process because the digitization requires the volumes to be completely flat," Shirley explains. "We made only emergency repairs that would have caused more damage if they had not been attended to. For this reason, some of the digital page images you see online look as if they have had no conservation work because the work had not yet been done."

Shirley provided oversight and advice about how to carefully handle the journals during the week that it took two technicians to digitize more than a dozen small travel diaries and 7,700+ pages of Anne's accounts of her daily activities, love affairs, correspondence, and social engagements. Once the digitization step was finished, the journals were safely returned to the archive service's Wakefield studio for the team to complete the 12-month conservation process.

"So often I say that we've done all this work and you can't see any of it," Shirley recounts with a smile. "The paper repairs get hidden, the new sewing gets hidden, the clothings on the spine get hidden. We put new leather on the spine, and then we hide it with the old leather so the journals look like they would have when Anne wrote in them."

Conservation of the journals was just the beginning. Next came tailor-made boxes to safely store them in the vault. Shirley and then-archivist Dan Sudron selected a page from one of Anne's journals to replicate on screen-printed fabric that Shirley then used to make cushions to cradle the journals when they are on public display. The fabric includes a memorable quote from Anne's entry on 16 September 1823: "I can tell my journal what I can tell none else."

Before *Gentleman Jack* aired, Shirley says the journals were rarely publicly displayed. Anticipating the possibility of an explosion of interest in Anne Lister, her journals, and various documents related to her wife, Ann Walker, as a result of the television series, she recognized the need for the journals to be fully restored and made available for people to see.

"We know we have to mitigate any risk to them, and we can rotate them to minimize any light damage," she says. "What are preserving and keeping the journals for if not for viewing? We have to remember that we at the archives are the only way people can see them because the journals aren't available anywhere else."

Shirley's foresight proved to be true.

"I have been quite amazed by the passion of interest. We are a provincial part of a large archive service, and we're punching at something of national weight here," Shirley notes. "It's taken over our lives as well. We're doing handcrafted merchandise, and we're not used to our talks selling out. What I've been surprised about is that people are actually interested in the conservation work, so I'm heartened by that because it has been such a team effort."

In 2011 Anne Lister's journals were added to the national register of the UNESCO Memory of the World Programme in recognition of their worldwide historical significance, an honor so far bestowed on fewer than 400 sets of documents in the world.

But aside from their incalculable historical value, Shirley also has observed firsthand what the journals mean to individuals.

"When I have done talks, it is a very moving spectacle to see a line of people queuing up to see one of the journals and just wanting to stroke the book," she says. "We've obviously appealed to very many people from the LGBTQ+ community, but women of all types and a few chaps have been interested as well. The journals have quite a profound effect on people, and they are very emotional when they see them in person. Seeing the journal entries on a computer screen cannot give you that experience."

Never in her wildest imagination could Anne Lister have foreseen that the two dozen blank books she filled to chronicle her daily life would become the global treasures they are today. And because of the efforts of a handful of dedicated conservators and archivists, they'll be around for future generations to cherish too.

For a list and description of Anne Lister-related handcrafted items available from the West Yorkshire Archive Service, email conservation@wyjs.org.uk.

DANIEL SUDRON

Halifax, West Yorkshire, England, UK

PRESERVE THE PAST, PROTECT THE FUTURE

*S*eventeen years ago, a young man fresh out of university with a degree in heritage management reported to his first job as an archive assistant in Leeds at one of the five offices that make up the West Yorkshire Archive Service (WYAS). Dan Sudron was fascinated by the centuries-old paper trails that people in northern England have left behind and the many stories they tell. He still is.

As lead Calderdale Archivist based at the WYAS Halifax branch, Dan's fascination with history hasn't waned. In recent years, Anne Lister captured his professional and personal admiration, so he took on the task of creating an online exhibition of Anne's journals linked to the WYAS website and led a team effort to make her five-million-word diaries accessible to an eager global audience.

Thanks to *Gentleman Jack*, interest in Anne's journals has never been greater.

"Anne's diaries and travel journals are fully digitized and available on the WYAS website," Dan says. "People can use the diaries for detailed research, and when they are able to visit the WYAS search room in Halifax in person, often the diaries can be put on display so they can look at them and can read them. Visitors can view and handle many of Anne's papers, such as her letters. Of course, access to the original diaries is limited to ensure their long-term survival."

While all 24 volumes of Anne's journals are now online, there has been a major drawback: most have never been fully transcribed. Unless one is able to read her challenging handwriting and decipher her secret code, many details of Anne's remarkable life remain hidden in the tiny scribbles and symbols she scrawled on the 7,700+ pages of her journals.

"The Archive service has long known the value of increasing access to Anne's diaries, particularly since their inscription on the UNESCO UK Memory of the World Register, and I always had it in my mind how good it would be to get completed transcriptions of the diaries," Dan says. "But it became clear that the level of interest in Anne Lister herself was increasing so much as a result of *Gentleman Jack* that if there was ever going to be a transcription project, it was time to launch it."

That's exactly what he did. On the heels of Season 1's final episode of *Gentleman Jack* in July 2019, the #AnneListerCodeBreaker project officially got underway.

"The level of interest was much more than I anticipated," Dan admits.

"To get so quickly to over 160 volunteers in 17 countries that are engaged in the project was really fantastic."

"As transcription projects go, this was a complicated one," Dan explains. "With Anne's handwriting, her extensive abbreviations, and that incredible code of hers, it was quite a tricky undertaking. We sent the same block of 10 pages to two transcribers, so when the transcriptions come back, there are two transcriptions to compare to each other. There may be points where there are slight differences, so those will be checked to confirm the text for the final transcriptions that will be posted online."

Anne's tiny handwriting fills 7,722 pages, and thanks to the small army of volunteer codebreakers, all have now been transcribed, and *Gentleman Jack* fans and researchers will substantially benefit as a result. In addition to having the image of each diary page that is already posted on the WYAS website, they'll also soon be able to see two versions of the final transcripts.

"The first version aims to show as closely as possible the text as it appears in the diaries," Dan explains. "It will be marked up with square brackets to show extended abbreviations and italics to show the text which has been translated from the code. It will be made available as a PDF attached to the WYAS online catalogue for each complete volume. The other version will be a keyword searchable version, without the square brackets for the extended abbreviations, and will be embedded into the entries on our online catalogue for each individual page alongside the images of the diaries."

Dan points out that the new transcriptions linked to each image on the WYAS website are an important addition.

"Now people will be able to search by place name, by person, even by a particular word. For example, someone might search for mining and see how many times an entry comes up that contains mining, or perhaps they might want to enter Mariana Belcombe Lawton's or Ann Walker's name and see how often each one pops up as well."

Anticipating the challenges that the transcribers would face and intent on providing the support they might want and need, Dan also took steps to ensure that the group, all working remotely, could easily connect with one another. Created and maintained by WYAS, the project's Twitter page—#AnneListerCodeBreaker—gave volunteers throughout the world an active social media community for seeking transcription advice and sharing stories from the diaries. A private Facebook group also served the same purpose.

Dan believes the information in Anne's journals has significant historical value beyond the telling of the riveting story of an unconventional woman in the 19th century.

"Because of the level of detail Anne records in her diaries, I certainly envisage that once the final transcripts are complete, many researchers will use them when they're looking at Halifax because Anne has so much to say about local history and what's going on in society," Dan says. "They will also have value for people interested in a wide variety of other topics. For example, someone contacted WYAS from another country that had no formal records of the weather during a time when Anne was visiting that country. Since Anne, of course, recorded the temperature almost every day wherever she was, her diaries could fill in the missing details."

Anne's journals have also sparked a new sociological interest in the late Georgian/early Victorian time period in which she lived.

"Learning about Anne, who is unique in very many ways, reflects a change in how people interact with history now," Dan observes. "They tend to want to know more about the social aspects rather than just the wider brushstrokes of history. They want to know stories about people, and I think it's the diaries and things like that that reveal personal information that most find much more interesting and which can add so much to mainstream history."

Though she started noting her activities on loose scraps of paper and in notebooks as early as 1806, it wasn't until 1817 that Anne began writing in her journals almost daily, a practice she continued until shortly before her death in 1840. Dan notes that Anne's diaries are unique because they provide 23 years of detailed records about what Anne herself is feeling and what she is doing.

"Not only do we see the LGBTQ+ aspect of her life, her many activities and many interests, and her perspective on the different places she visits, we see her viewpoint as a landowner just as the Reform Act was happening, and of course, her thoughts on politics," he says.

As complete transcriptions of Anne's journals become available, more fascinating details about her are emerging.

"I am constantly amazed about the different details she records, and how many times she seems to be firing a pistol or has a sword on hand," Dan says. "These references just kind of come out almost as a side comment. It's quite interesting just to see what potentially someone might think was a completely normal kind of living 200 years ago. Pistols and swords seem to come up a lot—Anne doesn't seem to be going after anybody with them, though she does fire them out the window occasionally."

In 2020, the Anne Lister transcription project was honored with the UK's Archives and Records Association's annual Volunteer Award for the invaluable contributions that its scores of volunteers were making to extend the reach of Anne's diaries and engage with a large online community.

"The award was a fantastic acknowledgement of the hard work of dedicated and enthusiastic volunteers and a great recognition of the huge significance of this important archive collection and the power of archives in general to bring people together," Dan says.

Though Dan originally anticipated that the transcription project would be a multi-year undertaking estimated to take 16,000 to 20,000 volunteer hours, by early 2021, all journal pages had been transcribed by enthusiastic volunteers, and reconciliation of differences in the transcriptions is currently underway. Until all are completed, *Gentleman Jack* fans and researchers can continue to view an online exhibition of Anne Lister's journals and their contents on the WYAS "cataBlogue."

"Anne's strength of character very much comes out over the many years that she keeps a diary," Dan says. "It is incredible to be able to see in such detail, in her own hand, how she is progressing. Now that so many more people know about Anne Lister, it's clear that her strength has become an inspiration for a lot of people. As an archivist, it was quite incredible and really special to care for these records that mean so much to so many and have a role in fully bringing them to the public."

An online exhibition of Anne Lister's journals can be viewed at wyascataBlogue. wordpress.com/exhibitions/anne-lister. Dan has changed jobs and is now Archivist at the North Yorkshire County Record Office in Northallerton.

∞

RACHEL WHITBREAD

Halifax, West Yorkshire, England, UK

MY MOTHER HAS MORE LESBIAN FRIENDS THAN I DO

*N*o matter the day of the week, no matter what else is going on, no matter the location, Anne Lister always manages to inveigle herself into at least one conversation a day at the Whitbread household. Rachel Whitbread can attest to it. It's been close to 40 years since Anne Lister became a commanding presence in her family.

It's what happens when your mum becomes an expert in her field, falls in love with the past and her research subject, and likes to share little tidbits about her historical discoveries.

It started when Rachel, the youngest of four children, was still a teenager. At 18, she already had moved away to attend university when Anne Lister first showed up on large, blurry photocopied sheets that Rachel's mother brought home from the West Yorkshire archives. It was 1983, and Helena Whitbread was just setting out to learn more about this woman from her hometown by transcribing Lister's journal entries––one page at a time, 50 pages per week.

"Every day my mum would sit on the sofa in the living room where she and my father lived," Rachel says. "Anne Lister was her hobby then, and she learned to read Anne's secret code and her handwriting. It didn't take long before Mum discovered Anne Lister wasn't like anyone else. When she came across a passage where Anne said she wanted to go to Russia to find herself a wife, that's when Mum realized Anne Lister was a lesbian."

VOICES FROM HALIFAX · **89**

Now Helena knew two lesbians: Anne Lister and her daughter Rachel.

"Since I had recently come out to Mum, I think discovering that Anne Lister was a lesbian helped her come to terms with my sexuality," Rachel reflects. "We were both finding our way. Mum was just beginning her research and finding out more about Anne, and I was trying to find my place in the LGBT community. We had some very interesting conversations during those days."

Just as Anne Lister had experienced two centuries before, it wasn't long before Rachel also got a taste of the enduring condemnation of same sex relationships. In 1988, Margaret Thatcher's Tory government passed a repressive law that outlawed local governments and schools in the UK from "promoting the teaching of the acceptability of homosexuality as a pretended family relationship."

"Section 28 was a step backwards just as we were getting to the stage where even TV soaps were being a bit brave and putting lesbian characters on TV," Rachel remembers. "I was living in Manchester at the time and studying for my Youth and Community Work diploma. It was scary that a law like this could get passed, and we were afraid if something as homophobic as Section 28 could get support, what might happen next?"

Rachel and her partner took their concerns to the streets in protest, as did thousands of lesbians and gay men throughout the UK. In 2003, the highly discriminatory law was repealed.

Like Anne Lister, both Whitbreads have a trailblazing gene.

With the publication of *I Know My Own Heart: The Diaries of Miss Anne Lister, 1791-1840* in 1988 when suppressive Section 28 took effect, Helena Whitbread was the first historian to reveal that Anne Lister was a lesbian. Reflecting the anti-LGBTQ+ hostilities of the times, one reviewer discounted the book on the grounds that the journals had never existed in the first place. Another questioned the book's validity because it was written by a straight woman.

"When things like this came up at her talks, I was Mum's defense," Rachel says. "If anyone asked why she was so interested in writing about a lesbian, she could say ,'My daughter is a lesbian' or 'I'm doing it for my daughter.' While I think writing for the first time about Anne's sexuality certainly did help her deal with the fact that I am a lesbian, it also was an intellectual pursuit that addressed her thirst for history and her love of Halifax."

Ten years later, in 1998, Rachel and her partner had a first of their own: they became the first lesbians under the Brighton and Hove authority in East Sussex county to be accepted as foster parents, taking in two school-age children.

Rachel says that no matter where she's lived (York, Manchester, Norwich, Madrid, Brighton, Leeds, or Halifax) or what career path she was following (youth worker, teacher of English as a second language, foster parent, librarian, civil service), Anne Lister has remained a constant in her life. Sometimes it's meant mother and daughter traveled together to explore some of the many places Anne had been. Other times it's been pitching in to help her mother with research tasks for her books.

"In the early days, I explored York's archives for the birth and death records of Anne's associates, especially the Belcombe family," Rachel says. "Mum and I were very interested in Mariana Belcombe, whom we both believe was the love of Anne's life, and to this day I'm still Team Mariana."

There was always something interesting to discover about Anne,

Rachel explains.

"For example, years ago when I was part of a small group transcribing sections of Anne's journals, I came across an entry about a man who visited her uncle at Shibden Hall," she says. "The visitor operated a slave ship, and naturally Anne wanted to know everything about the ship and what happened on it. She meticulously recorded the cost of different slaves in her journal and even noted that if a woman was pregnant the buyer would get more for his money because it was two slaves for the price of one."

Not only was it a fascinating though horrifying story, Rachel recalls, it was proof of Anne's unflagging curiosity about all subjects and her compulsion to record every detail.

Thanks to *Gentleman Jack*, interest in Anne Lister—and Rachel's mum—has never been greater. Of course, Rachel is still pitching in. She helps care for her mother, chauffeurs her wherever she wants to go, and attends all of her meetings. As she has done for many years, Rachel also accompanies her mother to the talks Helena continues to give about Anne Lister, events that draw capacity crowds of lesbian admirers and always end with a standing ovation.

In 2020, Rachel began leading a three-hour women's walking tour in Halifax highlighting the places that Anne Lister visited and telling stories about Anne and people familiar to viewers of *Gentleman Jack*.

"With my connection to Anne Lister, and having been born and bred in Halifax, it's a perfect opportunity to share the knowledge I've acquired over the years," Rachel says. "It's a way I can continue to learn more about Halifax myself and the characters in Anne's life too." (When tours resume after pandemic restrictions are lifted, Rachel expects to also guide a tour in York where Anne studied, lived for a time, and was married in Holy Trinity Church, Goodramgate.)

"I'm especially glad *Gentleman Jack* has led to more recognition for Mum's contribution to the Anne Lister historical record," Rachel acknowledges. "She's worked very hard for many, many years. Even at 90 years old, Mum still spends a part of each day on her Anne Lister biography and staying in touch with what is now a very large group of devoted lesbian fans."

It's no surprise to Rachel that *Gentleman Jack* is so popular.

"The show is entertaining but highly romanticized," she says. "When I watched it, sometimes I found myself thinking, 'I know that didn't really happen,' or 'I wonder if that's true, I'll have to ask Mum.' At the same time, I couldn't help being moved because I know it means a great deal to lesbians to be so positively represented and validated. I believe Anne Lister would like that too."

Information about women's walking tours in Halifax and other locations is available at HerOnAHill.com.

Tower Library, Shibden Hall

RACHEL LAPPIN

Hebden Bridge, West Yorkshire, England, UK

THROUGH ANNE LISTER'S EYES

*N*estled in the rolling Pennine Hills just eight miles (13 km) west of Halifax is Hebden Bridge, a charming small town filled with stone houses, cafés and tea rooms, pubs, shops, and a large concentration of gay women.

The former mill town, in the 19th century, was referred to as "Trouser Town" because of its many clothing factories. These days it's known as the "Lesbian Capital of the United Kingdom" because it's said to have more gay women per square mile than any other place in the country. Rachel Lappin and her longtime partner are two of them.

When Rachel is not at her desk at The Piece Hall serving as the part-time project manager of Calderdale Cultural Destinations, Hebden Bridge is her home base. Her longtime appreciation for Anne Lister make her the ideal point person for promoting Anne's nearby hometown and the dozens of other places of interest in this Northern England metropolitan district.

"I got a dream job during a nightmare time," Rachel jokes, having assumed this role during the coronavirus lockdown. "I've probably had more Zoom meetings since the pandemic began than I've eaten hot meals," she says about her efforts coordinating with local cultural heritage organizations to promote and publicize the Calderdale area ahead of the influx of visitors who'll pour in when pandemic travel restrictions are lifted.

Rachel knows that high on the list for women making their way to Halifax, aka the new lesbian mecca, are Anne Lister-focused destinations. As one of a handful of Lister aficionados going back to the 1990s, she can relate to the appeal of walking in Anne's footsteps. Historical lesbian information was scarce when she first discovered Anne Lister, long before *Gentleman Jack*'s top-hatted version of her strode into the hearts of millions and created a global community of Anne's enthusiasts.

"Anne Lister has always been part of my adult life," Rachel says. "I must have been in my late teens or early 20s when I first learned of her, and then picked up Helena's *I Know My Own Heart*."

"Helena," of course, is Helena Whitbread, and her groundbreaking book, published in 1988 as the first chronicle of the same sex love affairs of a little-known 19th century English woman, initially was the main resource about Anne's explicit journals for those who happened to run across it.

"In those early days, I did a lot of research myself and just got hooked on Anne's whole story," Rachel says. "I loved what she did, how brave she was, and what courage she had. I was already comfortable with myself when I found out about her, but Anne Lister validated my being who I am. I thought if someone could do what she did nearly 200 years ago, surely to God, I should be able to do it now."

Shortly after reading about Anne, Rachel found herself drawn to Shibden Hall, Anne's home and, for many, the place where Anne's presence still lingers.

"I remember the very first time I saw Shibden," Rachel says. "It was so magical, even before I went inside. Shibden still just speaks to me from the second I see it, and it always has. It tells me to give it a big hug, and metaphorically, that's what I try to do. It's the place I've always gone when I just need a bit of quiet and mindful thinking time."

In those pre-*Gentleman Jack* days when so few were aware of the unconventional woman who once owned the estate, Shibden Hall attracted the occasional visitor interested primarily in local history or Tudor architecture.

"It's a rather small house really, and it's not grand like some of the other historic homes in this country," Rachel explains. "There were many occasions over the years when I would go to Shibden and there wouldn't be a single soul around."

To visit Shibden Hall is to experience Anne's imagination and handiwork firsthand by way of the extensive renovations she made to the house and its grounds. As a former volunteer docent, Rachel learned some of the ins and outs of this 600-year-old home. She is one of the lucky few who has been allowed into the two-story library tower that Anne added to Shibden in 1839 as her private haven, where she could read and write surrounded by her extensive, eclectic collection of books.

"The tower is so special," Rachel explains. "It literally wraps itself around you. It's so small and intimate you can't really swing a cat around in there. I love the tower because it is absolutely Anne Lister. She inherited the house as it had been built by other people, but the tower was all her. She designed it, and she oversaw everything about it down to the millimeter probably. When I looked out of the tower windows, I was actually looking at something she purposely and very specifically designed. Since she left for Russia just as it was being finished and wasn't able to really enjoy it, I felt like I was looking at the view for her. That's unbeatable."

That *Gentleman Jack* was actually filmed at Shibden Hall and in and around West Yorkshire is among the reasons the television series has been so impactful, Rachel thinks.

"You've got this woman who is basically saying I'm going to do what I want to do and not care about the consequences, and you're seeing all of that play out where it actually took place," Rachel says. "There is no question that Sally Wainwright's scriptwriting is genius. UK audiences are very familiar with her work and with Suranne Jones, so we knew *Gentleman Jack* would be good. And it was very, very good. I was just excited that so many people were learning about Anne Lister for the first time."

Rachel believes the effect of *Gentleman Jack* has been profound.

"An entire supportive community has sprung up that didn't exist before," she says. "Anne's legacy is remarkable for many people all around the world, but particularly for gay women. She's given so many of us a sense of purpose, and validation of our own sense of who we are. Her story also has given many a level of confidence they've never had before. Isn't this simply priceless?"

She's also noticed it's not just gay women who've been touched.

"Even my mum was captivated by it!" Rachel says. "Many women in their late 60s and 70s were gripped by the show. When I was volunteering at Shibden, I was surprised by how many older, heterosexual couples were coming to visit, and when I would ask 'What brought you here today?' the answer was often '*Gentleman Jack.*' I remember one bloke telling me he and his wife really liked the show. 'My wife was proper into it, and I had to even cook tea sometimes because you couldn't pull her away,' he told me."

As Rachel sees it, *Gentleman Jack* has made an enormous contribution to global well-being by introducing Anne Lister to people around the world.

Tower Library Interior, Shibden Hall

"We simply can never underestimate the impact and how it may have affected everyone who has seen it," she observes. "You know to a great extent, it even will have saved people's lives because during the last two years, especially with Covid, there have been people who have had really dark moments and dark times, and they have been able to look at and lean on *Gentleman Jack* to get them out of some pretty deep holes."

Rachel wonders if a program like *Gentleman Jack* will change the general public's attitudes toward gay women.

"I think most people are wary, if not scared, of people who are 'different,'" she says. "If they see groups of women like us en masse, we are probably not what they normally see. But because *Gentleman Jack* was on during a Sunday night dream time slot on BBC, and it was Sally and Suranne, it did mainstream female homosexuality. It explains a bit why so many women felt recognized and sort of puffed out their chests a little bit from believing we're worth having a prime time TV program written about one of our people."

Rachel says from her professional point of view and also as a proud local resident, she's delighted about what *Gentleman Jack* has done for the area.

"It's told Anne's story to millions of people who didn't know about it before, and now millions of people are interested not only in Anne Lister and Shibden, but the wider area where she was from," she says. "You can actually go, and be in, and walk around Anne Lister's home and hometown. That's phenomenal."

Rachel's interests in Anne Lister aren't limited to just her day job. She's also a good friend of Jill Liddington, the author of two definitive books on Anne Lister's life in the 1830s. As Jill's occasional assistant, Rachel helps out with Jill's website and presentations, and the two have recently launched a new YouTube video interview series called *A Walk in Anne Lister's Footsteps*. In addition, Rachel is part of the working group supporting the new Anne Lister Society, and she's a key behind-the-scenes player for 2022 Anne Lister Birthday Week events.

"For me, *Gentleman Jack* was completely entertaining, and I can't wait for Season 2," Rachel says.

"But I have been totally absorbed and engrossed by Anne's story for many, many years. This whole *Gentleman Jack* phenomenon is something we've not known in our lifetimes. Anne Lister will live on through all of us, especially when we go into her home and look out of the windows she looked out of, or when we go to the Minster and feel she's with us there too, or wander around the many places she went. This 'lady woman' keeps us all occupied in so many different ways. I often think what she has left us, and I'm delighted that a story as important as hers is no longer a secret."

Recalling a scene in *Gentleman Jack* when Anne attends the wedding of her friend Vere Hobart, who has abandoned her to marry a Scotsman, Rachel says television Anne Lister's words are especially relevant today: *Our time on earth is brief and we should all strive to make the most of it and be as happy as we can be.*

Rachel wholeheartedly agrees with the sentiment.

"Anne Lister made the absolute most of her considerably shortened life," she says. "We should all try to do the same and be as happy as we can be too."

No cats were harmed during Rachel's visits to the Shibden Hall library tower.
Visit http://www.jliddington.org.uk/anne-lister-AV for Rachel's interviews with
Jill Liddington. You'll find a 3D tour of the library tower at https://museums.calderdale.
gov.uk/visit/shibden-hall by selecting Inside Shibden Hall under the Virtual Tour tab.

∞

JENNIFER GRANT

Hastings, East Sussex, England, UK

WE'LL SHOW YOU AROUND IN STYLE

*W*hat would it be like to have a job where you get paid tell to people to take a hike, or exactly where to go, and where to get off? As the founder of Diva Destinations, Jennifer Grant does it all the time. Her lesbian travel company has been pampering and guiding women around the world on once-in-a-lifetime group excursions and customized tours since 2013.

From its humble beginnings, Diva Destinations mushroomed from a one-person labor of love to a thriving operation, so much so that Jen turned to friend and former colleague Caron Morton for her sales and management expertise.

"Caron is a whiz at drumming up excitement for our bucket list trips and helps keep our business humming and growing," says Jen of her business partner since 2018. "There are many gay women who want to have everything taken care of for them. They know we're going to look after every detail. A host is on every tour to take care of anything that needs attention, and they'll be in the company of friendly, like-minded women. What gay women like about our tours to wonderful destinations is that we bring them together on holidays where the memories and friendships formed will last forever. It's the most amazing feeling for me after the first evening of a tour to sit back and watch everyone already just having a fantastic time."

One of her company's most popular trips is a 7-day or 14-day

Blue historic plaque unveiled at Shibden Hall on 3 April 2019,
Anne Lister's 228th birthday

excursion to Skala Eressos, a picturesque beach village paradise on the
Greek island of Lesvos, which also goes by the name Lesbos. Every year,
Jen escorts dozens of lesbians to an annual international women's festival
for a holiday of sightseeing, beachcombing, and swimming in the Aegean
Sea by day and beachfront dinners, entertainment and live music, and
dancing by night. The idyllic island, where the word lesbian comes from,
was home to Sappho, the ancient poet in 600 BC whose reputation for
relationships with women has secured her a place in queer history.

Thanks to the explosion of interest in Anne Lister, Diva Destinations
now is also offering special year-round guided tours to the new lesbian
mecca: Halifax, and nearby York.

Jen gets it. She recognizes the fervor that is driving thousands of
ardent *Gentleman Jack* fans worldwide to pull out their roller bags, dust
off their passports, and set off for northern England.

"Anne Lister is a real person who has left us this amazing diary,
who had an amazing life, who was true to herself in a time when it
was unheard of, and she managed to steer her way through her life not

deviating from who she was," Jen says. "Finding love, finding adventure, documenting it so we can feel it through her diaries—no one has left anything like that. The fact that she was a lesbian just adds an extra layer to her personality."

As a seasoned tour operator and die-hard Anne Lister enthusiast herself, Jen also knows just what it takes to delight fans with hassle-free arrangements, lovely accommodations, and an unforgettable experience at must-see Anne Lister/Ann Walker venues.

In addition to visits to Shibden Hall, Halifax Minster, and other points of interest in Anne Lister's hometown and environs, Jen offers what independent travelers can't swing on their own, such as a private talk from author and historian Helena Whitbread and special access to Holy Trinity Church where Anne Lister and Ann Walker were symbolically married, each arranged exclusively for *In the Footsteps of Anne Lister* tour participants.

"Oh my word, we've had people in tears on our *Gentleman Jack* tours," Jen says. "When we took our group into the Bankfield Museum in Halifax and there was Helena sitting behind the desk, we had women almost dropping at her feet to thank her for what she's done. When we got private entrance just for our group to the chapel in York where Anne and Ann made their vows to each other, we had women wandering around the church who were just speechless. Our amazing guides took us to places related to Anne Lister that most of us didn't even know existed. The feedback was phenomenal, and many said the experience transformed their lives."

It's one thing to look at photographs of the locations where Anne's life unfolded, and it's quite another to see them in person and connect to the very places where Anne Lister lived, loved, learned, and prayed.

"I had the same reactions as the women on our first tour had," Jen says. "I was blown away, myself, by all I saw. You know, if you're a *Gentleman Jack* or Anne Lister fan, it does almost take over your life to a degree because it's the most amazing true story that has come to the lesbian community. What's wonderful is that it's possible now for people to live and breathe every part of Anne's life."

Besides overseeing Diva Destinations' escorted group tours in England, Europe, and elsewhere, Jen is a co-organizer of the Anne Lister Birthday Week (ALBW), and she'll be taking on an even greater role in managing the event in the future. For the much-anticipated inaugural gathering in 2022, she's in charge of putting together more than a dozen affordable half-day and day-long tours of points of interest in Halifax, and beyond, for attendees. She has selected prestigious Blue Badge Tourist Guides, professionally trained and accredited to conduct tours in selected regions throughout England, to deliver the inside scoop on locations familiar to *Gentleman Jack* fans and Anne Lister enthusiasts.

"I'm so looking forward to ALBW in 2022 after the pandemic forced us to postpone it twice," Jen says. "It's been an amazing journey working on it, and it will just get bigger and bigger. What is exciting is that we know we'll be bringing Anne Lister to a new audience every year as *Gentleman Jack* continues its run and women who are young now will be discovering Anne far into the future."

While *Gentleman Jack* not only has had a huge effect on Jen's business and led to her involvement in ALBW, finding out about Anne Lister and her haunts has touched her personally, too. Jen says it's a hand-in-glove fit.

"There are so many things about her that I admire," she says. "Anne Lister was strong, she was successful, and she stood up against the men in those days when it was unheard of. She was resilient, romantic in her way, and always true to herself. A lot of people have got strength from her from what she went through, thinking if she can do that and be okay and love and be at peace with herself, then so can they. For me and many others, learning about Anne Lister has been life-altering. I wish we could just say 'thank you' to her for all she's done for us."

Besides four or five prepackaged tours available through Diva Destinations each year, the company also can create bespoke tours for smaller groups with particular interests in the United Kingdom and throughout the world. For more information, visit divadestinations.co.uk.

NICKY CHANCE-THOMPSON DL

Halifax, West Yorkshire, England, UK

COME SIT BY ME

When The Piece Hall opened to tremendous fanfare in Halifax in 1779, it was a lively, bustling market with more than 300 separate rooms where wool merchants displayed and sold 30-yard lengths of their handwoven textiles known as pieces in its iconic courtyard. The good times rolled until the 19th century, when factories mechanized fabric production and The Piece Hall began its long slide into obsolescence and disrepair. Fortunately, this sole survivor of Britain's network of great cloth halls was recently rescued and transformed with a £22 million restoration project and a new Trust charged with operating the building.

Now a major international tourist attraction, The Piece Hall is alive again as more than two million visitors come each year to marvel at this expansive, one-of-a-kind-in-the-world Georgian building. Both international tourists and locals delight in strolling among its many independent shops, sampling a variety of cuisines and treats at its bars and restaurants, and enjoying an ever-changing program of concerts and live music events. Nicky Chance-Thompson DL, The Piece Hall's Chief Executive since its reopening to the public in 2017, says this isn't the only famous Halifax attraction making a comeback.

The Piece Hall, established in 1779

Anne Lister is having a revival, too.

"How I came to find out about Anne is quite a fascinating journey," Nicky says. "I discovered her quite by accident 13 years ago when I was helping the canon of Halifax Minster (where Anne is buried) update their website. I found the story of this incredible woman hidden deep in the church's archives."

Nicky was fascinated to learn about a local historical figure whom she instantly recognized as a woman ahead of her time, living bravely and unapologetically two centuries ago. As it happened, around the same time, Nicky's mother-in-law invited her friend and local author Helena Whitbread, a leading authority on Anne Lister's diaries and secret code, to tea. Nicky wondered out loud why more people didn't know about this incredible woman. During their tea time conversation, it became apparent that Anne's scandalous life as a lesbian had been hush-hush for decades, in order to protect the town's reputation.

A dozen years would pass before Sally Wainwright's *Gentleman Jack* let the cat out of the bag and millions of television viewers around the world learned about Anne and her remarkable, unconventional, and, to many, inspirational life.

Thousands of tourists from around the world began pouring into Halifax to experience Anne's hometown, her 600-year-old ancestral home, and her parish church. Included in their itinerary is the town's signature architectural wonder, The Piece Hall, a center of culture and commerce that Anne mentioned in her journal and likely visited during her lifetime.

"Not long after *Gentleman Jack* aired, I met with Sally Wainwright," Nicky says, "and I just said, 'What an amazing thing you have done! You've created a spiritual home for the female gay community. You've done something wonderful for Halifax and created some kind of alchemy here with this incredible story. Anne Lister had always been Halifax's dirty little secret, and you've given her her rightful place in the sun. Well done!'"

As a former Mayoress of Calderdale, Nicky has seen pre- and post-*Gentleman Jack* versions of Halifax up close.

"In a very short space of time, we've had a wonderful moment where the town has gone from one thing to another," she observes. "Due to investment in culture by the Council and the combined Piece Hall and *Gentleman Jack* effect, we have witnessed the transformation of Halifax. What I see now is a tremendous amount of pride in our town, and pride in Anne Lister. I just think she's an incredible role model who's been left out of the history books and taken us all by surprise."

Along with other local dignitaries, Nicky, with her husband Marcus Thompson, then Mayor of Calderdale, was on hand at Shibden Hall on April 3, 2019, on Anne Lister's 228th birthday, where he unveiled the Halifax Civic Trust's historical plaque noting that diarist, businesswoman, traveler, and lesbian Anne Lister had lived at this Halifax landmark from 1815 to 1840.

Anne's once-"scandalous" life is now celebrated during the annual Anne Lister Week, with events and lectures taking place at The Piece Hall and other venues around town. Private guided heritage tours are on offer for those eager to literally follow in Anne Lister's and her wife Ann Walker's footsteps around town.

"It's also important to me that we tell the stories of strong women," Nicky says.

As a great admirer of Anne's important place in the history of all of Yorkshire, she is planning to permanently memorialize Anne with a life-sized sculpture at The Piece Hall, expected to be installed sometime in 2021. She's tapped awarding-winning British sculptor Diane Lawrenson, who previously created the likenesses of Anne's fellow Yorkshirewomen, the three Brontë sisters, for the job of bringing Anne to life in bronze.

"When Diane creates sculptures of her ladies, she absorbs them," Nicky says. "She reads about them, she reads their letters and their books so that she starts to imagine them as if they're in the room with her."

Although Anne Lister is not often thought of as the pensive type, Diane's vision of her has her seated, cross-legged, in a thoughtful pose. The sculpture will have a prominent place in The Piece Hall courtyard where it can be accessible to Anne's many admirers, and visitors can easily interact with it.

"Anne's going to sit there on a bench so that people can sit next to her and be with her, have their picture taken with her, and perhaps even imagine what it would have been like to meet Anne as she was in the 19th century," Nicky says, joking that Anne Lister, as inherently class-conscious as any other gentlewoman of the 1800s, would probably thoroughly disapprove.

"When I found Anne Lister in the archives, I thought she was really intriguing and utterly amazing," Nicky explains. "I think learning more about her gives you confidence to be yourself. She is a really strong, powerful role model, incredibly inspiring and really funny and very witty. The fact that she did what she did in a time when living like she did was frowned upon and considered sinful when it absolutely wasn't, and she just did it anyway—that's something I really like about her."

The ripple effect of Anne Lister's new status in Halifax has touched both locals and tourists. Nicky says it's noticeably boosted local pride, and along with The Piece Hall, has turned Halifax and Calderdale into a vibrant tourist destination with all the economic benefits that come with it. She notes that Anne has left another important mark.

"What's happened since *Gentleman Jack* has been very healing," Nicky says. "Around town we've had some great conversations about Halifax, and of course, prior to that Hebden Bridge, in that both have become a spiritual home for women who have perhaps struggled to have a place they feel connected to, where they are connected to history, and where there is someone they can identify with. It's like Anne's spirit has come alive again. She's actually got her correct place in history now. All of that happened here, and I think it's tremendous. We're very proud of Anne, and we're very proud of Sally."

In 2019 Nicky was appointed as a Deputy Lieutenant by Her Majesty's Lord Lieutenant of West Yorkshire to assist him with his duties as the Queen's representative.

ANGELA CLARE

Halifax, West Yorkshire, England, UK

MY SEXY NOVEL ABOUT ANNE AND ANN

What do you get when you combine an insider's view of history, a steadfast interest in Anne Lister, lesbian sensibilities, and a vivid imagination? If you're Angela Clare and writing under the pseudonym Clara Barley, you get *The Moss House*, a historical novel with 200+ pages of alternating soliloquies delivered by Anne Lister and Ann

Walker. In it, they portray their evolving relationship, beginning in 1832 and through the June night in 1839 when they slip away from Shibden Hall for their final trip together to Russia.

Anne's and Ann's first-person fictional musings in Clara Barley's first published novel depict what their inner thoughts and emotions might have been. It's a stark departure from what Angela Clare conveys in her professional life as the collections manager for the Calderdale Museums Service, which oversees Shibden Hall and three other museums in the borough.

"My job is to share stories," Angela says. "With Anne Lister, we have so many different elements to talk about. She was so clever, she left diaries, she climbed mountains, and then of course we have her house. And she was gay. I am really glad we can talk about so many different aspects of her life. She checks lots of boxes."

Angela can't help but be touched by working at Shibden Hall, she says.

"I think Anne's diaries bring you close to her and what she was doing," she explains. "To me, there's also something very interesting about being where somebody lived and slept and had their emotions and even lost people. Walking through the Hall and realizing I see something that belonged to her, or these were portraits of her relatives that she had reframed, or this was her room—it just brings me even closer to her."

It's Angela, the historian, who uncovers and presents engaging facts about Shibden's most famous and infamous owner. She's written a guidebook to Shibden Hall and a short biography about Anne Lister that are available online or at the hall. She coordinates exhibitions and events that shine a light on the 19th century context of Anne Lister's life and accomplishments. In 2016, she produced *The Anne Lister Story*, a

26-minute interview with Lister authority Helena Whitbread, that gives visitors to Shibden Hall or its website a glimpse into the life and times of the remarkable Miss Lister.

"Helena knows so much," Angela says. "The things she was telling me were amazing, and many of them hadn't even been included in her books. I literally ran home afterwards and started making notes. I started to write about Anne and Ann then, and over the next few years I realized what I was writing was turning into a novel."

The setting Angela had in mind for her book was as real as its characters. In the late summer of 1832, Anne Lister built a *chaumière* on the grounds of her Shibden estate as a private and safe refuge where she could woo Ann Walker—an intimate place she herself often referred to as her moss hut. In *The Moss House*, Angela takes creative license to imagine and express each woman's perspective on life, love, and the struggles they faced during their initial courtship, eventual marriage, and often tumultuous life together at Shibden Hall.

"I wanted to tell Anne's story in my own way," Angela says. "The thing about Anne's journals that hooks a lot of people is sex and the fact that Anne Lister writes about it. Not only was she gay but she was having sex regularly, and a lot. Most writings skirt around the topic. Two women get together and they go into the bedroom. You don't get details. That's what's missing in most women's stories. Or some writings are about sex with no story. I thought it was important to bring those two together, so I included some steamy parts in this love story because Ann and Anne had quite a passionate relationship that I wanted to bring to life."

A chance encounter with Sally Wainwright in the kitchen at Shibden Hall led to a rewarding outcome.

"Sally mentioned she was working on a television show about Anne

Lister," Angela says. "Of course, that piqued my interest. I decided I'd better get on with it and finish my novel. And since I'm an actress, I also hoped perhaps I might even be able to audition for a part."

Good things came Angela's way. She did land a small role in Wainwright's *Gentleman Jack* series in 2019, appearing in Episode 7 as Mrs. Watson, Mariana Lawton's ladies' maid. *The Moss House* also was published the same year, and Angela began working on her next novel, one she anticipates will be available first on Kindle.

"It's called *The Meer House*, and it's a prequel that again uses first-person voices, but this time for Anne Lister and Mariana Lawton to talk about their love affair," Angela explains. "Meer is the name Anne gave to the lake she created on her estate. When they took the sacrament together to cement their relationship, Anne wanted Mariana to live with her at Shibden. In my story, I imagine she told Mariana—whom I believe was the love of her life—that she was building a little house by the lake and would call it Meer House so they could be together in total privacy. It was never built, as Mariana married someone else, but Anne's idea came to light again when she met Ann Walker and created *The Moss House* for her. My next book covers Anne and Mariana's complicated relationship from 1812 to after Anne's death in 1840."

With so many new stories to tell about Shibden Hall, Angela showcased many of them in a new exhibition for Shibden's 600th anniversary in 2021. While the exhibition celebrates the many families over the centuries who've called Shibden Hall home, no one has left a more indelible mark than Anne Lister.

"Two hundred years on, Anne's touch defines Shibden today," Angela notes. "She landscaped the grounds very much the way we see them now. She built the lake, the waterfall, the gatehouse, and wings on both sides of the house. She expanded the house body and added the carved Lister lion and even her initials to the house's staircase. But her legacy is more than the property she left behind. The courage she showed to live her life as she chose continues to inspire women all over the world, and her experiences of love, life, and loss are as relatable today as back then. I'm so pleased my job is to share her amazing story."

To order publications about Anne Lister and Shibden Hall or to view Helena Whitbread's video about Anne Lister, visit www.calderdale.gov.uk/museums. The Moss House is available on Amazon and at The Book Corner in Halifax.

KIRSTY DAVIES

Halifax, West Yorkshire, UK

MY RAINBOW TRIBE

For many of us, time can be measured in two ways: BGJ (Before *Gentleman Jack*) and AGJ (After *Gentleman Jack*). Kirsty Davies' BGJ life was quiet and happy. She and her husband and teenage daughter enjoyed their lovely home overlooking the moors of Halifax just minutes from Shibden Hall. She enjoyed her job as a teaching assistant. Her friendship circle was wide and well-established.

Then *Gentleman Jack* appeared, airing first on HBO in the United States in April 2019 before its debut in the United Kingdom four weeks later.

"I saw the very first episode when it was shown on the BBC in May, and I just couldn't wait for the rest," Kirsty says. "I downloaded a streaming site so I could watch what was already showing on HBO. At first, I was taken with the show because of the script, the humor, the scenery, and the fact that Shibden is just down the road from me. But watching it over and over again, I began to have more appreciation for Anne Lister as a person, businesswoman, as somebody who stood out from a crowd and did her own thing and lived her life authentically."

Growing up seven miles (11 km) away from Halifax in nearby Huddersfield, Kirsty had heard of Anne Lister. As a child, she'd gone on school trips and regular Sunday afternoon family outings to Shibden Hall. As an adult, she'd seen the 2010 Maxine Peake film and the Sue Perkins BBC documentary about Anne Lister, and she'd read Helena Whitbread's book *I Know My Own Heart*. While she found all of it interesting, Anne Lister's story was easy to set aside.

Then her long hiatus from Anne Lister came to an abrupt end when she joined the *Gentleman Jack* Fans (HBO and BBC One TV Show) private Facebook group, and her AGJ life took off like a rocket.

"The membership was very small at first," Kirsty recalls. "Early on people would introduce themselves and say they were from so and so, and I'd say, 'Hi, I'm Kirsty from Halifax,' and the response would be, 'Oh my God, how lucky you are, and if we ever come to Halifax, would you like to meet for a coffee?' and I'd say, 'Sure, why not?' That's how I got the request from two women in Wales to meet up and show them around some of the filming locations because they didn't know where they were."

The trio got together at Shibden Hall, launching a cascade of events that transformed Kirsty's AGJ life.

"When I walked into the reception hall I was engulfed in an enormous hug from a complete stranger," Kirsty says. "And we hit it off straightaway, like a house on fire. We had a lovely day seeing the sights, and we got on so well that we arranged to meet again later for the heritage weekend that the Calderdale Council organized."

When they met again—this time standing in line to get into Shibden Hall—Kirsty and her new Welsh friends struck up a conversation with other women in the queue, and the group, now numbering 10, ended up going to lunch together and visiting other Halifax points of interest. They all made plans to meet again in two weeks for the Anne Lister Walk.

"I was really nervous because I worried how we might all get on outside of the confines of Shibden," Kirsty admits. "But we all just hit it off, and we've met each other at least once a month ever since. We message each other every day, and we talk all the time. We call ourselves 'the tribe,' and it's just been brilliant. We had a lockdown barbecue in my garage a few months ago, and when we couldn't do Pride in 2020 because of the coronavirus pandemic, we did Pride in my garage too."

While the tight-knit tribe is now an important and permanent fixture in Kirsty's AGJ life, her outreach to other *Gentleman Jack* fans hasn't stopped, and her role as a self-appointed, one-woman Halifax Welcoming Committee and Occasional Guide Service continues. She estimates that she has personally met more than 100 women making their pilgrimages to Halifax, and she can count another 20 that she's met on Zoom.

Every day Kirsty's inbox is filled with messages from her new friends from around the world. She participates in Lister Sister gift and postcard exchanges. She meets up with women touring around Halifax, York, and other locations in *Gentleman Jack* territory. Her daughter has even coined a new phrase for Kirsty's newfound passion—she calls it "Listering."

"I'm very lucky," Kirsty says. "My 'Listering' is fabulous and a lot of fun. It has massively affected my husband and my daughter, but they've been very tolerant. I am mindful of taking care of my family, so we balance it."

Reflecting on her post-*Gentleman Jack* life, Kirsty says the TV show opened up a world to her that she didn't know even existed nor ever imagined she would be part of.

"If you asked me two years ago where I'd be in 2021, I never would have thought I would be where I am now with these amazing women that I adore. I've learned so much from them that I didn't know much about. I was puttering along as a perfectly contented 50-year-old housewife, and suddenly I'm in the middle of this LGBTQ+ community, and they've taken me on board as their token straight woman and made me one of their own."

Through the tribe's eyes, Kirsty has been exposed to a world she has never experienced.

"I sat up in my ivory tower with my nice, middle-class white privilege, and I've since come to see and realize the difficulties I perceived for gay women are far, far worse than I knew, and it really breaks my heart," Kirsty says. "Now I wear my rainbow bracelet with pride, and I see that sometimes in the supermarket people look at me in a strange way. Just that little gesture reminds me of the really serious trials and tribulations that my friends still face. It means the world to me that one of the tribe recently sent me a rainbow badge with the word 'Ally' on it, and I am glad to be a jolly good one."

For Kirsty, the effect of *Gentleman Jack* has had personal repercussions well beyond making new friendships and developing a more enlightened view of LGBTQ+ experiences.

"I consider it an absolute privilege and pleasure to be part of this wonderful global community of fabulous people," Kirsty says. "Besides that, Anne Lister has definitely changed my attitude toward difficult situations, and I stand up for myself far more. I used to be a bit of a lame duck, and I would let people walk all over me. Not anymore. *Gentleman Jack* has brought new life into my world."

BRIAN HILDRED

Ovenden, West Yorkshire, England, UK

MEMORIES OF SHIBDEN HALL

In the late 1940s, in the midst of enduring postwar austerity, people in England, Wales, and Scotland had something celebrate. At midnight on July 5, 1948, the United Kingdom became the first nation in the world to offer its citizens free healthcare. Just ten minutes later, Brian Hildred was born in Calderdale, West Yorkshire, the first national health baby in history.

"That's my claim to fame," Brian jokes. "Every time there's a party to celebrate the National Health Service (NHS), I'm the guest of honor."

Of course, Brian has his own reasons for celebrating these days, and the NHS has played a role in that as well. In the past two and a half years he's survived two bouts with life-threatening cancer, and says, thanks to the UK's healthcare system, he feels lucky to be alive.

"I just feel fortunate that I can do what I can do now," he says. "Every day is a bonus."

What Brian can do, and what he most likes to do, is paint. One of his favorite subjects is Shibden Hall, located just two miles (3+ km) from his home in the village of Ovenden.

"When I were a boy, my dad used to take me to Shibden Hall," Brian explains. "We used to have picnics and go boating. Boating were brilliant when you're only about 7 or 8. I also liked the barn because there were always a coal fire going in the corner because that were back in the 50s and 60s. Shibden were a joy of my early life."

His affection for Shibden hasn't faded in the ensuing 65 years. He and his wife of more than 50 years still regularly walk around the grounds, and he continues adding to his collection of photographs that he uses as reference for his acrylic and watercolor paintings. He has his favorite vantage points of the old house and its grounds.

"You can paint it in many different ways," Brian says. "There are certain views, like the front of the house, that are very popular that you can show in the most wonderful way. It can be in autumn or summer or winter. In watercolor, you can use different sorts of washes to make it looser. You can make it as detailed as you want, and that's what I like to do. All of my paintings are originals, and none is exactly the same."

Brian wasn't always an artist. He spent his career keeping track of stock at a local

Exterior Lister Lion,
Shibden Hall

brewery before retiring and taking up painting full-time at the age of 60. He went to night school and took a few art classes, but he says over the years he has perfected his skills and taught himself how best to capture a landscape or a building. Among his subjects are popular Halifax attractions, including The Piece Hall and Halifax Minster.

"I'm painting better now than I've ever done," he says. "I don't know why that is, but perhaps because it's because of my relaxing and taking my time. I've gotten more professional as I've gone on, and I have an agent and a gallery that represents me so I can just focus on painting. I paint what I like now because I'm not chasing money like I used to do when I were younger."

In those bygone days, Brian recalls, few tourists visited Halifax, and it was mostly locals who came to Shibden Hall to make use of its park land, lake, and small café. He recalls a time when a mock Tudor house sat on the edge of the lake that Anne Lister added to her property in the 1830s.

"It were amazing," Brian says. "I used to do pictures of the little house and everybody loved them. The building didn't have a purpose and you could walk in front and around it. It were pulled down in the 60s, which were a big shame. I think they were trying to modernize things, but sometimes you've got to be better and leave things."

There wasn't any talk of Anne Lister's sexuality back then, Brian recalls, and her reputation revolved around her unique role as a female landowner and strong-minded woman. He says he's glad that the fact that she was a lesbian can come out now.

Naturally, Brian is a big fan of *Gentleman Jack*.

"Suranne Jones does a really good job of showing Anne Lister as a strong woman, tough as nails, but she's got this tender side," he says. "I really like that. Now when you're at Shibden Hall, you can just imagine what Shibden were like with Anne Lister in it, and it's really nice. She's brought the whole place to life, and this program has brought something to Shibden in a big way."

As a proud Yorkshire native, Brian thinks *Gentleman Jack* has been a boon for Halifax. He appreciates the many improvements he sees at Shibden Hall now, too.

"It's been brilliant for the town," he says. "It's made Halifax talked about when it were just a little backwater. With more filming, it's going to continue for some considerable time, which will be good."

Brian adds that *Gentleman Jack* has rejuvenated his interest in Anne Lister, too.

"Before, we'd never had a visualization of her apart from a picture of her they kept somewhere else," he observes. "Now there's a human feel to the place as opposed to it being a museum, and I really like that."

As he reflects on the role Shibden Hall has played throughout his life, Brian says it's been both an inspiration for much of his artwork and a source of joy.

"I think a lot of it has to do with where my parents used to take me when I were little," he says. "We always had good times at Shibden. Always. So I have good childhood memories that stick with me. And not only that, when my sister had children, we used to all go together with her children and with my son. We've just passed it from one generation to the next if you like. Shibden Hall is super—really super."

Fans interested in Brian's work can visit his page on Pinterest or contact Studio 9 in Elland, West Yorkshire (studio9.photography).

∞

COMMUNITIES & FRIENDSHIPS

CONNECTIONS AMONG GENTLEMAN JACK'S PEOPLE

PAT ESGATE

Nyack, New York, USA

A MOMENT AT THE MINSTER

From her vantage point in the third row at the Halifax Minster, Pat Esgate watched as hundreds of women streamed in and took their seats in the gated pews of the 12th century church. It was a bright summer evening in July 2019, and they'd all come to hear from Helena Whitbread and Jill Liddington, preeminent Anne Lister scholars.

The excitement was palpable. *Gentleman Jack* had just wrapped up its final episode on the BBC, and freshly minted Anne Lister fans from around the world were eager to hear accounts of this remarkable 19th century woman whose spirit, intelligence, and self-acceptance of her nature had vaulted her to instant heroine status among them.

As the program and accompanying Q&A session drew to a close, there was time for a final question. Sensing that this was her opportunity, Pat stood up. The audience was church-quiet and still.

"This isn't a question," Pat said. "It's more of a comment. If you follow social media, read the posts from people who've seen the show, who now read the diaries—*you are actively changing people's lives.*"

Pat continued to direct her remarks to Helena and Jill.

"People talk about increased confidence. They talk about the things they set out to do that they are now doing. They are *proud* of themselves. You have taken a major step forward for women, and I thank you for that," she concluded, and the audience burst into applause.

Pat turned around and saw a sea of tear-streaked faces.

"It was astounding—I could actually see the impact this show and this evening had on every woman in that audience," she says.

Following the talk, she was inundated with thank you's from women eager to share their excitement. Later, over a pint at the centuries-old Ring O' Bells pub across the street from the Minster, Pat wondered how she might share that collective experience with others.

"I want everyone to be in the Minster," she explains. "I want everyone to feel the power of being in the place where Anne Lister was baptized and buried, where she came—regularly—to commune with God, certain in her knowledge that she was exactly who God had intended her to be, had *created* her to be."

Anne's confidence, Pat believes, came from her inner certainty that she had the right to be who she was meant to be, regardless of what others might think or say.

"That's a huge realization, especially if you've been born and raised in a society that says you should feel shame, that you should seek help, that you are not acceptable," Pat says. "It's really quite phenomenal, and it is breathtakingly life-changing. Life-*affirming*."

The die was cast.

Pat returned to her home in the United States and couldn't put aside the excitement of what she'd felt in the Minster. She began to weigh options for organizing a similar event at the Minster in 2020, wanting to allow plenty of time for fans to plan ahead. She says her initial idea was to organize a reprise of Jill's and Helena's talks, but when each woman accepted her invitation to speak—moments that left Pat stunned, she admits—she began wondering what else she might add to make the journey worth it for those who'd be spending a tidy sum to get to Halifax. Never being one to shy away from a challenge, Pat reached out to Sally Wainwright, asking if she might come to the Minster as well.

"I sent her several paragraphs, certain she'd need all sorts of coaxing," Pat says, "But five minutes later, there was an email in my inbox that

Halifax Minster

simply said, 'I'd be delighted,' and that's how the Anne Lister Birthday Weekend (ALBW) was born."

Over the course of the next few weeks three days of activities fell into place, and Pat recruited an enthusiastic group of women to help.

"They had to be volunteers," Pat says. "ALBW was never meant to be a money-making venture. It always was a work of heart. I'm still astounded by their response, and I thank my lucky stars every day for my wonderful team."

On a Saturday in early November 2019, 800 ALBW tickets went up for sale on an online ticket exchange.

"I was hoping we'd sell 200 tickets," Pat says, "just enough to cover our costs at the Minster for three nights of use."

She laughs now when recalls what happened next.

"It was like watching an avalanche. We were completely sold out in 20 minutes!"

Pat kept adding events to make sure everyone would have plenty to do. As soon as more tickets were posted, they also were quickly snatched up. Pat, her team, and more than 1,000 *Gentleman Jack* fans were beside themselves with anticipation and excitement at the prospect of a joyous gathering of women from all over the world.

Then the Covid pandemic struck, shutting down the world and forcing postponement of ALBW.

"You can't imagine the disappointment," Pat sighs, her dejection still fresh. "But I've never been one to stop at the first roadblock."

As Pat was toying with options for a new date, the phone rang.

"Sally Wainwright called and said she knew how disappointed I must be, having to cancel after all the work we'd put in," Pat says. Could she lighten the blow a bit? Maybe do an online interview instead of being at the Minster?

"You could have knocked me over with a feather," Pat laughs. "Sally Wainwright. *The* Sally Wainwright, caring enough about our event to make that offer."

Suddenly ALBW 2020 was back and under a new name—ALBW Live—with Pat hosting livestreamed interviews with every presenter on the original program. Sally had two more surprises to add to the online mix: actor Suranne Jones, who had brought Anne Lister to life in *Gentleman Jack*, and O'Hooley & Tidow, whose jaunty "Jack the Lass" hallmark song wraps up every *Gentleman Jack* episode.

The revamped weekend was a rousing success, leaving the expanding *Gentleman Jack* (and Anne Lister) fan base still hungry for more information about the historical figures in the series and insights about the making of the show.

Next, Pat and her team created a vital lifeline to fans during the pandemic with even more livestreamed interviews. A welcome staple during 2020 and 2021, Pat's conversations included members of the *Gentleman Jack* production team, authors, historians, researchers, and others. To date, ALBW Live has offered more than 20 livestreams, and even more are scheduled in the future.

The online Anne Lister Birthday Weekend officially cemented Pat's relationship with the worldwide audience of *Gentleman Jack* fans. This assertive American, so charmed by Anne Lister that she felt compelled to host a big 229th birthday bash for her, has become the leader of the pack of women as enamored of *Gentleman Jack* and Anne Lister as she.

"I wasn't expecting what happened as a result of ALBW," Pat says. "It started out as a simple destination event, something that would allow all the people online to meet one another in person. But the ongoing passion for it has been a real amazement to me. Never doubt the power of real connection!"

While the ALBW in-person event was rescheduled for 2021 in Halifax, Pat and her crew faced the possibility of another postponement as they continued to navigate tricky pandemic waters.

"We are fully committed to ALBW, and it *will* happen," Pat says with fierce determination. "It will definitely be back in all of its planned glory in 2022. There are just too many of us waiting to be reunited in the Minster. You can only interact on social media for so long!"

With the demands of ALBW, ALBW Live, and her role on the steering committee of the newly formed Anne Lister Society, Pat says it's been a nonstop, two-year whirlwind.

"I never expected, when I first walked into Shibden Hall in 2019, that my little UK side trip would lead me anywhere other than the satisfaction of my own curiosity," Pat reflects. "But it's so much more than that."

Pat says it was Anne Lister's authenticity—her intense focus on being exactly who she was, to the greatest extent she could be in her own time—that really touched her.

"I absolutely identified with Anne Lister right from the get-go. I felt that she was like me, and I was like her. I feel a very real and very deep connection to Anne. Meeting her in *Gentleman Jack* prompted me to think about how we find our authentic selves. Even in my own life—and I've been out since 1969, always politically active—I've had to work to discover who I really am, and that's an ongoing discussion. Anne Lister offers such an intriguing roadmap, especially to such a work in progress as myself."

Pat speculates where the *Gentleman Jack*/Anne Lister path may take her.

"There comes a time," Pat says, "later in life—I will be 70 in 2021—where one starts to wonder what footprint she might leave behind, what good one may have done for others. I'm proud of what I did during that early Gay Liberation part of my life, opening the door to a closet that people now slam right through. ALBW and the Anne Lister Society I'm involved with feel like the opposite end of that journey for me, a sort of legacy to leave behind. I hope they have value, that they help people in their own struggles to come to terms with who they are. I hope it all leads to each and every one of us realizing that, like Anne, we have every right to be as and who we were created to be. I hope it encourages others to find their own inner Anne Lister, and their own mission in life."

Pat's commitment to celebrate Anne Lister's life and its impact on women in general, and lesbians in particular, isn't lost on fans who now recognize Pat Esgate as an icon in the *Gentleman Jack* community. Their gratitude, respect, and admiration isn't lost on her, either.

"The reaction that people have had to ALBW, and to me, has been overwhelming. It opened my eyes, again, to what kind of impact you can have on other people with a positive point of view," Pat says. "It rekindled my sense of community and my feeling that I had a duty to help others on their path to self-acceptance. I don't think that mission ever ends, and ALBW gave me a new megaphone for that."

Pat can take pride in what will surely be among ALBW's long-lasting contributions. She's hosting forums that have greatly expanded our knowledge about the exemplary Anne Lister and other strong women who played a role in Anne's life. She's reminded us that we have a right to be who we are and live accordingly. She's established a much-needed safe community for women to be themselves, make new friends, and support one another. All of this has happened in the short span of two years—without a single person having yet been a guest at the much-anticipated Mother of All Birthday Parties in Halifax.

Pat's assessment of what draws us to Anne Lister rings true.

"Anne Lister is at the top of my 'who would I like to have had dinner with' list," Pat says. "I don't think there could ever be enough time to pick that woman's brain. Her curiosity—there was hardly anything she wasn't interested in—and her self-confidence is just so inspiring. Any time she faced a roadblock, she found the workaround. No matter what, she just kept right on going."

Pat's global fan club could say the same thing about *her*.

ALBW and ALBW Live have been a team effort from the start. Jennifer Grant, Cheryl MacDonald, Rachel Lappin, Steph Gallaway, Livia Labate, and Kat Williams are unsung heroes, and Pat extends kudos and her appreciation for their hard work, tech savvy, and good humor.

JESSICA JOHNSON

Felton, California, USA

POSTS, COMMENTS, REACTIONS, OH MY!

Seven days after the debut of *Gentleman Jack* on the HBO network in the United States in April 2019, the first fan page for the series—*Gentleman Jack* Fans (HBO and BBC One TV Show)—popped up on Facebook. In less than 90 days, membership had surged to 8,000 people worldwide.

Among the fan page's earliest members, Jess Johnson didn't take long to find herself as one of three captains of the *Gentleman Jack* social media mother ship, a position she holds to this day.

"I joined the fan group shortly after it was formed and was fairly active," Jess says. "I wanted to be a site administrator to give back to a community that I felt was so positive. It is a group that is so nontoxic and such a good collective of folks. Some of our members live in environments that are hostile toward the LBGTQ+ community, so this site is a place of support and where people can express themselves."

Growing up in the 1990s, Jess weathered her share of inhospitable conditions, both inside and outside her home. But it didn't hold her back from donning a helmet and a pair of quad skates as a blocker on the Santa Cruz Derby Girls, a roller derby team in California, that boosted her confidence and secured lifelong friendships. Jess proudly skated under the name of Sally *Pride* #1983 in honor of Sally Ride, the first American woman in space and the first acknowledged gay astronaut.

"I was a very awkward teenager, and I carry that sort of social anxiety with me to this day though now I understand it better and can deal with it," she explains. "Like many, I didn't have the level of engagement or social support that would have made such a difference for me. I was drawn to *Gentleman Jack* because it is the story of two women who learned to be who they are and be accepting of that, and forge a path in a society that didn't welcome them. I was drawn to the fan site because I could relate to these characters, I really enjoyed the show, and I felt very connected to it."

Jess has found plenty of kindred spirits among *Gentleman Jack* enthusiasts. The fan site's membership has grown to more than 10,000 members representing 100 countries on every continent except

Antarctica. The fan site sees an average of 3,500 posts, comments, and reactions every day. Since its inception, it has logged more than 2 million engagements.

Jess acknowledges that the show's storyline, its production quality, the fourth wall breaks, and the contributions of every person who had a role in it—from producers and crew to its writer and actors—are reasons why she and thousands more remain engaged with *Gentleman Jack*.

"We all want to see ourselves reflected in art and media and to feel validated in that way," Jess says. "Having powerful and strong women, especially queer women, so positively represented is still too rare. *Gentleman Jack* is just not typical of what we see on our screens every day. *Gentleman Jack* is what art should be. The story of Anne Lister and Ann Walker builds on the perception that love is love—and that it's normal, and it's okay. It shows their relationship as just another example of the cornucopia of life, which is infinitely diverse and creative. Art opens all of us up to a wealth of experiences, and it should give us the ability to reflect on what we are seeing and grow from it."

That growth takes many forms. For die-hard fans, it has often meant expanding their knowledge and finding out more about the real Anne Lister and Ann Walker. Jess is happy to see so many posts on the site from members involved in transcribing Anne's diaries.

"Our isn't a fandom of a fictionalized character," Jess notes. "There is a tenacity among fans to know more about Anne Lister and to go through the scraps of history that are left to find out more about her. That's very cool to see. I'm also hoping more information comes out about Ann Walker, what she went through and how she coped in such a difficult time after Anne died."

Jess is especially glad that the fan site has served as a go-to place for camaraderie and conversation. For herself, it's also meant the development of close ties with Robin Trousdale, Taryn Abbott, and Rachel Newman, who also manage and moderate the fan page.

"Ours is definitely not a one-person operation. I get to work with awesome folks who are very welcoming and very accepting, and it's nice that we have the same intentions," Jess says. "It doesn't matter that we've never actually met in person. It's like so many other relationships that have come out of our site. They may have started out with the love for *Gentleman Jack*, but that has expanded to the creation of many new friendships."

Jess believes that the storytelling in *Gentleman Jack* has had a dramatic impact on its many fans. She sees the show's portrayal of Anne Lister's depth of character as an opportunity for women to discover a piece of Anne—or Ann Walker—in themselves. She says the value of the support that the fan site offers can't be underestimated.

"I think continued representation always will be good for the LGBTQ+ community," Jess says. "If the single effect is that people just feel better about themselves, that's big. It's like gay icon RuPaul says: 'If you can't love yourself, how in the hell you gonna love somebody else?'"

As thousands of comments posted on the Facebook site bear out, the online community that has sprung up in response to *Gentleman Jack* reinforces the sense of self-acceptance that many in the LBGTQ+ community now feel.

"The community resulting from *Gentleman Jack* has been nothing short of phenomenal," Jess says. "And it's so important in these times to see the good that humanity can collectively do together. For some of our members, this is their first exposure to being part of a gay community. Our group offers a place where people finally can be themselves."

The *Gentleman Jack* Fans (HBO and BBC One TV Show) Facebook page remains the largest social media platform devoted to all things *Gentleman Jack.*

"There are lots of amazing splinters of all forms, like other Facebook groups, Twitter, Instagram, and podcasts," Jess says. "I'm glad about that, and I hope that our group continues to serve as a kind of hub, not just for our site to continue to build and grow, but also to bring in these other groups and just share in a passion for *Gentleman Jack.*"

Jess expects a big surge in members when Season 2 airs and more new viewers discover Anne Lister and Ann Walker and the online community that is so crazy about them.

"I'm excited about that," she says. "There's always something engaging and fresh to see when somebody falls in love with what you fall in love with. Finding this community has gone a long way toward making me and thousands of other people feel more accepted by society. I believe there is a ripple effect from a series like this and a community like ours. It is a momentous thing, even if it's singular, to feel comfortable in your own skin and to feel your own self-acceptance. From that point, you're able to grow outwards in every interaction you have. You can never put the genie back in the bottle, can you?"

∞

LEANNE MERTZMAN & MARY SCHWARTZ

Los Angeles, California, USA & Tallahassee, Florida, USA

CAN WE TALK?

*L*ooking back, Leanne Mertzman and Mary Schwartz agree it was their total fan girl freak-out that launched one of the most popular *Gentleman Jack* offshoots. Leanne couldn't stop making *Gentleman Jack* GIFs and posting them on Tumblr. Mary couldn't stop replaying every scene from *Gentleman Jack* in her head.

"I felt so connected to Anne Lister—it was like, 'she gets it, she knows I'm here,'" Leanne says. "My wife really wasn't all that interested in watching the show, so I didn't have anyone to talk to about it for so long. I went on Tumblr, and Mary showed up."

"After I watched *Gentleman Jack*, I needed to find other lesbians to talk to about this," Mary says. "I immediately thought, 'This is our story,' and I landed on Tumblr because it was the only place I could find where people were talking about the show. I saw Leanne's blog, and I just messaged her to see if she had any interest in doing a podcast."

This is what *Gentleman Jack* does to us: a woman in Florida just picks up the phone on a Monday and calls a complete stranger in California who's just as entranced by *Gentleman Jack* as she and says, "How about doing a podcast with me?" and, of course, the complete stranger in California says "OK!"

Four days later, these 30-somethings are recording their first episode of Shibden After Dark (SAfD) dishing on Episode 1 of *Gentleman Jack*, offering enthusiastic analysis of Marian Lister's rolling eyes, the High

Flyer scene, and the genius of fourth wall breaks.

So what that they don't even know each other, that they're on opposite sides of the country, and that neither has ever done a podcast before? *Gentleman Jack* inspires us to take chances and do things we've never done before.

It's no surprise that Shibden After Dark was an instant hit. It appeared at the dawn of unbridled *Gentleman Jack* obsession sweeping around the world, and it was exactly what many viewers wanted and needed. We could listen to two queer women talk about all aspects of *Gentleman Jack* while taking comfort that we weren't the only ones having such a baffling and unfathomable reaction to a TV show and rejoicing that we'd finally found *our people*. Once Leanne and Mary got the SAfD Facebook group going, it was easy to engage with people from around the globe.

Leanne and Mary's Sunday podcasts kept everyone connected before and during the coronavirus pandemic lockdowns, sometimes with as many as 8,000 people listening to a single episode. Topics were always changing.

"*Gentleman Jack* and what it's doing to us was something that needed to be talked about," Leanne says. "But we also wanted the podcast to be a forum to talk about things our community has never talked about before."

In the beginning, Leanne and Mary used their podcast to dissect each *Gentleman Jack* episode. From there, the pair moved on to talking about their favorite movies and TV shows, and one thing leading to another brought them to discussions about what it's like to be queer. No subjects were off limits.

"The show gave us a platform on which to talk about issues that matter to other lesbians and bisexual women," Mary says. "One of my favorite episodes was the 'sexpisode'. Sex is something a lot of gay women are uncomfortable talking about because there aren't many people to have that conversation with, so it was a perfect topic for us."

"It wasn't just talking about sex and things that always have been so taboo," Leanne adds. "It's about normalizing what gay women feel and do, and ways that women get turned on. Of course the sex part is great, but it's also the buildup and the slow burn. I think we captured the giggly excitement of that."

In the first conversation Leanne and Mary had about their format they talked about what their podcast might do.

"We thought it would be successful if just one person listened to it and didn't feel alone—like some kid in the middle of Nebraska would hear it and be like, 'this isn't the rest of my life. I can grow up and get out of here and find somebody to find love and it will be ok,'" Mary says. "We wanted queer people to know we're completely normal, there's nothing wrong with us, and there are other people in the world who feel like we do who are successful, happy, and functioning gay adults."

"We also wanted to make something for 15-year-old Leanne Mertzman, who needed a show like *Gentleman Jack*," Leanne adds. "And we wanted this to be a podcast that we, as young gay women, would have wanted to listen to."

Shibden After Dark quickly grew beyond a weekly podcast to become an online global community of more than 2,000 gay and straight women, and counting. The private SAfD Facebook group is like a small town with different neighborhoods and a diverse population of women, from 20-year-old Gen Zs to 80-year-olds of the Silent Generation, all with eclectic interests and a variety of experiences. Within the community, any and everything goes. There's cyber Anne Lister University, Zoom hangouts, watch parties, finance and fitness groups, and even an ongoing discussion about vibrator recommendations. The Shibden After Dark website has a store for *Gentleman Jack* merch and a Patreon that keeps the Zoom Rooms open and the website up and running.

The complete Shibden After Dark package has had a far-reaching and unexpected impact on its enthusiasts and its creators.

"Did we have any idea that it was going to turn into this family of people all over the world who feel like really, really close friends now, or that people would meet and fall in love, or they'd give advice and help each other with all kinds of problems?" Leanne says. "No, I had no idea that would happen."

Leanne and Mary have been witnesses to a variety of changes among their followers.

"We're seeing women who are more liberated, more willing to have open conversations, even willing to investigate their sexuality," Mary says. "Our podcasts also incited such an appetite for women to find their place in LGBTQ+ history."

"Personally, I know I am a more confident person than I was before all this started," Leanne says. "I think our community now has more confident people who feel like they can be a little louder and are a bit more comfortable with who they are. We all want to live our most authentic selves, and our Facebook group has helped people be able to do that. The really cool part is that your authentic self is the best version of yourself, and you don't have to worry about reining yourself in because you think you're too gay, or too much of this or too much of that."

Their podcast undertaking has paid off for Leanne and Mary in personal ways too.

"What I got from Shibden After Dark is Mary," Leanne says.

Mary echoes the sentiment.

"Definitely Leanne's friendship is the No. 1 thing I've gotten out of Shibden After Dark," she says. "This is probably the first time in my life that I've had a gay friend, and especially one as close to me as Leanne is. Just sitting down every week and having a focused time for us to talk has brought up a lot of things I have previously been unwilling to talk about. It's hard to know how to be a gay person when you have no representation, and you grow up like I did in the deep South where homosexuality is such a big sin. Being able to talk about painful things and not just ignore them and keep on going—I'm very Anne Lister in that 'I'm always alright'—has been great for me."

The success and popularity of Shibden After Dark has led Leanne and Mary to believe they're doing something bigger than themselves. They say they feel a certain moral and ethical responsibility to continue providing information and encouragement to their fan base.

"At this point, what we're doing feels almost like a calling," Leanne says. "Mary and I recognize our place in a long line of people who have come before us and have had to make huge sacrifices. We feel like we're the next ones to be carrying the torch to make things better for our community. It's rewarding to feel that we are contributing to incremental changes in people's lives and changing people's minds. At least I hope we are."

"What kept us going week after week was hearing the stories of how our audience was feeling so validated," Mary says. "They knew they weren't the only ones having such an intense reaction to *Gentleman Jack*, and as gay women, they weren't alone. That became such a driving force for us to keep doing what we're doing even when it felt so exhausting."

It's the rare lesbian who escapes the scourge of gay pain, a condition that some psychologists have begun referring to as gayngst (a mash-up of gay and angst). Whatever its name, the ache derives from fear, shame, family rejection, self-doubt, loneliness, and social disapproval that plague so many of us whose nature and preferences dictate whom we love. For thousands of its fans, *Gentleman Jack* has been an antidote to this darkness. Shibden After Dark is medicine for its symptoms. Leanne suspects the reason why.

"I think Shibden After Dark is filling the holes in our hearts with love," she says.

Gentleman Jack *merchandise and a library of 46 podcast episodes are available at ShibdenAfterDark.com.*

STACEY BROOKS

Norman, Oklahoma, USA

THE LISTER SISTERHOOD

*I*n the Before Time—those heady, glorious days of first watching *Gentleman Jack* in 2019, before countless global friendships formed around shared interests and newfound 19th century heroines, before Covid appeared in 2020 and upended meetups and everything else—fans began turning to social media to connect with one another and share information about their new favorite TV show.

The rules that governed the original private *Gentleman Jack* HBO and BBC One Facebook fan page restricted comments to those having a direct tie to *Gentleman Jack* or to the real historical figures it depicted. Since *Gentleman Jack* enthusiasts had plenty of other things to talk about, a thread soon opened for conversations on wildly tangential topics. Without warning, one day it morphed into a Messenger chat group with more than 200 participants.

Stacey Brooks was at work when her phone blew up.

"All of a sudden, it was just bling, bling, bling, bling, bling," she says. "Messages were coming in so fast I couldn't even read them. So I just pulled up Facebook on my computer and created a new group. I pasted the link into the chat. That's how the private Lister Sisters Off-Topic Group got started, and everybody just started joining it."

The origin story of Stacey's founding of the off-topic group actually began several weeks before its official June 19, 2019 birthday. Intrigued by a trailer for *Gentleman Jack* and raves about it on Tumblr, Stacey tuned in and met Anne Lister. It was love at first sight. And the second, and the third, and the 17 more times she watched the show. Obsession was the word of the day for her and thousands of other gobsmacked fans.

"To see a butch-presenting lesbian, a strong character full of confidence in 1832, was huge for me," she says.

Stacey couldn't help but identify with Anne Lister's unconventionality because she, too, had made some nonconformist choices for herself.

Like Anne Lister, Stacey grew up in a small town. Appearances meant everything to her family, especially her Southern mother who insisted that her teen daughter wear makeup, dresses, and pantyhose in spite of Stacey's hating every second of it. But she had good reason to go along.

"When I was around 12 years old and didn't fully understand my sexuality, it was a time when AIDS was being talked about," she says. "One day I heard my mother talking with her friends, and I heard her say, 'Well, it's killing all the right people.' At that moment I remember thinking to myself that I can never let her know who I am."

Her secret lasted until she was in college in the 1990s, a period when the gay community in the US was starting to make itself a political and social force in American culture, though homophobia remained a real and present danger.

"When I got to college, there was an LGB group—we didn't know about T's then," Stacey recalls. "For National Coming Out Day, the group chalked the sidewalks on campus, and I watched students go ballistic. Guys peed all over the writing on the sidewalks. It was scary for me to think what might happen if they knew I was a lesbian. I decided I'd better let my hair grow out, and I began dressing differently."

Stacey was facing a dilemma. She wanted to be her authentic self, fully share her life with a woman, and also fulfill a dream she had always had: Stacey wanted to have a baby and be a mom.

A solution involving a gay male friend from school landed on her doorstep. He had been a donor for a mutual friend who had wanted to get pregnant but who became ill and wasn't able to take care of her baby after she was born. He turned to Stacey for temporary help in caring for his new daughter. After being a regular part of the baby's growth from newborn to toddler, Stacey hoped to make the arrangement permanent.

"In Oklahoma, I couldn't adopt her if her biological father and I weren't married," Stacey explains. "So we got married, though we didn't live as a married couple, and I still had girlfriends and he still had boyfriends. The birth mother's health improved, so she was back in our lives. The adoption plans fell through, but we worked things out so the little girl we both loved would have two mothers."

Seven years later, Stacey's "husband" became *her* donor, and after her son was born, they divorced and went their separate ways. When Stacey met and married her wife, who had a little boy close to the age of Stacey's son, her family expanded again. The nest is empty now, with all three kids grown and on their own.

"During those crazy years when the kids were growing up, my social circle got smaller and smaller," Stacey says. "I was too busy to notice that something was missing. I only had few lesbian acquaintances and even fewer lesbian friends. *Gentleman Jack* changed that almost overnight."

Thanks to her spur-of-the moment creation of the Lister Sisters Facebook group, Stacey acquired an army of friends who are like-minded souls.

"It's been so cool to meet people with similar experiences and see multigenerational experiences," she says. "I love the age ranges in our group, and the different points of view and the different experiences from different time frames. It's been a huge thing for me to meet all of these people and wonderful to see all the support."

Now 550-strong, the members of Lister Sisters Off-Topic Group come from 27 countries and stay connected not only on Facebook but also through the annual postcard, Christmas card, and gift exchanges that Stacey organizes.

"We're more than a bunch of people who just chit chat online," she says. "We're people who really care about each other."

Stacey still marvels that the *Gentleman Jack* series and Anne Lister's actual story as a historic figure have touched her in other unexpected ways too.

"First of all, just knowing that lesbians have been around forever is life-affirming," Stacey says. "To see somebody from that era who says 'This is who I am. This is how God made me' is very impactful. I feel like I've seen myself represented, and it's been a big confidence builder. Most of all, it's given me the courage to be more outspoken and be a butch woman without being ashamed of who I am and how I feel."

As someone who always wanted to be a mom, Stacey got her wish. Now, in addition to her three adult children, she also can proudly claim another title: Mother of the Lister Sisters Off-Topic Group.

LESLEY BROWN

Harrow, London, England, UK

ANNE LISTER UNIVERSITY, AND MORE

Some people just have a knack for tending to people and things. Lesley Brown, mom to three adult kids and married to her husband for 43 years, is one of them.

As a professional gardener, she nurtures flower beds and rose bushes to full bloom to create lush urban oases for her many longtime clients.

As a cricket coach Auntie Les, as the young lads affectionately call her, teaches sportsmanship to 6- to 9-year-olds and makes sure they learn the ins and outs of the game she loves and calls "chess on grass." Prior to 2020 when a local ladies' team emerged within the Harrow St. Mary's Cricket Club, she was the only woman ever to play for the 140-year-old club in league matches.

"I'm not a great player, but I love the game and was always happy to make up the numbers if the team was short of players. Now I stay busy with coaching and doing the club newsletter," she says.

These days, as the founding Dean of Anne Lister University—just one of Les's offshoots of the Shibden After Dark (SAfD) Facebook group—and the Head Buddy of the Shibden Survivor Society, maître d' of the Shibden SAfD Lunch/Coffee Club, Mother Hen of the SAfD Singles Fellowship League, and co-captain of the SAfD Wednesday Walkers fitness group, Les stays busy supporting *Gentleman Jack* fans throughout the world as the 2020 coronavirus pandemic begins easing up.

The seeds for her many new roles were planted on an ordinary spring evening at her home in the London suburbs.

"There were four reasons I watched *Gentleman Jack* in the first place," Les says. "First, dramas on the BBC on Sunday evenings are traditional TV viewing in the UK. Second, Suranne Jones, because I've never seen anything on the telly or on stage that she hasn't been good in. Third, Sally Wainwright's writing, and last, I love period drama."

Of course, *Gentleman Jack* didn't disappoint.

"I loved the whole package, the cinematography, the little details and things, the story of a woman of that age living in that era being so certain about how she was going to live her life," Les elaborates. "What stood out for me was that Anne Lister was a woman in a man's world, and she stood up to men at a time when women just didn't do that, or if they did, we just don't hear about them because they didn't leave diaries like she did."

Enamored of Anne Lister, Les followed a path familiar to thousands of *Gentleman Jack* fans. She read the Choma/Whitbread/Liddington books. She became active on social media. She joined a fan group for the first time. She made a pilgrimage to Halifax.

But where she broke rank was in her crafting a creative and welcoming response to the global coronavirus lockdown that played havoc with many in the burgeoning *Gentleman Jack* community.

"When Covid struck, a few messages popped up on the page of the Shibden After Dark fandom group I had joined from people saying they were finding it hard to deal with Covid and lockdowns and were feeling isolated and struggling," Les says. "I had the idea of pairing people up as support buddies. If someone wanted another person to talk to, they could message me, and I'd randomly put them with someone."

About 100 fans responded, the Shibden Survivor Society was born, and now buddies can check in with each other when they need to. When Les came across a photo online of a couple having a Zoom lunch together, she saw an opportunity for more fans to chat in small groups, and she formed the SAfD Lunch/Coffee Club. Forty people participate in small online groups over a meal or a cup of coffee or tea from their homes.

What came next was an even bigger and more far-reaching undertaking.

"I was struck by the vast diversity of the SAfD group," Les says. "With all of those teachers, historians, musicians, photographers, medical professionals, and others, I thought there must be a way to share all of their knowledge. I offered to set up online classes where everyone could learn from one another if anyone was interested."

Again, responses poured in, and Les winnowed down suggested class topics from nearly 100 to an eclectic mix of 35 subjects, from languages such as French, German, and Welsh to anatomy, birds, camping, creative writing, geology, art appreciation, poetry, trees, cooking, and almost two dozen other areas of interest. The reasons for various topics are as varied as the people requesting them.

"The sign language group was asked for by someone who said she's going deaf and would like to learn to sign while she can," Les says. "Someone in New Zealand who can sign sends the group of 14 videos to learn, and in a recent chat, she was showing them basic things, like how to count, say hello, introduce themselves, and other practical phrases."

Some groups also have found online courses in their subjects that they are now taking together.

The Shibden Hall Campus Class of 2020 at the cyber-based Anne Lister University is still up and running. Groups gather using Facebook chat or meet on Zoom (after working out time zones). Currently more than 100 "students" span the globe from the United States, the United Kingdom and Europe to Australia, New Zealand, India, Israel, and the Philippines.

Responding to a request from a "friend asking for a friend," Les next proceeded to organize 50 SAfD singles into random groups to promote new social connections through online meetup sessions that change every two weeks. At the end of 14 days, participants have the option of continuing to chat privately after Les disbands the groups and creates new ones to encourage people to keep expanding their social circle.

"I told people not to come looking for love but just to chat away and find a new friend or two," Les says. "I always remind everyone of

Ann Walker's observation that 'sometimes a good friend is better than a marriage.'"

While she professes to love all of her groups, Les admits she has a particular soft spot for the Wednesday Walkers, a 75-member irreverent bunch she co-founded in early 2021 to promote physical and mental well-being during lockdown through weekly walking challenges and friendly teasing.

"I've generally always enjoyed walking, but never had any incentive to take it 'that extra step further,'" Les says. "The reports from the group about what we all see during our walks, plus our friendly challenges to see how far we can walk, have given me new focus. It all started when Lisa Cutler, one of the Blister Sisters climbing Vignemale, and I started walking together—I'm in London and she's 60 miles (97 km) away in Kent—and chatting through WhatsApp. We walked a combined 1,000 (1,609 km) miles in 100 days, randomly talking, singing to one another, being heartfelt about our lives, laughing until it hurt, and never once had an awkward silence, all before we ever met face-to-face. Now we're the very best of friends."

Les says the walking group has members in about 15 countries and notes that the daily banter between them starts when New Zealand first wakes up, and then the photos start coming in as the sun rises around the world, from Europe, the UK, and the US. The Wednesday Walkers are also participating in a fundraiser for the Alzheimer's Society, in appreciation for the joy that Suranne Jones, ambassador for the charity, has brought to *Gentleman Jack* fans with her portrayal of Anne Lister.

Having secured donations totaling more than £3,000 in less than a month, the group challenge now is to continue fundraising and encourage interested members to set a goal to walk 850,000 steps, each, in three months. Les and Lisa, as the group's co-founders, are stepping up the pace for the cause, on their way to logging at least *one million* steps, approximately 500 miles (805 km), in 90 days.

"All I ever wanted to do was to be able to help just one person out there who might want to connect with someone else and just say 'hi,' but the five groups I set up have turned into something I'm quite proud of," Les says. "What is good for me is that I am being educated by the world, I've got free education on 35 subjects, I'm fitter than I've been in years, I've met tons of wonderful people, and I've got a new friend in Lisa!"

When she's not being the registrar and booster for her groups, Les has other Anne Lister-related interests. Among them are investigating some of the many places Anne visited in London.

"I once spent an entire Sunday afternoon going down a rabbit hole looking up silversmiths in London because Anne was searching there for a silver tea pot to give to Vere Cameron," she says. (Fans will remember a scene in *Gentleman Jack* when Anne discusses a shopping trip for this wedding gift for her former love interest.)

Les is also the adopted "mum" to a group of 14 *Gentleman Jack* fans in London who began regularly meeting at a pub before the coronavirus put a stop to social gatherings and they had to revert to online meetups.

"I'm the oldest in the group, and we have great fun," Les says. "We all have nicknames and at Christmas, they gave me a cup with my nickname on it. It says Les *'Wildly Inappropriate' Brown*, a name I try to live up to!"

Les says her post-*Gentleman Jack* life has undergone many changes. "I wake up in the morning thinking of Anne Lister and I go to bed thinking of her, and all in between," Les says. "A new bunch of friends landed in my lap when I didn't think I needed any other friends. We talk every day and have been a lifeline to one another during these times.

I've done things I've never done before, like deciding to go away for a long weekend to Halifax with two women I've only met twice in a pub. My codebreaker friends entertain me with updates as they're decoding Anne's—and now Ann's—journals, and they often begin with 'You won't believe what she's doing now.'"

Les says it's never too late to make new friends and join any of her groups, but she does have a caveat.

"Have fun," she says. "And remember, it's all because of Anne."

To sign up for the Shibden Survivor Society, the SAfD Lunch/Coffee Club, Anne Lister University, the SAfD Singles Fellowship League, or the Wednesday Walkers, you need to be a member of the private Shibden After Dark group on Facebook and send a direct message to Lesley Brown.

LAURIE SHANNON

Chicago, Illinois, USA

ADVOCATING FOR ANNE LISTER

*E*xcept for the relatively small number of people who knew about Anne Lister beforehand, almost everybody who watches *Gentleman Jack* comes away asking the same thing. *Why have I never heard of this amazing woman before now?*

If Laurie Shannon, Franklyn Bliss Snyder Professor of Literature at Northwestern University, and her colleagues have their way, Anne Lister will soon get the name recognition and broader scholarly attention she deserves. The newly formed Anne Lister Society (ALS) is committed to ensuring that Anne Lister has her rightful place among the ranks of the world's most celebrated women in history—the suffragettes and activists, the writers and artists who've rocked the boat, anyone who's dared to break barriers and defied conventions.

Before she became the coordinator of the new Anne Lister Society in March 2020, less than a year after *Gentleman Jack's* broadcast around the world, Laurie's engagement with Anne Lister began as an enthralled viewer of the show.

"I was first a fan of the series—appreciating the heart-stopping performances and the unbelievable cadences of the script," Laurie says. "But what also stuck with me about *Gentleman Jack* is the way the diaries, as written documents, become a virtual protagonist, a shaping power for the show. That really got my attention, because Sally Wainwright makes the literary significance of the diaries so palpable."

As a Shakespeare expert and former chair of the English Department at Northwestern University, when she learned that the West Yorkshire Archive Service was organizing a diary transcription project staffed by volunteers, Laurie joined right away. She wanted to read Anne Lister's journals directly.

In the fall of 2019, Laurie was on research sabbatical as a fellow at the Warburg Institute at the University of London when she decided she would also pursue an Anne Lister-related inquiry while in England. She was particularly keen to visit the Calderdale archives to take a look at the lecture notes Anne took at the scientific presentations she'd attended during her time in Paris, in order to write about Anne's engagement with natural history.

With Halifax an easy three-hour train ride away, Laurie headed north for her first visit.

"I had no idea that the arc of my scholarly activities would take up new directions as a result of the visit," she says now. "Besides time in the archives, I had arranged to have coffee with the amazing Helena Whitbread, and she generously spent two hours with me, just talking about Anne Lister—and also guiding me toward unpublished parts of the diaries that speak the most about my topic."

As chance would have it, when Laurie was back at the same coffee shop on the following day, she ran into Sally Wainwright.

"I hesitated to intrude on her privacy," she says, "but *Gentleman Jack* is such a mind-blowing series, so I said I was a Shakespeare professor from the States doing archival research on Anne Lister as a result of *Gentleman Jack* and just wanted to congratulate her on the truly singular achievement of the show."

It was a friendly, brief interaction, and, with that, Laurie assumed the conversation was over.

On Day 3 in Halifax, Laurie took another fateful coffee break at the same coffee shop.

"I saw Helena talking very animatedly with someone across the room. I sat down to read over my archive notes, when I felt someone walking directly toward me," she recalls. "I looked up and I saw Pat Esgate, the organizer of the Anne Lister Birthday Week (ALBW). She introduced herself, and she said, 'Helena suggested that you're the person Sally might speak with about starting an Anne Lister Society.'"

Laurie says that the timing of the proposition was auspicious.

"Something like that was nowhere on my radar, but like every other fan, I'd felt profoundly and gratefully affected by the show," she says. "Since I was able at this point in my career to take on something new, and it would mean a lot to help gain due recognition for Anne as a thinker, I was very interested."

Fired up by this new purpose, Laurie spent hours with Sally Wainwright, series consultant Anne Choma, and Pat Esgate (mostly on Zoom), brainstorming possibilities and plans for a new organization—an idea Sally and Anne had first had long before *Gentleman Jack* made its debut. She met again with Helena and with historian Jill Liddington, and over several months she consulted with 18th and 19th century scholars and others in her academic orbit. Thanks to input from so many who are committed to preserving Anne Lister's legacy, within months the essence of the Anne Lister Society coalesced around Sally's original vision to provide space for "serious conversation about Anne Lister."

"One of the unique things about Anne Lister and the aftermath of the show," Laurie observes, "is that there are any number of fan groups and codebreakers organizing various kinds of conversations, and hunting for facts and collecting details in timelines and spreadsheets. So what we felt still remained to be organized were venues for sustained analysis and the interpretation of what Anne Lister means, with an aim to establish her rightful place in cultural history."

By the summer of 2020, the Anne Lister Society had taken shape as a working group with a mission: to foster knowledge of Lister's extraordinary life and writings and to interpret her legacy. Although subscriptions and memberships will eventually be open to anyone, anywhere, the organizers are committed to keeping the Society connected to Halifax, given that it's Anne's hometown and where her voluminous body of writing is archived.

"We do not imagine this as scholars-only," Laurie says. "It's a mistake to classify 'academics' and 'fans' as two, non-overlapping groups. I got started on this as a fan, and our meetings will welcome everyone who's interested in what Sally first called 'serious conversation' about Anne."

Like so many Anne Lister enthusiasts, Laurie's admiration runs deep for the prolific writer that she views as a polymath with a ferocious intellect.

"My own passionate view is that we should classify Anne Lister's journal as *a masterpiece of English writing*, a monumental text we now must reckon with in terms of literary history," Laurie points out. "She always talked about publishing something, though she never did. But she has written and left us a masterpiece. It's perhaps not the one she imagined, but it's a masterpiece nevertheless. I also like to think of her journal as a belated inheritance that arrived just on time for our time—we find ourselves holding this sudden legacy we didn't know to expect, and we still need to explore it in all its aspects."

As part of their focus on raising the general public's awareness of Anne's intellectual achievements and her importance in English history and letters, the ALS working group was involved in the University of York's decision to name one of its ten colleges after Anne Lister—the first there to be named after a woman, and probably the first to be named anywhere for an unapologetic lesbian.

"We thought our nomination was a long shot, in a way," Laurie admits. "Would the university name a college after someone already known to be LGBTQ? On the other hand, given Anne's remarkable lifelong pursuit of knowledge and her powerful connection to the city of York, maybe the timing was exactly perfect. When we learned Anne had been chosen, we were just basically delirious. Anne Lister College! It was one of the utter high points of our first months."

The Society is also currently involved in a working group at the Halifax Minster, considering Anne Lister's final resting place inside the church.

"We are really excited to be participating in this project," Laurie says. "Both the University of York nomination and the Minster effort highlight what it is that we, in particular, can do, which is to focus on the institutional establishment of the importance of Anne Lister for the long run and in larger cultural contexts where she should have a presence."

Next on its agenda is the first two-day Anne Lister Society conference in April 2022. In conjunction with Anne Lister Birthday Week, the event will bring together academics and Anne Lister enthusiasts to present research papers on a wide variety of Lister-related subjects.

"We put out a call for papers not knowing how many to expect," Laurie says. "Immediately we received 20 submissions, and we're still in conversations with several more people. About a quarter of the presentations to be given are from people who are not university-based scholars."

Laurie reiterates that it's all part of the Society's role to promote conversations and publications about Anne Lister and engage scholars of all ages and specialties in support of their work in areas where new research is just getting underway.

"Besides scholarship, our focus also involves advocacy," Laurie says. "The way to assure Anne Lister's legacy is to get her into the college curriculum, so she's read by people across the spectrum of identities who need to know about one of the superheroes of our history and literature. That's partly how Anne can be established in the place that I think she deserves. It's going to take *all* of the modern academic disciplines to begin to grapple with the phenomenon of her life."

While there is no doubt that Anne Lister appeals to Laurie's intellectual sensibilities and has influenced her career path, she's also left another mark.

"I'm so taken with the way Anne pulls herself up after whatever blow or disappointment," she concludes. "Something untoward happens. She doesn't repress an emotional reaction. She has it, but she doesn't stop there. Her brain engages, she moves on, she learns from it how to be differently defended next time. I think about that especially in Covid time. Every day there's been something difficult that you have to absorb and still keep going, and I know of absolutely no better model for that than Anne Lister. No document on our planet lets us follow somebody doing that, almost in real time, like her journal. We're privileged to listen to the thinking, as someone keeps firmly deciding that she wants to *live*. I find that moving every day."

As she collaborates with the Society's movers and shakers to institutionalize Anne Lister's place in history, Laurie has special praise for Helena Whitbread and Sally Wainwright.

"Our gratitude goes to Helena, such a generous figure across the Listerverse, for first bringing the amazing phenomenon that is Anne Lister out of the archives and into a world of admiration," she says. "And also to Sally, whose writing in *Gentleman Jack* not only makes award-winning television, it's also an inspired act of scholarly curation. I think it's fair to call the series itself one of the great 'editions' of Anne's diaries."

Putting a new organization together takes many minds and hands. Special thanks go to the dedicated team giving advice and support to bring the Society to life. They include Dan Sudron (former archivist at West Yorkshire Archive Service), David Glover (president of the Halifax Antiquarian Society), Caroline Gonda (St. Catharine's College, Cambridge University), Chris Roulston (University of Western Ontario), Ros Ballaster (Mansfield College, Oxford University), Rev. Jane Finn (Curate, Halifax Minster), Rachel Lappin (Calderdale Cultural Destinations), and Joan Burda (attorney and member of the Anne Lister Diary Transcription Project). For information about the Anne Lister Society, visit https://english.northwestern.edu/about/anne-lister-society.

HAZEL CLINK & JOANNE MONK

Essex, England, UK

WE'RE JUST US

*H*azel Clink knew the drill. As a young woman living in a small Scottish village in the 1990s, being a k.d. lang fan wasn't easy in those days long ago, before the internet made it simple to get your hands on scarce recordings. So, for love of the Canadian singer-songwriter, Hazel was prepared to do serious sleuthing, track down word-of-mouth leads, scour fan magazines for tips, and even drive to meetups hours away to locate someone who had *the list*.

The list was the vital treasure trove of names of people who could procure hard-to-find records and tapes. In her dogged pursuit of rare k.d. lang cassettes and videos, Hazel not only found what she was looking for, she also found the love of her life.

"Fate dealt me a hand," Hazel reflects. "Jo Monk's name was at the top of *the list.*"

Though she lived almost 500 miles (805 km) away in England, Jo was the right person to contact.

"I was running a free service making tapes of videos of rare stuff that an American friend sent me that wasn't available here," she says. "That's why I had 43 k.d. lang pen pals at the time."

"Jo was quite popular because she could convert US videos to UK format," Hazel adds. "We exchanged a few letters and a couple of phone calls and agreed to look for each other several months later when we were both in London at a k.d. lang convention."

"We actually met at a photo stall at the convention," Jo says. "Without even opening our mouths, she knew instantly who I was, and vice versa."

Besides being attracted to her music, Hazel and Jo were attracted to k.d. lang—and each other—for another reason: k.d. lang is a butch lesbian, and so are they. After 18 months of taking turns shuttling back and forth between countries, Hazel said goodbye to Scotland and moved to England so she and Jo could be together. Now middle-aged and happily married, they reflect on 28 years as a couple and their latest fan crush.

"We started watching *Gentleman Jack* on an app on my phone that allowed us to see it while it was on first in the States," Jo says. "Every week we could hardly wait for the next episode, and then of course we watched it all over again when it started here."

It wasn't lost on avid TV viewers like Hazel and Jo that a series about an unconventional historical 19th century female landowner intent on finding a wife had snagged the coveted 9:00 Sunday night time slot on the BBC. An entertaining program about lesbians in love was representation at the highest level. It also was 100% addictive.

"I was hooked from the minute Suranne Jones appeared in that jacket and jumped down from the High Flyer," Hazel says. "I needed to see more. It became a bit of an obsession."

For both Hazel and Jo, their mutual preoccupation translated into a summer of nonstop, exclusive *Gentleman Jack* viewing, especially watching Episode 8 again and again and again.

"To me, the hilltop scene is the best telly I've ever watched," Hazel says. "It's remarkable and incomprehensible that we were so entertained by a lady who has been dead for 181 years. She was single-minded, and she was not prepared to conform. I take my hat off to Anne Lister because she was ahead of her time. She was a clever, clever woman held back by society, and she left us such a legacy."

"Seeing the representation of a butch lesbian really appealed to me the most, especially that it was on prime time Sunday night television," Jo says. "I'm also a great admirer of Anne Lister, but it's Suranne Jones's portrayal that's done it for me. Kudos to her for the acting and completely transforming herself in the way she walks and her mannerisms as Anne Lister."

Considering the treatment endured by those who don't conform to traditional expectations of how women should look and act, it's no wonder that Hazel and Jo are dazzled by the story of Anne Lister's determination and courage to defy those expectations. They find it both validating and inspirational.

"I always say that if you had a button in the back of your neck which said gay or straight, you'd probably have switched to straight because it's an easier life," Hazel says. "As it is, you're fighting all the way for everything. We're an instant draw to the curious mind, and we see the way people look at us. We're not feminine at all, and people cannot get their heads around that."

Disrespect, rejection, and verbal abuse are standard fare for most butch lesbians. It happens in families, at the workplace, on the street, everywhere. Hazel says she was turned down for a job because she wasn't "girly" enough—couched in the phrase "wrong cultural fit"—and on another occasion, she was outed by her boss to a new employee with the insulting and backhanded compliment that "she's gay, but she's good at her job." Wisecracks, snide remarks, and unwelcome comments about Hazel's and Jo's appearance are unending. They've even been confronted by a complete stranger wanting to know what goes on in their bedroom.

Jo disagrees with those who believe we're living in a modern, more enlightened era. Even going for a walk in the neighborhood has its perils.

"Some people just can't seem to comprehend that two women can love each other," Jo points out. "Even now when we're out and about, we get abuse on a daily basis."

She says she and Hazel make a special effort to do nothing that might attract attention to themselves. They avoid eye contact with those they pass, and they're careful not to touch each other when they're outside. Still, it isn't unusual for young men driving past to honk and shout "Dykes!"

"I wonder how many straight couples carry their civil partnership or marriage certificate wherever they go?" Hazel says. "Because I do. At any time, I may have to prove I'm Jo's next of kin. It's happened before at the reception desk in a crowded hospital. I don't really have a chip on my shoulder, but I think the world should just be 'live and let live.'"

While being misgendered is an aggravation, there are times when Hazel and Jo can get past the annoyance and even find humor in what life throws at them.

"The greatest was when we were on holiday in the Canary Islands and this old couple asked if we were brothers," Jo recalls.

"I had to laugh," Hazel says. "I had on quite a fitted polo shirt showing all the curves, and quarter length trousers and mules. I mean, you don't see many guys that look like that."

The tale of Hazel's sister's wedding brings smiles too.

"My mother was insistent that I wear this pink frock," Hazel explains. "Neighbors that I've worked beside took the day off from work to see me in it. My mum said I had to grow my hair and lose some weight. I said, 'I think you want somebody else.' I wanted to change into a tuxedo for the reception but mum didn't want any of that. So I ended up stuck in this bloody pink frock the whole time, wearing size 9 pink shoes dyed to match. On top of that, the best man even asked me out at the reception. Really, what woman like me in her right mind wears a frilly thing and goes through any of that? I've always been quite flexible, but that was just a bridge too far."

In light of their experiences, Hazel and Jo agree that *Gentleman Jack* has been transformative for them on many levels.

"For me, *Gentleman Jack* has increased my confidence a hell of a lot," Jo says. "I've always been quite shy and reserved, but I just feel much, much more confident now. I can't really describe why, but I know I just do. I can only imagine what we'd be like now if we had this sort of confidence back in our early 20s."

Thanks to *Gentleman Jack*, Hazel and Jo are now part of a new world of kindred spirits who share more than their enthusiasm for the show. Through social media, they've found a supportive community of like-minded lesbians that has eluded them all of their lives.

"There's an element of loneliness that goes with this life," Hazel concludes. "Years ago, I went to a k.d. lang concert, and it was full of sensibly-shoed women who all disappeared after the gig. Where did they go? I just didn't know. Many, many years later, lo and behold, this TV program comes along, and suddenly, we're friends with hundreds of people and regularly meeting up with folks at Shibden Hall. We've discovered there are swathes of people who are our age, and they look like us. *Gentleman Jack* has brought a whole community together. Long may it continue."

New allies and friends make it easier for Hazel, Jo, and millions of other lesbians to navigate a still-hostile world.

"We're just us," Hazel says. "We're not some sort of novelty. If you're feeling a bit down, people in *Gentleman Jack* Facebook groups will pick you up, which is something we've not had before. Everybody's got a voice, and I like that."

When Hazel and Jo began their love affair almost three decades ago, *Constant Craving* was k.d. lang's breakout hit. Regardless of century, its opening lyrics ring true for every woman who has ever loved and been in love with another woman: *"Even through the darkest phase, be it thick or thin, always someone marches brave here beneath my skin."*

∞

JOLENE COADY & GENEVIEVE McGARVEY-TANENBAUM

Waterford, Ireland & Sacramento, California, USA

BEST FRIENDS FOREVER

*O*n August 21, 1823, 32-year-old Anne Lister wrote that her "journal has amused and done me good. I seem to have opened my heart to an old friend, and I can tell my journal what I can tell none else." That pretty much sums up the way Jolene Coady, from Ireland, and Gen McGarvey-Tanenbaum, from California, feel about each other.

"The one thing that brought us together in the beginning was Anne Lister," Jolene says. "We're an ocean and 16 years apart, so how would we have met or even been introduced without *Gentleman Jack*?"

"Divine intervention," says Gen. "It's amazing that two complete strangers could mean so much to each other."

Social media kickstarted Jolene and Gen's friendship through a private Facebook page that drew them together in the afterglow of *Gentleman Jack's* first season. Both gravitated to the Lister Sisters page to find like-minded fans to gush about the show, lavish praise for the performances of its lead actors, and rehash the storyline that touched them in so many ways.

As Jolene tells it, "Gen noticed me first when I responded to her post for a free copy of Anne Choma's book about *Gentleman Jack*—I was second in line, so I missed out on the book, but wound up with a new best friend. We began exchanging casual messages soon after I sent her a voice clip message when she commented on Facebook on a picture of my dogs, and then we really starting getting to know each other. We talk every day now, and we've exchanged reams of messages, letters, and gifts over the past two years. It's a very expensive friendship!"

"But so worth it," Gen says with a laugh.

The packages flying back and forth across the Atlantic have introduced Jolene and Gen to each other's food tastes, quirky senses of humor, and gift-giving prowess. Both have been recipients of an assortment of *Gentleman Jack*/Anne Lister merchandise, books, t-shirts, American or Irish sweets and junk food, family photos, and even doggie treats. A standout for Jolene? Gen designed and stitched a special weighted Anne Lister quilt for her—it's like a big hug, she says—to help Jolene cope with anxiety.

It still amazes them that an ex-drag king (Jolene) and a former university dean of students (Gen) could wind up as each other's go-to source for lively banter, serious discussions, and mutual support. But conversation comes easy, and Jolene and Gen are never at a loss for words on any subject, whether it's dogs, current events, politics, Jolene's daily walks by the sea, Gen's two sons, or the minutia of everyday life.

It did, however, come as a surprise when they discovered that each woman had been in the vanguard for marriage equality. What Jolene and Gen both have in common with Anne Lister, who boldly married Ann Walker at Holy Trinity Church in 1834 without benefit of clergy, is that their weddings have chipped away at homophobic attitudes toward same sex unions.

Jolene tells her story first.

"My wife, Àine, and I were among the first lesbian couples in Ireland to be married after Irish voters approved the country's constitutional amendment in 2015 legalizing same sex unions," Jolene says. With a majority of 62%, Ireland was the first country in the world to authorize gay marriage by popular vote.

"Our first wedding, which we had been planning for quite awhile, was on August 28, 2015, not long after the referendum passed but before it became effective in November," Jolene says. "It was a beautiful and simple ceremony with about 50 people in attendance. My little brother walked me down the aisle, and Àine's dad gave her away. Because we were the first lesbians and same sex couple married at the Theatre Royal in Waterford, the venue put us up on their website, a local radio station interviewed me about growing up gay in Ireland, and *Irish Wedding* magazine, which until then had been predominately straight, did a feature story on our wedding. We were thrilled with all the attention."

But the couple wasn't done with the formalities. Minus Jolene's black and red rock-a-billy wedding frock and Àine's crisp white shirt, black pants, bow tie, and red Converse tennis shoes, they snuck off six months later and got married again on April 4, 2016 to exchange their civil partnership certificate for an official marriage certificate.

"During our civil ceremony, neither of us was allowed to say 'I take you as my wife,'" Jolene explains. "That's why our second wedding, with just us, was so important. It meant we had full, *equal* rights."

Two weddings down, three to go: Gen tells her story.

"Terry and I have been married three times—to each other," she says, beginning with wedding No. 1, in 1996, when Gen and Terry were joined together in a private commitment ceremony that, much like the union between Anne Lister and Ann Walker, was "in the eyes of God" rather than legally binding. Eight years later, they jumped at the chance to give their partnership an official government seal of approval with wedding No. 2. It was 2004, and Gen and Terry accepted the invitation of San Francisco's mayor to come to his City Hall to obtain one of the municipal marriage licenses being issued to same sex couples under his orders at a time when gay marriage was not permitted by California state law.

Gen and Terry had been married for less than a month when the California Supreme Court annulled all of the San Francisco marriages, theirs included, on the grounds that the mayor had overstepped his authority. It would be another four years before the court declared California's ban on same sex marriage to be unconstitutional, and Gen and Terry could once again formalize their union. Wedding No. 3 occurred in July 2008, but it too was put in legal jeopardy when, later that year, California voters passed a constitutional amendment to ban same sex marriages once and for all. Only the state's last-ditch concession allowed thousands of gay marriages that had already taken place in 2008, like Gen's and Terry's, to stand.

It wasn't until 2015, the same year that Jolene and Àine were first married in Ireland, that the United States Supreme Court struck down all state bans on same sex marriage, thereby legalizing gay and lesbian marriage in all 50 states and upholding the unions of couples, such as Gen and Terry, who had previously wed in states where legality had already been established by state statutes.

"We toyed with the idea of getting married a fourth time then," Gen says, "but it seemed like that would be over the top." Gen and Terry celebrate July 27, the date of weddings No. 1 and No. 3, as their multi-marriage anniversary.

In addition to withstanding years of bureaucratic assault during the fight to legalize her marital status, Gen has also battled and survived ovarian cancer. Likewise, Jolene has proven her own mettle as she contends with PTSD (post-traumatic stress disorder) brought on by an extremely abusive childhood.

Having a sympathetic and steady best friend through hard times has been a godsend for both women. As Gen says of her wife of 25 years and three weddings, "Terry loves *Gentleman Jack*, but she doesn't *love* it like I do. I'm sure she was relieved when I met Jolene because she was like, 'Thank God, you have someone to talk to.'"

In January of 2020, when no one knew that the world was on the brink of a year of the plague, Jolene's wife Àine gave her a plane ticket to travel from Ireland to the US to meet Gen and her wife in person for the first time. They spent a delightful week of sightseeing, laughter, and talks late into the night. Gen even helped Jolene scout out locations for the Irish couple who are weighing the possibility of emigrating to California. It seemed natural, back then, to make plans for the future, which included a repeat visit to America in the next few months. But the coronavirus pandemic shut down international travel, and "the future" became a moot point. Phone calls and video chats became the stand-in for in-person contact.

Gen found herself particularly isolated.

"Because of rheumatoid arthritis and the immune suppressant medication I take, leaving me especially vulnerable to the virus, I had to be a hermit throughout the pandemic," she says. "Jolene was a life raft for me. Having her in my life on a regular basis, she was my touchstone, my anchor, and my long distance connection. Our friendship has been more important to both of us than I think we even realized back in January of 2020."

As the pandemic year wore on, another close friendship emerged— this one between Àine and Terry, Jolene's and Gen's spouses. Now the two couples even sport the same tattoo—"I rise above it." Jolene displays this new maxim of lesbian pride and endurance on her left foot whereas Àine's is on her left arm. For both Gen and Terry, the words are, literally, close to their hearts.

Jolene's and Gen's personal interactions around the subject of Anne Lister never abated during the lockdowns. Jolene says that she drew strength from a specific moment in *Gentleman Jack's* third episode.

"What I always think about is Anne Lister's line to Ann Walker when she says, 'Why do you have such a poor opinion of yourself?' and what an impact that had on me," she says. "My therapist had told me to stop and just listen to myself, and I realized I had had this negative narrative in my head for years and years. Now I have a much nicer dialogue with myself, and because of that, I'm starting to build a little bit of confidence. I feel healthier, mind and body, than I have in a long while. I'm starting to not give a shit about what other people think. I even let myself go gray during the pandemic."

Gen has felt an internal shift too.

"When I look back, I think it's really incredible that in the early 1800s, Anne Lister had such self-assurance in herself and her true nature that she did not allow culture or peers or family or stigma to keep her from living the life she wanted," Gen says. "Though she had social mores to contend with, she was artful in her way of managing her situation and staying so strong and true to who she was. That has just reinforced for me that there is no reason that I can't be as solid and confident in who I am."

Now, as they eagerly await Season 2 of *Gentleman Jack*, Jolene is hopeful that having a positive story of a lesbian couple on mainstream TV will make a big difference for members of a new generation coming to terms with their sexuality.

"What I loved about *Gentleman Jack* is that it's about a beautiful, butch, androgynous, out lesbian," she says. "The future is bright for young gay people because now they have the representation in the media that I never did. I didn't know anyone who was gay, and I was too afraid to tell my parents, the school, even my best friends. Now people can talk more about themselves and who they want to be with, and it's not such a stigma."

Jolene has only to look to her own life to assess the everlasting benefits of the *Gentleman Jack* effect.

"I think *Gentleman Jack* has had a massive impact on people's lives," Jolene observes. "First of all, it gave me Gen, so that's brilliant. And *my* wife has *her* wife as a good friend. With social media, we feel like we're all part of a bigger community that came together because of Anne Lister.

I rise above it.

It's just amazing, and it still surprises me to this day how important *Gentleman Jack* has been to me and to so many other people."

Gen agrees.

"I'm appreciative of all the inspiration Anne Lister has provided, plus the strength and role modeling, but when it comes down to it, I got a lifelong friend out of this," she concludes. "And who could have imagined two years ago that I would have this person who means so much to me, living 5,000 miles (8,047 km) away from me, who is part of my everyday life? And you know, for that, we'll both be forever grateful to *Gentleman Jack*."

CAROL GOULD

London, England, UK

THE MIRACLE OF GENTLEMAN JACK

*L*ife is filled with delightful and horrific surprises. When petite Carol Gould arrived in England from Philadelphia in 1976 to pursue her studies in film and theater, she never expected she'd be an ex-pat making her home in London for the next 40+ years.

She didn't anticipate that she would have a long and distinguished career in television—rubbing shoulders with A-list celebrities, bringing P.D. James's mystery novels to the small screen, or being credited on 65 international drama productions. She didn't know she'd become a regular commentator on BBC television and radio on American and Israeli politics and current events. She didn't expect to be fascinated with the role of women pilots in the Air Transport Auxiliary in World War II and write the book *Spitfire Girls* to document their heroic service.

And the very last thing Carol Gould counted on was receiving the grim news in 2016 that she had Stage 4 metastasized breast and lymph node cancer and had six months to live. It's no surprise, however, that this strong, outspoken American was determined to stay alive in spite of the odds against her. Besides participation in clinical trials and years of debilitating chemotherapy and immunotherapy, she says other powerful medicine was in play.

"I am convinced that *Gentleman Jack* and the new friends I made from around the world not only have inspired me but also sustained me through brutal cancer treatment," Carol says. "I adore the series, and it changed my life."

She says that even though she had been a successful network drama executive for the bulk of her career, she had forgotten how stunning a well-devised, multi-episodic TV series can be and that *Gentleman Jack* was the closest to perfection she'd seen in decades.

"*Gentleman Jack* struck me to the core as soon as Anne Lister, portrayed with explosive vigor by Suranne Jones, jumped off the High Flyer and put a male passenger in his place," she recounts. "Then the series unfolded with a stream of bold, gorgeous, and sexy 19th century female characters expressing their passion through Sally Wainwright's finely honed scripts. In light of the taboo of the time, the ability of these gay women to sublimate guilt and shame was one of the most powerful aspects of this captivating production."

Carol found herself especially drawn to Episode 2 when Vere Hobart, another of Anne Lister's failed love interests, opts to marry a Scottish military officer.

"Watching the wedding, I relived every romantic disappointment of my life in a few minutes of seeing the profound pain on Anne Lister's face and in her eyes," she says. "When I say *Gentleman Jack* changed my life, that scene replays in my mind's eye at least once a week and has afforded me the realization that I am not the only fool of a woman to mess up, lose a great love, or think that great love is real but actually isn't. It gave me the courage to come out to many old friends who, perplexed at having attended my wedding to a man some forty years ago, to this day cannot fathom why a 'TV show' would have such a profound effect on me. But 'hey ho,' as Anne would say."

Carol says she fell in love with *Gentleman Jack's* many unforgettable punch lines, such as Anne's admission to Ann Walker that "I only went to Paris to study anatomy," followed by a jump cut to naked Anne pleasuring her lover Maria Barlow.

"It was one of my favorite scenes in the entire series," she says. "Others were the scenes in a bar with a platoon of soldiers as a young Anne beats them at cards, puffs away on a cigarette, and bangs her hands on the table in glee. Even more amusing is her father, American Revolutionary War veteran Captain Jeremy Lister, at the dinner table recounting such incidents to the rest of the family, talking about Anne in the third person."

The dinner table scene alone paid off in big dividends.

"I had been suffering from protracted writer's block for over two years, but watching Sally Wainwright's masterful series made me realize that there is so much to write about," Carol explains. "When I picked up a reference by Anne in Episode 1 about Captain Lister's military service in the American Revolutionary War, including the Boston Tea Party, I thought 'God, I must do some research on this and write about it.' Indeed, I spent the rest of the summer of 2019 plowing through his book, *Concord Fight*, and with the help of Halifax archivists and historians, compiling a screed about the Listers in early 18th century America and Captain Lister's compelling, death-defying tour of duty in the colonies in the 1770s. Since then, I have continued to write other articles and can thank the sparkling words of *Gentleman Jack* for curing my writer's block."

Gentleman Jack has provided hours of welcome diversion for Carol, especially Anne and Anne's Episode 8 hilltop reunion and subsequent "wedding" in York that she's dubbed the two most beautiful scenes she's ever witnessed in British television drama. The online community that has sprung up around *Gentleman Jack* also has been a source of emotional and economic support for her as she endures never-ending cancer treatment. Now contending with chronic pain and loss of income from her inability to work, Carol's pressing need for financial support hasn't fallen on deaf ears. An American friend set up a GoFundMe account that has raised thousands of pounds from fans around the world eager to pitch in and help out.

"Not a day goes by that I do not smile to myself as a warm feeling washes over me, or a memorable line from the show pops into my head, or I watch the news and I wonder, 'What would Anne Lister think of *that*?' And I so appreciate the help I've received from *Gentleman Jack* fans," Carol says, who can often be seen in her selfies on Facebook, Instagram, or Twitter fashionably clad in a selection of Anne Lister/Ann Walker apparel.

"As I await Season 2, now I can only pray that I live long enough to see the genius of Suranne Jones, Sophie Rundle, and the *Gentleman Jack* production bringing the brave Anne Lister and Ann Walker to life once more."

∞

Lister Coat of Arms

MYTH BUSTERS & ARMCHAIR DETECTIVES

UNCOVERING FACTS & FILLING IN THE BLANKS OF 19TH CENTURY HISTORY

STEPH GALLAWAY

Kearney, Nebraska, USA

ONCE SEDUCED, ALWAYS SEDUCED

*B*logger. Researcher. Codebreaker. Packed with Potential website co-founder and contributor. Anne Lister Research Summit organizer. ALBW Live (Anne Lister Birthday Week) technical director.

If all of her *Gentleman Jack*-inspired activities were musical instruments, Steph Gallaway would be a one-woman brass band.

Steph had heard of Anne Lister before *Gentleman Jack* aired, and was, in the spring of 2019, eagerly anticipating the new television series about her. What she *didn't* know was that her life would never be the same after watching it.

"After I saw the show, I started reading every Anne Lister-related book I could find," Steph says. "By October of 2019 I had run through the gamut of everything I could get my hands on, and it seemed inevitable that going to the diaries themselves was next. But I'm in grad school and working full-time and really didn't have time."

However, Steph did find the time to assemble an authentic Anne Lister costume for Halloween that year—top hat, waistcoat, a wig to replicate Anne's hairstyle, cravat, the works—and as a nod to Anne's journal, she accessorized her outfit with a small binder of photocopied diary pages.

"The pages were just sitting around my house one weekend, so I decided to give it a try and see what I could make out of them," Steph recalls. The random pages she had downloaded just happened to detail 29-year-old Anne Lister's nightly escapades with Miss Mary Vallance and others at Langton Hall in 1820.

"I was like, 'Oh my God, I have to keep going, I *have* to know what happens next," Steph says, and that led her to plunge headfirst into the codebreaker rabbit hole. Within a few weeks, she was submitting a batch of transcriptions to the West Yorkshire Archive Service for approval and acceptance into the official volunteer codebreaker project. In the many months since, Steph reports she's transcribed about 400 diary pages containing an estimated 400,000 words.

"It's been a really interesting journey," Steph says. "In the beginning, it was taking me about three hours to read and decipher a single diary page. Now I'm at about half an hour per double-sided page. It's a little bit like getting fluent in a foreign language."

As many other codebreakers have discovered, viewing Anne Lister's life through the lens of her handwritten words casts her in an entirely new light and creates a special bond.

"It's so much more impactful to have gotten to know Anne Lister this way," Steph says. "You pick up on her writing pattern, so you can begin to kind of predict the way her mind is working. You learn her vocabulary, her speech patterns, the phrases she uses over and over again, and you can even figure out what's coming next. It's the first-person perspective that makes reading her entries different from reading them in someone's book. You begin to feel like she's a friend, or someone you know and love, and that makes her so much more real than just a historical figure you're learning about."

The truth is there is no end in sight to all there is to learn about Anne Lister, Steph says, and she sees many years ahead of delving into the life and times of such a remarkable woman.

"One of my favorite things that Helena Whitbread told me is, 'If you've once been seduced by Anne Lister, in bed or on paper, you remain seduced.'"

Seduction, of course, is one of Anne's particularly notable skills, and her sex life has become one of Steph's areas of interest. Steph traces it back to those first journal pages she transcribed from Anne's coded entries of her nighttime experiences with multiple women at the home of Isabella "Tib" Norcliffe, with whom she also had been romantically involved.

"I was thrown into having to figure out a little bit more of what Anne was talking about, and the language she was using, or what she meant by certain things," Steph says. "People who were reading my blog were asking about things in the transcriptions—there were a lot of questions about the meaning of grubbling, for example—so I just kept making lists, transcribing, researching, and cross-referencing what I was finding in the diaries."

What started out as a 12-page summary of Anne's sexual vocabulary and proclivities eventually became the detailed *Anne Lister's Sex Guide* that now resides on the PackedwithPotential.org website. It includes a glossary of Anne's terms for sexual activities, their definitions and interpretations, and specific journal entries about her amorous encounters with various lovers.

In fact, a sizable amount of Steph's time is dedicated to providing content for this information-packed website. As one of the co-founders of PackedwithPotential.org, she's contributed to its pictorial travel maps of Anne's visit to London in 1824 that detail where Anne went, what she saw, and what she thought about it; the compilation of books about Anne Lister; the list of bloggers publicly sharing their transcriptions; and the meticulous article reviewing where Anne might be buried at the Halifax Minster. She also uses her considerable IT skills to help keep the site up and running.

"One of the coolest parts is the collaborative spirit that has come about from *Gentleman Jack* and the interest people have in Anne Lister," Steph points out. "We're so lucky this show happened to attract an international audience. People around the world have been working together to make Packed with Potential a useful resource, and it's one of the huge reasons we've been able to do so much so quickly."

The enormous amount of research being conducted by Anne Lister enthusiasts prompted Steph and her Packed with Potential colleagues to go a step further to support and encourage continued collaboration.

They organized the first online Anne Lister Research Summit in September 2020, held remotely during the height of the coronavirus pandemic, to bring together 300 people from around the world for two days of presentations from self-styled history detectives, academics, codebreakers, graphic artists, and others discussing their research discoveries about Anne Lister and Ann Walker.

"It's important to us to make it easier for people to connect and work together to pursue their interests," Steph says. "We're all feeling the effects of *Gentleman Jack* and recognizing the impact it had on us. It made us realize that what we've learned needs to be shared, so other people can discover Anne Lister for themselves or experience what we've felt. There are so many people that are doing independent research in service of finding out more about Anne Lister and Ann Walker, and it's important for us to invite and encourage them to share the stories that they've discovered."

Steph sees storytelling as a powerful force that connects us to our past and to people with whom we can identify. She believes that acknowledging queer representation in history is an important component of elevating queer visibility in today's media because it validates where we've come from and how we feel about ourselves.

"Growing up as a queer person in the rural Midwest meant if I wanted to learn anything about the world or anybody that's different from me, I had to turn to media," she says. "So, I've always looked for positive and authentic representation in queer pop culture. There was something in *Gentleman Jack* about the portrayal of this 19th century person that really resonated with me. Seeing the representation of a butch woman, her more masculine mannerisms, seeing somebody that sits the way I do or walks the way I do—I felt a connection that I hadn't felt to a character in TV or film before. Then what attracted me to the real Anne Lister is that she had the audacity to be herself, whatever that self was, in her time, and that she was able to write about it in her *crypthand* so she could be honest about it."

Steph says *Gentleman Jack* has touched every facet of her life.

"The way my life has changed on a day-to-day basis is immense," she explains. "I do something having to do with Anne Lister every day. I'm involved in lots of projects and much more invested in history. I help out Pat Esgate with her ALBW livestreams a couple of times a month. After I stopped playing roller derby, I lost the female community I'd had for seven years, and I really missed it. Now I'm part of a large Anne Lister community and have a lot of new friends. I've added a women's studies minor to my graduate degree in communications, and I'm questioning my career plans and what might lie in the future for me."

Two years in, Steph continues to enjoy and learn from her Anne Lister passion project.

"What we all get from Anne Lister is the example to just be yourself and have the confidence and belief that you can do it," she says. "Nobody has to give you permission. Just seeing this woman who was going to do what she wanted to, whether it was traveling extensively, or studying science, or doing anything else, reflects the many sides of her personality. Anybody can be drawn to her, and that becomes the hook that reels you in. Still, sometimes I do wonder why I am so obsessed with this dead woman, and I realize I'm still trying to figure it out."

Helena Whitbread nailed it: Once seduced, always seduced. And Steph isn't the only one.

To see Steph's 2019 Halloween costume in action, visit her website at skgallaway.com and check out the Gentleman Steph video that mimics the opening Gentleman Jack sequence. Her blog also can be found on her website.

∞

JANE KENDALL

Richmond, Virginia, USA

ANNE LISTER'S GUIDE TO AUTHENTICITY

For more than 50 years the famous Muppet amphibian, Kermit the Frog, has been singing to the world that "It's not easy being green." Change *green* to *gay*, and it could be the anthem for an entire community.

As a lesbian in her late 60s who grew up constantly hearing that she was "too masculine," Jane Kendall has spent a lifetime honing her defenses against harsh judgment, unwelcome criticism, and offensive comments.

One of 13 children, she got the message early on that she was way out of step with how she was supposed to be.

"I was a misfit, and growing up, I felt like something had gone dramatically wrong with me," she says. "As a girl, I didn't walk right. I didn't talk right. I didn't like the right toys. I felt absolutely, completely unlike my sisters. I was insanely jealous of my brothers' lives and how they were permitted to dress and play and be interested in whatever appealed to them. On my sixth birthday, I asked for a Winchester toy rifle, so I could run around and play 'cowboys' with my brothers. My parents, in their infinite wisdom, gave me a bride doll instead. It was clear how they wanted me to be."

By the time she was in high school, Jane's best friend had pegged her as an "in-betweeny," and she says the uglier names then—queer, butch, dyke, bull dyke—quickly followed. Bewildered and unnerved by her steady stream of female crushes, she says she felt it was a necessity, in the 1970s at the age of 19, to get married as fast as she could to prove everybody wrong about her, and demonstrate that all the things that had been said about her were false.

"So I absolutely threw my youth away," Jane says. "By the time I was 27 and got out of that marriage to a man I was not in the least attracted to, I had wasted one third of my life trying to be someone I was not."

Therapy was a lifesaver, and it wasn't long after the end of her dismal husband experience that Jane fell in love with the woman who has been her partner for 39 years and three times wife. They first married in Canada in 2003 when same sex unions became legal, then in New York in 2012 after gay marriage was legalized there, and finally in 2014 when they could officially marry in their home state of Virginia.

"You can't be too married these days," Jane says with a smile.

After a long career in insurance and law, Jane was happily ensconced in the rhythm of retirement when the *Gentleman Jack* bombshell dropped.

"The first time I watched *Gentleman Jack*, it took off the top of my head," Jane says. "I was absolutely spellbound. My first reaction was the realization that, all those years ago, this amazing woman had been able to navigate the challenges of life as a lesbian better than I had. If only I had known about her when I was younger! It produced a period of melancholy for my lost youth, followed by a compelling need to find out all I could about Anne Lister. Nothing, absolutely nothing I had ever read or seen on TV or in the movies before has affected me this way. I have lived, eaten, slept, and breathed Anne Lister since the moment I first watched the program. The impact of the show has been so great that I now think of my life in two parts—Before Anne Lister and After Ann Lister."

Historical Anne Lister was news to Jane. Here she was, face-to-face, with a power-walking, take-charge superwoman, bursting with intelligence, humor, courage, and suited up in clothing of her own choosing, who made no apologies for her nature, a nature exactly like Jane's.

"I feel such a strong sense of admiration for and identification with Anne Lister," Jane explains. "She says so many things that I could have said, and she describes just how I felt when I've been in the same situations. How many times have I been mistaken for a man? Thousands. It happens to me every time I leave my house. Anne 'pleads in her own defense' that she was born this way, that if she seems to be masculine, so be it. She can't help it. It's who she is. It's how she was made, and how I was made."

Jane says a huge part of Anne's appeal is that she knew her own heart very early in life, and she wasn't going to let anybody talk her out of it. She marvels that Anne lived a life as true to herself as a lesbian could in her day, exceeding the boundaries of propriety as much as necessary to preserve her integrity. And she did this even when she knew she might be taking all kinds of heat for it.

"No matter what, Anne was going to be herself," Jane says. "What so many of us have gained from *Gentleman Jack* and our knowledge of Anne Lister is a powerful affirmation of our own struggles and a strengthened resolve to continue trying every day to be our authentic selves too."

Jane has gotten an insider's look at her new 19th century heroine through transcribing more than 700 pages of Anne's journals. Like other codebreakers, Jane agrees that mastering Anne's secret *crypthand* code and her scrawling penmanship is challenging, but reading Anne's words firsthand creates a special bond between the reader and the writer. She says it makes the heartache Anne describes more wrenching, her loneliness more pronounced, her determination to improve in every way all the more inspiring.

"I see three common themes in Anne's diary entries," she says. "I believe Anne's journals, ultimately, are about love. Her love of life—you can't miss that. Her love of learning is on every page, and of course, there's her love of women. Without question, transcribing and participating in the West Yorkshire Archive Service (WYAS) codebreaker project has been the most uplifting, fulfilling, and worthwhile activity I've ever been engaged with, and it's just plain fun. *Gentleman Jack* and the transcription project have introduced me to a wonderful online community that has embraced me. The supportiveness, enthusiasm, and camaraderie of the group gives me a treasured feeling of inclusion and belongingness, of having 'found my people.'"

Reasons for her all-consuming fascination with Anne Lister are often difficult to articulate so, in January 2020, Jane set about to express artistically what she was unable to explain in words. Every day for 10 months, she labored over a needlepoint tapestry that she calls "Kindred Spirits," her 131,712-stitch love letter to Anne Lister.

"This piece is meant to be a testament to the importance of Anne Lister in my life, and also to express how Anne Lister's words about her experiences, her thoughts, and her feelings so often mirror my own," she explains. "Creating this piece has truly been a labor of love, as well as one of gratitude to all the women whose collective brilliance, perseverance, dedication, and hard work have come together to bring Anne Lister out of the shadows, where she had been hidden for most of two centuries, and into our culture where she belongs."

At the center of this intricate and symbolic work of art is a portrait that combines half of Anne's face with half of Jane's, to represent their shared emotions and experiences. Surrounding them are keywords—strength, courage, dignity, and love—and lines from Anne's journals which Jane has embroidered in both Anne's *plainhand* and *crypthand*, thoughts and words that she says "almost seem to have come right out of my own mind."

Kindred Spirits © 2020 by Jane Kendall

Anne's pocket watch, which forms the backdrop to the Anne/Jane portrait, is the device that Jane uses both as a nod to Anne's lifelong preoccupation with noting times of day and also to signal the passage of time represented in the changing colors that form the interior frame. The bright hues of the Pride rainbow flag are a joyous transition from the dull sepia and gray tones of the 19th century and also reflect what Jane feels as she thinks of the past.

She can't help but look back on the sadness and isolation of her childhood and misspent 20s with regret.

"Suppose my mother, when I was a kid being mocked and made fun of and called names, had said to me, 'You know, there was a woman a long time ago in England, and she was a lot like you. Only she figured out it was okay to be just the way she was because that's the way God made her. So it's okay for you to be just the way you are too.' How life-changing would that have been? It could have saved me so much misery."

Just as she observed in the journals how Anne's thoughts evolved over time, Jane says her exposure to *Gentleman Jack* and the real Anne Lister have given new fuel and energy to her own lifelong evolution into the woman she was born to be.

"Even though my wife and I have been visible and out of the closet since 1982, I realize I still had the vestiges of those feelings of isolation and faking it and trying to be what other people think I should be, like fitting in at work and in my family and in my neighborhood. These days, like Anne Lister, I no longer adjust myself to try to make people accept or like or love me. I spent far too much of my life doing that. In *Gentleman Jack* and in real life, Anne Lister had the guts to fully be her authentic self. One of her gifts to me has been the affirmation, in no uncertain terms, of my own ongoing endeavor to do the same."

Jane says she hopes to continue working with WYAS as it wraps up its project to get all 24 volumes of Anne's transcribed journals ready to post online. She's helping to compile *Anne Lister's Dictionary* for the PackedwithPotential.org website to catalog Anne's extensive vocabulary with its abundance of obscure and invented words. In spite of her paralyzing fear of flying, Jane's pilgrimage to Halifax is coming up.

"I sometimes struggle to express the depth of the effect that *Gentleman Jack* has had on me, but it has to do with affirmation and a sense of validation and belonging," Jane concludes. "I feel my life has been so enriched by *Gentleman Jack* and everything the show caused to happen to me. As I've learned, Anne Lister was *both* a paragon of strength, confidence, and self-acceptance *and* a person who inwardly experienced feelings of vulnerability and self-doubt like we all do. So I see her as this larger-than-life person, the greatest lesbian of all time, but also, in some way, as every one of us. I cannot adequately express the magnitude of the pride it gives me to be among her tribe."

MARLENE OLIVEIRA

Évora, Portugal

FOLLOWING THE FACTS

The reward for completing her studies in computer science was a promise to herself to take at least a 10-year hiatus from any kind of academic research. Master's degree in hand, Marlene Oliveira happily settled into her career as a software engineer, but it didn't take long before her new position lost its sparkle and boredom and monotony set in. Marlene longed for excitement to make up for her lackluster job and repetitive days of walking the dog after work, going on a bike ride, and watching TV.

On a Sunday evening in the spring of 2019, she got her wish. Marlene was thunderstruck by *Gentleman Jack*.

"Anne Lister barged into my life. All of a sudden, I'm meeting others through social media, and then I got started as a codebreaker, which gave me all these interesting people to interact with," she recalls. "We got chatting, one thing leads to another, and suddenly Packed with Potential happens, and after that came Halifax, and then there was the Anne Lister Research Summit. So, it's been kind of a roller coaster for a couple of years."

That's quite an understatement from someone who, in defiance of her original stay-out-of-the-library-for-a-decade plan, has become a researcher extraordinaire and a codebreaker with 500 pages of diary

transcriptions to her credit. She's also a core maintainer of the influential Packed with Potential website, and she's a member of the "summit squad" behind what's shaping up to be an annual gathering of Anne Lister enthusiasts all sharing their latest research findings.

Given her interest in cryptography and her experience in deciphering codes, it's no surprise that Marlene turned to Anne Lister's journals to satisfy her insatiable need for more information about the historic characters she met through *Gentleman Jack*. She soon realized that the journals not only tell intriguing stories about Anne Lister and Ann Walker, they also provide a unique bird's-eye view of the 19th century.

"They are a treasure trove of information for all sorts of research, not just the historical research about Anne and the people she writes about but also research about the times," Marlene says. "But the journals aren't the only thing I've worked on. There are many more sources, like legal documents, letters, even random slips of paper that are needed for research."

While she remains intrigued and inspired by Anne Lister, Marlene says her interests have veered toward Ann Walker, who has received far less attention in history's annals.

"Sometimes I think people get blinded by the characters they see in *Gentleman Jack,* and they miss the gold under the surface," Marlene says. "They might think Ann is this frail lady because they get too stuck to the sweet, fearful thing, and later they might even read about Ann referred to as the 'poor lunatic lady.' But she is actually quite adventurous. And with the discovery of one of Ann's journals, we now can see that Ann takes time to pay attention to things that Anne Lister doesn't seem to notice."

Marlene's fascination with this wealthy heiress has led her to take a closer look at Ann's relationship with Anne Lister and what happened in the years following Anne's death. Among her many articles on the PackedwithPotential.org website, Marlene (with co-author Livia Labate) writes about the months leading up to the couple's final trip together to Russia, Ann's subsequent legal entanglements when she is living alone at Shibden Hall, and the Lunacy Commission, which declares Ann to be of unsound mind. Their articles are elightening and required reading for Team Walker fans.

Transcribing the entire 24th, and final, volume of Anne's journals, covering 1840 and the trip that she and Ann Walker made to Russia, particularly captivated Marlene.

"It's better than many adventure books," she contends. "The whole thing is so insane. It makes you stop and think about what they were doing and the people of all sorts that they were meeting, like military, government, academics of all sorts, and then they went on to royalty."

Marlene's transcription of Anne's entry on March 5, 1840, for example, recounts the tale of a harrowing middle-of-the-night experience on the frozen Volga River. As Anne and Ann were headed toward Volgograd (known then as Tzarizine and decades later as Stalingrad), their Russian guide stopped on the ice for an unknown reason. Suddenly the ice breaks. One of the horses pulling their *kibitka*, a carriage fitted with sledges for easy travel on frozen rivers and roads, screams, and they begin to sink into dangerously frigid waters.

"What starts as an unexpected stop becomes a fight for survival," Marlene continues. "But they were so lucky that they were close enough to the bank of the river that the horse's feet could touch the ground under the ice. The servants in their separate *kibitka* heard the commotion and went back to rescue them. After switching horses, they just went on ahead. Of course, that's just one of many adventure stories in the journal."

Besides travel escapades and the minutia of their day-to-day lives, what also emerges from the journals are insights into Anne and Ann's complicated relationship and the evolution of their strong partnership. In spite of their ups and downs and Ann's ongoing struggles with depression, their shared interests and deep affection were enough to keep them together. Marlene believes that some of the things that Anne writes about her frustrations with her wife were merely her way of blowing off steam, especially in her entries calling it quits with Ann Walker.

"Obviously, it's a normal marriage," Marlene observes. "They have disagreements. Sometimes one spouse is right, sometimes the other is right. Sometimes nobody is right. They are both very stubborn ladies. Sometimes you need to just look at Anne's actions and not so much her words. Obviously, anyone can say 'I want to be rid of her,' but then she never leaves. When the opportunity arises, the reaction is not 'Finally I am free.'"

Glimpses into the couple's activities also prompted Marlene to dig deeper into what was happening socially, politically, and historically in the 1800s to better understand the real lives of both of *Gentleman Jack's* main characters.

"The women depicted in *Gentleman Jack* were complex people who lived in a time very different from ours," Marlene says. "I like to think about the TV versions of them as sort of unicorns on a pedestal, given how many people seem to believe that the real women were exactly as their fictional versions. It is a big responsibility for us as researchers not to paint them as we would like them to be. Our job is to let them shine and do their own talking. If you read our articles on PackedwithPotential. org, we provide context, but we don't put words into people's mouths. Our job is to let them be judged as they were, provide the framework for people to understand their circumstances, and then let people come to their own conclusions."

That "framework" that Marlene and her fellow researchers are constructing is a comprehensive overview of the first half of the 19th century in England. Understanding the times, traditions, and details of life in the 1800s is where Packed with Potential's wide range of "trackers" comes in handy. Information on a variety of topics is extracted from the pages of Anne's diaries and sourced by the site's contributors.

Want to know what books and magazines were on Anne Lister's bookshelves and reading list? There's a tracker for that. Curious about the fashion statements that Anne Lister and the ladies and gents of her class were making in the 1800s? Tracked, and covered. Interested in what food was served at Shibden Hall and the many places Anne visited? Dished up in a tracker. As for the sketches Ann Walker drew, the letters Anne wrote and received, Anne's religious practices, and yes, even Anne's bodily functions, there's a tracker for that, that, that, and, yes, that.

"The purpose of the trackers is to provide researchers with a way to get quick references to what they need or are interested in," Marlene explains. "It's important that everything we say is supported by facts, or else we have to indicate it's just a theory or speculation. Research is neutral in the sense that science is science. Even if you don't agree with it, it's still there. Of course, every person has their way of looking at things, and every person has their way of researching. I keep an eye out for unsubstantiated or improperly referenced claims, and I will investigate further to verify if these are accurate. All the articles I have written have one thing in common: there is a story to be told, and it's not a story told by me or by the Packed with Potential team. It's a story told by the people who lived it."

It's one thing to plow through archival documents. It's another to actually experience the places where Anne Lister and Ann Walker lived or traveled. A cheap plane ticket, put into effect just days before the coronavirus would shut down global travel, was the impetus Marlene needed for her first reconnaissance trip to northern England in March of 2020.

"The train from Manchester to Halifax passes through several stops that are talked about in the journals, so I knew I was getting closer and closer," Marlene says. "I was laughing when I got out of the train station in Halifax, and I look to my right, and there's the Minster. 'I'm here!' I thought, and I'm going to make the most of it."

The solo travel adventure that Marlene had long dreamed of was officially underway. Of course, days at the archives in Halifax poring over dozens of historical records were first on the list. Next came a traipse down the muddy paths around Shibden Hall and a self-guided tour inside Anne's home, plus a stroll through the Minster, each giving Marlene a firsthand experiential context of Anne's domestic life. Then she headed to York and Holy Trinity Church, and she says that's when reality hit.

"I knew Anne and Ann had been there to take the sacrament together, and I knew there was the rainbow plaque," Marlene recalls. "I took some pictures outside, but then I turned to look at the church and stopped. The significance of the moment hit me."

She elaborates.

"When you are reading the journals and you haven't gone to certain places, sometimes it is hard to imagine what they are doing and how they might have felt. But those two women whom I had read so much about had stood in the same place, and probably they thought, 'Oh my God, this crazy thing we're about to do!' What a happy day it was for them, and it was a happy day for me too. It's when and where their story became *real* for me."

That spur-of-the-moment trip to England is just one example of how life has changed for Marlene, courtesy of what *Gentleman Jack* unleashed.

"Anne Lister has inspired me to take chances on things I would not do before," she says. "I've always wanted to travel by myself, and I simply have never done it. But I saw Anne having all of her adventures, so I thought, 'Why can't I have adventure too?' And when I was in York, I decided to keep a travel journal for my observations like she did on her trips."

Marlene says Anne Lister was her ticket to a much broader and more interesting world.

"One of the best things that happened because of *Gentleman Jack* is that it got me into this research, and now my life is completely different. After working my day job, I have reading to do and materials to review. I have Anne's journals to transcribe and read. I have friends and a support group to discuss things with. What I do now is rewarding because I'm putting pieces of a puzzle together."

There is no question that Marlene has been instrumental in contributing to a more complete picture of Anne Lister and Ann Walker.

"I keep telling people I'm no expert and I think of myself as the translator," Marlene says. "I'm more like an observer and I don't judge them. It's like you're in a conversation with someone and they're telling you a bit of their personal history. Because of Anne's journals, I had the privilege of meeting Ann Walker through the eyes of someone who actually knew her. I hope people get to know Anne Lister better because that's my crusade: understanding her and Ann Walker better, how they interact, and why they are as they are. Anne Lister and Ann Walker have legacies, and the best way we can honor them, in my opinion, is letting *them* tell their own stories."

Transcriptions of Anne Lister's journal entries during her Russia trip in 1840 are available on Marlene's blog at anne-lister-adventures.tumblr.com.

∞

AMANDA PRYCE

Ely, Cambridgeshire, England, UK

THE MAGIC OF ANNE LISTER

*A*s devotees of *Gentleman Jack* and Anne Lister know firsthand, Listermania has a predictable list of diagnostics. Binge-watching episodes again and again. Hours frittered away on Facebook, Twitter, and Instagram. Compulsive reading of every available book and scrap of paper that mentions Anne Lister. Immersion in diary transcriptions and hard-core research. A pilgrimage to Anne's birthplace and stomping grounds.

Recovery times vary, but for many, Listermania may be a permanent condition. Just ask Amanda Pryce, top-notch researcher and creator/guardian of the Anne Lister timeline on PackedWithPotential.org.

"I think about Anne Lister constantly, and she has become an obsession," Amanda says. "There is certainly no other person in history who has written as much in a journal as she, while identifying as queer in some way and being explicit about her experiences with other women. I feel that we are looking back at our own history. There are many other women who were probably on the same path of self-discovery, but weren't as meticulous in documenting their lives so they don't get remembered."

Amanda will be the first to admit she didn't see it coming, that her life would be upended by a lesbian who's been dead for close to 200 years. It all began with *Gentleman Jack* and its portrayal of Anne Lister, sparking her insatiable desire for a more complete understanding of the real Anne's passions, love interests, and adventures.

"LGBTQ+ people are constantly looking for some sort of representation in the media, whether it's good, bad, or in the middle, so when I first saw an advert for this show, it just screamed like something I need to see," Amanda says. "Then after I saw the show and read all the books about Anne Lister, I still needed to know more about her. When I progressed to reading academic papers, my wife was like, 'What's going on?'"

Amanda's virtual walking in Anne Lister's boots soon became the real thing with a trip to lesbian mecca. For Amanda's 32nd birthday in 2019, she and her wife celebrated the occasion in Halifax. Amanda was profoundly touched by her strolls around the beautiful grounds at Shibden Hall and exploration of each room in Anne Lister's house.

"It's really hard to put it into words," Amanda explains, "because it's so magical. You can't really believe this is where the woman lived, and she walked these halls and these rooms, and around the gardens, many that she landscaped herself. All that you see has her influence. Then you think, 'Oh my God, this is *her* in the form of a building,' and it's so grand and homey and just wonderful. It's the closest to being in her presence that will ever be, isn't it?"

Once back home, the wealth of Lister information that was being newly discovered, transcribed, and presented in a multitude of online and offline forums made it hard for Amanda to keep up and process all that was coming to light. Her solution was to create an interactive timeline to show, at a glance, what was going on in Anne's life. With Jenna Beyer, she created the Anne Lister 1791–1840 Timeline, a one-stop resource to track Anne's almost half century of activities, travels, and relationships. It made sense for this valuable tool to reside on the Packed with Potential website, the emerging go-to source for any and all things Anne Lister.

"We started with the basics and just built it up from there," she says.

"We've kept making a lot of changes because so much stuff is coming out of the transcription project. The timeline has images to go with the key dates, links to various resources, and I've started including birth and death certificates, burial certificates, and other documents. Plus I've added a lot of quotes from Anne's diary to emphasize an event or specific thing that shows up on the timeline, in an effort to allow Anne to tell her own story."

Of course, Amanda couldn't call it a day with only *one* big undertaking. Besides her ongoing work on the timeline, she signed up for the West Yorkshire Archive Service's diary transcription project.

"I was transcribing the diaries because that's all that was left," she says. "Even though the pages of Anne's journals looked really hard to read, I just had to do it. My curiosity was just too much, and I couldn't walk away from it."

Her big surprise was that deciphering Anne Lister's journals wasn't as daunting as Amanda feared. Here's where her job as a medical coder for the National Health Service—and the hours she's spent translating physicians' scrawl into comprehensible patient medical records—paid off. Experienced in reading difficult handwriting, Amanda could now apply her skills and sharp eye to decrypt what Anne wrote in her journals and piece together the puzzle of her riveting 19th century life.

Amanda's first foray into the diary pages was transcribing 33-year-old Anne's seduction of Maria Barlow in 1824.

"It was quite fun to see her in her stride," she says. "It was Anne Lister in action."

This graphic introduction to the secret world hidden in Anne's *crypthand* code piqued Amanda's interest in Anne's other girlfriends. She advanced to transcribing entries about Anne's Scottish lover Sibbella

MacLean, in 1828, then on to Anne's visit to Isabella 'Tib' Norcliffe at Langton Hall, Yorkshire a few years later.

"There's just something about reading the woman's handwriting, running across her making a mistake and crossing it out, recognizing her turns of phrase, seeing how her handwriting changes over time," Amanda observes. "There's a certain magic in it, and you just begin to get a sense of how she felt, and who she really was. She does a lot of maturing with Maria Barlow, and that relationship drags on and on for years. My goodness me, Anne was incredibly romantic, and you see that in some of the letters between her and Sibbella. By the time she's with Tib in 1831, I saw a different side of her that I hadn't really seen before, and I got the sense she was a little bit more melancholic at this time in her life."

Amanda discovered that her ability to quickly read Anne's diary was a game-changer for her.

"It was a landmark day when I could open a file from the archives and just read what Anne wrote directly off the page," she says.

It was like having a key to a chest filled with treasures, and it meant Amanda could easily skim Anne's journals for mentions of whatever topics grabbed her attention. Anne's accomplishments as a mountaineer were a particular interest, and so was investigating where Anne's grave may be in Halifax Minster. Both are subjects covered in articles Amanda has written or contributed to on the Packed with Potential website.

Aside from setting the historical record straight, Amanda says she can't help but feel a strong and intimate connection to Anne Lister based on their common experience of coming to terms with their sexuality.

"Personally, I feel that her journey to understand herself speaks to me on such a deep level," she elaborates. "When I came out, I wondered, 'Why me? Why is this happening to me? What is there that can explain this?' I think Anne Lister went through the same thing, obviously in a completely different time. The fact that she did it, like 200 years ago, just blows my mind that she was going through exactly the same experience."

Amanda still struggles to explain her own experience of Listermania.

"I've been thinking about this obsession from the beginning and trying to verbalize it and understand my fascination with Anne Lister," she says, "because it has very real consequences and it affects my time. But I believe it is because it speaks to something fundamental in me about understanding my own queer identity by looking back at a woman who was on the same path."

Thanks to *Gentleman Jack* and learning about Anne Lister, Amanda says she is a different person.

"I'm doing things I never, ever thought I'd be doing, like writing for a website and transcribing journals," she says. "I never imagined I'd be going to libraries and archives and digging through historical documents. It's opened up a whole new world of people that I never imagined I'd be friends with, and I've found a community I didn't know I needed, a community that I absolutely adore."

There is no end in sight to Amanda's time travel back to the 1800s. The expanding list of to-do projects for Packed with Potential contributors like herself could keep her motivated and occupied for years.

"I think it's because for so long Anne Lister just sat alone in the archives, and we didn't know about her," Amanda concludes. "Many of us are a bit sad that the codebreaker project is going to be over once all the journal pages have been transcribed. But everybody has said they plan to continue reading about certain times in Anne's life anyway, and I've got my own list of years I want to check out. We all take our research very seriously, but we also have so much fun doing it. I am literally reading Anne Lister's 200-year-old handwriting and breaking her code to reveal this powerful history that speaks directly to me as a lesbian woman in 2021. That's just incredible. If I could do this as a full-time job, I absolutely would."

SHANTEL SMITH

Kansas City, Missouri, USA

CAPTAIN, TEAM MARIANA

When it comes to all things *Gentleman Jack*, Shantel Smith is all in. She's made close to 15 trips from the United States to England in 24 months for sightseeing, fun, and research. She's active on multiple *Gentleman Jack*-related social media platforms. She's got two Anne Lister-inspired documentaries in the works. She's been to meetups of *Gentleman Jack* fans in nearly a dozen American cities. She's an administrator and regular contributor to the PackedWithPotential. org website brimming with information about Anne Lister. She was one of the organizers of the 2020 Anne Lister Research Summit, and she's part of the group climbing Vignemale in the summer of 2022.

But of all her pursuits, her favorite is making sure that Mariana Percy Belcombe Lawton gets the credit she deserves by shining a bright light on her and the entire Belcombe family.

Fans, of course, know that Anne Lister and Mariana were longtime lovers, having been introduced to each other by their mutual friend Isabella "Tib" Norcliffe when they were in their early 20s. As Anne had previously done with her first love, Eliza Raine, Anne and Mariana exchanged rings and took communion together to symbolize their forever commitment to each other. But their plans for spending a lifetime together were dashed when Mariana's father set about to secure his daughter's financial security by marrying her off to wealthy landowner Charles Lawton. Since Lawton was 18 years older than Mariana and believed to be in poor health, Anne and Mariana expected their separation to be short-lived and vowed to pick up where they left off "when Charles dies."

Charles, however, failed to pass away on schedule. He lived until he was 89, and, in fact, he outlasted Anne by 20 years. In spite of Anne's and Mariana's deep and passionate love for each other, their on-again-off-again relationship of almost two decades ended when Anne married Ann Walker, though they continued to correspond until Anne's death in 1840.

Fans reacted to Mariana, as she was portrayed in *Gentleman Jack*, with equal parts disdain (for breaking Anne's heart by agreeing to a loveless marriage with a man) or sympathy (for trading her happiness with Anne Lister for financial stability as a rich landowner's wife).

"I certainly didn't expect the #TeamMariana route to happen," Shantel says. "It just slowly began to take shape when I was going back and forth to England, learning more about Anne Lister, and starting to search for graves, including Mariana's."

It took months and three different trips before Shantel discovered Mariana's resting place in a small, iron-fenced area in the old graveyard at

Church Lawton in Cheshire, the markings on Mariana's large tombstone so faint that Shantel had overlooked them in previous searches.

"In the process of looking for Mariana's grave, I was learning more and more about her and the Belcombe family," Shantel explains. "Because of society and the time when she lived, Mariana had to make some choices she probably wouldn't have made if she were alive today. After I spent an afternoon in the archives reading the words straight from her pen, that just solidified my wanting to know even more about her. I was like, this is a fascinating woman who is never going to get any credit, so I will do what I can to figure out her story."

During the months of research that followed, Shantel says she discovered Mariana was an amazing writer capable of beautiful passages, dry humor, and sarcasm. Anne Lister's journals reveal she and Mariana exchanged more than 1,000 letters, though fewer than a dozen remain and are in the care of the West Yorkshire Archive Service in Halifax. After hardy Charles finally died in 1860, Mariana moved to London and lived with one of her sisters until she passed away eight years later at the age of 80.

Shantel's curiosity about the lives of all of Mariana's relatives led to the discovery of surprising details about Mariana's niece, the daughter of her brother Steph. Also named Mariana Percy after her aunt, she was sometimes called Little M and went by the name Percy. Mariana Lawton and Anne Lister were Percy's godmothers.

Like her aunt, Percy also had a close relationship with a woman, one that spanned more than 50 years.

"In census records, I found out that Elizabeth Hopkinson started out as Percy's ladies' maid and in later years was listed as Percy's companion,"

Shantel says. "Over the years, they were active in their community and often mentioned together in multiple newspaper articles. When Percy died, she left her home to Elizabeth, and Elizabeth commissioned a large stained glass window in St. Olave's Church in York in Percy's honor. They're even buried next to each other in York Cemetery, which is situated just outside the city walls."

Shantel says her research has not yet verified the nature of their relationship.

"Were Percy and Elizabeth just besties and gal pals?" she speculates. "I like to think these women got to have the life together that Mariana and Anne wanted but didn't have."

Shantel's fervent preoccupation with Mariana Belcombe Lawton and all the Belcombes manifests itself in multiple ways.

"Mariana has become my only hobby," Shantel admits. "I write a blog about Mariana and her family. I have a fantastic full-color Mariana tattoo on my left arm that stretches from my shoulder to my wrist. There is a standing Zoom room for meetups and a bunch of us play a game called Division on PlayStations and Xboxes. We've got Team Mariana running around the streets of Washington DC shooting bad guys and collecting supplies. And I used Mariana's initials and named my film production company MPB Productions after her."

Before *Gentleman Jack*, Shantel admits she wasn't a history buff.

"I didn't think history was exciting until now," she says. "But history is fun when you can relate, and I can relate to Mariana, Anne Lister, and many of the other women in this true story."

Shantel's interests extend beyond searching for historical documents or traipsing through English cemeteries. When the chance to climb

Anne Lister's mountain in France with a group of *Gentleman Jack* fans presented itself, Shantel says it sounded like fun and something worth doing.

"I'm excited about the camaraderie with all the other people, but I'm the type who will always say 'challenge accepted,'" Shantel says. "I used to run in ultramarathons and I started that just to see if I could do one. Now I just want the personal challenge to see if I can climb a mountain and check that off my bucket list. I think Anne Lister is amazing, but I'm not one of the people climbing Vignemale because Anne Lister did it. Now, if Mariana had climbed the mountain with Anne, I'd so be taking a sign and putting it up there for Mariana!"

In reflecting on all that has transpired since *Gentleman Jack* hit the airwaves in 2019, Shantel says this television show altered the trajectory of her life.

"I had just gotten out of a horrible relationship, and I didn't feel like myself," she says. "A month after I started watching *Gentleman Jack*, I was in another country, making new friends, and finding out about all of this historical stuff. If it hadn't been for all of that, I wouldn't have come back to myself so soon and experienced so many positive changes."

Shantel is at the center of a large and fast-growing international group of women initially connected by *Gentleman Jack* and the historic figures on whom it is based.

"I don't think we all would have become friends without the Anne Lister connection," Shantel says. "It's brought together people from every single walk of life from all over the world who probably would not have run across each other in any other situation. Everyone is welcome and every single person can join in and help with finding information if they're interested and just be part of this big, supportive community. It's where people can connect with themselves or discover things about themselves that they never even considered. It's amazing that this entire global community has risen from a TV show and that's not going to end any time soon."

Visit Shantel's website at herstoryinthearchives.com. for her take on All Things Mariana. Scroll through her many posts to find the delightful six-minute video, "All the Marianas," narrated by Lydia Leonard who plays the part of Mariana Lawton in Gentleman Jack, to learn about Mariana and descendants who share her name.

Interior Lister Lion, Shibden Hall

JANNEKE VAN DER WEIJDEN

Hilversum, North Holland, The Netherlands

A WOMAN BEYOND HER TIME

*T*ime travel is the stuff of science fiction and fantasy. What would it be like to go back a century or two and meet members of our family, or experience historic events in person, or eavesdrop on the conversations of our heroines and accompany them on their escapades?

Janneke van der Weijden knows. For two years she has transported herself back and forth to the 19th century by immersing herself in Anne Lister's journals and travel diaries.

"I was enthralled by *Gentleman Jack,* and I watched it on repeat for at least a year," Janneke says. "It drew me into a fandom, which I've never been part of, and it made me want to know much more about Anne Lister. I started reading all the books about her, but I didn't make the jump to think I could read her journals myself because I'm not an academic, and I'm not someone that would normally go and delve into old books."

Still, Janneke had questions that no one had yet answered. Did Anne Lister enjoy classical music? What was Anne's reaction to a performance of Handel's *Messiah* in York in 1823, a choral piece that Janneke, an accomplished singer, has herself performed? Where did Anne go and what did she see during her travels in the Netherlands, where Janneke makes her home?

Answers were surely buried in Anne's diaries and travel notes. With encouragement from Anne Choma, the author of the companion book to the *Gentleman Jack* television series, Janneke decided have a look at the source material to find out. With trepidation, she signed up to participate in the West Yorkshire Archive Service (WYAS) codebreaker project that was enlisting the help of volunteers to transcribe the millions of words in Anne's journals—roughly 20% written in her secret code—in batches of 20 diary pages at a time.

"It was tricky at first," Janneke says. "The code isn't that difficult to read, but her tiny handwriting can be a pain. But as you get into it and practice, you can sort of read it without thinking about it too hard—until you come across things where you need to ask for help."

Early on in the transcription process, Janneke realized that deciphering Anne's journal entries didn't have to be a solo activity. She and fellow codebreakers meet each other online—they call themselves the Lister Nerds—to revel in their finds about Anne's shenanigans while offering support and commiseration on the challenges of interpreting Anne's often illegible scribbles, her puzzling abbreviations, and many unfamiliar names of people and places.

"What I love so much is that there also is continuous cooperation on the Facebook website for codebreakers, and in the Twittersphere," Janneke says. "There are always people who want to help each other with questions related to research, events, and anything else."

Janneke discovered that a fuller and more complex picture of Anne Lister began to take shape as she read the words that Anne had inked upon the pages of her diaries.

"If you only watch the TV show, you might have a warped view of her," she says. "It may be too positive. You can have pink-tinted glasses about her because she is a lesbian, and she knew it. But I think it's fair to say she wasn't the easiest person either. You have to allow her to have her weaknesses. She's no saint, and I could see that in what she is writing."

Acknowledging Anne's flaws in no way diminishes her appeal.

"What strikes me as most interesting is her strength of mind and just the confidence she has in herself that never wavers," Janneke says. "I find that admirable and something to look up to. That she is not perfect is good because obviously we're all human, and so is she."

Anne's handwritten words touched Janneke in ways she didn't anticipate. While the typed transcripts of Anne's journal entries provide factual details about her activities, travels, business dealings, and private thoughts, Janneke believes they don't convey the vulnerability and humanity that comes across when gleaning the information directly from Anne's own hand.

"Anne's handwriting is a personality in itself," she explains. "You feel connected to Anne, and it probably sounds weird, but you really feel like you're listening to her firsthand. You're going into her head and you get to have more understanding of what's happening with her. Seeing her personality on the page really made me feel closer to her."

Transcribing Anne's dairies catapulted Janneke back to the 1800s and gave her an intimate view of Anne's life as an estate manager, businesswoman, and world traveler 200 years ago.

"I find it very interesting to read about her situation because it's so different from ours and so historically fascinating," Janneke says. "You're seeing her thoughts, and you're following what she is doing at Shibden. You're reading about some of her questionable business decisions, like investing 6,000 pounds to get a return of 250 pounds a year, and you think, 'What is this that you're doing? That can't lead to any good.' You see she was interested in how people in other countries did their business and made their money, which seems a fairly unusual thing at that point in time for a woman to be concerned about."

What especially drew Janneke to Anne was her passion for seeing the world.

"I love doing the transcriptions of where Anne is traveling and the way she describes everything," Janneke says. "She had an enormous sense of adventure, and she has an opinion about absolutely everything. She'll say this inn was brilliant, and the other inn was terrible, and be very vocal about it. Sometimes as I read about where she was going, I often think I would never do that."

Janneke was so captivated by Anne's travels in 1831 through the Netherlands with Mariana Lawton (née Belcombe) that she collaborated with codebreaker Adeline Lim to create an online story map tracing the couple's round-trip itinerary from Halifax to Amsterdam. Excerpts from Anne's travel diaries provide a running commentary on their accommodations, meals, and the weather of course, and reveal her impressions of the 40+ towns and villages they visited during their 21-day trip. To this wealth of material Janneke and Adeline have added contemporaneous 19th century paintings and engravings to illustrate what Anne and Mariana might have seen at each stop along the way.

"My motivation for documenting her Dutch trip was literally because I wanted to know where they had been in my country and what Anne wrote about it," she says.

To her delight, one day on her way home from work Janneke found herself taking an unexpected trip into the past. She was stuck in a traffic jam, and her navigation app redirected her off her usual motorway route to a narrow country road alongside a small meandering river.

"I was passing through all of these villages with little churches that I remembered Anne had mentioned seeing from the carriage as she and Mariana were traveling between Amsterdam and Utrecht," she recalls. "It's actually within 15 kilometers (9+ miles) of where my wife and I live.

Now it's like a favorite little detour I sometimes take."

Janneke says the affinity she feels for Anne Lister would never have happened without *Gentleman Jack* and what it initiated. She even found Anne's musical tastes match up with hers. In her journal on September 24, 1823, Anne noted that she and her entourage attended a performance of the *Messiah*: " . . . *our seats were excellent, the music and singing capital, the Hallelujah chorus transcendently fine, the leader says there will never be such a thing again during the life of this generation.*"

Transcribing the words of Anne Lister has been pure joy, and it's something she plans to continue after the WYAS project wraps up, just to stay in contact with this intelligent, funny, and complicated woman whose company she enjoys so much.

"Even when we didn't know about her, Anne Lister has been here all along, and she's proof that women like us have always been around, for centuries," Janneke concludes. "Anne has taught me what it's like to have inner strength, conviction, and self-belief, and she's boosted my confidence. There is a surprising love I feel for this person who is no longer here—because of who she was and how she inspires all of us so much."

The story map of Anne Lister's 1831 trip to the Netherlands can be found on the PackedwithPotential.org website, where Janneke is a regular contributor.

∞

JENNA BEYER

Sydney, New South Wales, Australia

A REMARKABLE TURNAROUND

*I*t's March 6, 1420, 416 years before Anne Lister will inherit Shibden Hall. An individual in the wool trade by the name of William Otes is the first recorded occupant of this south-facing house on a hill that once overlooked a lush landscape where rams, ewes, and lambs grazed. Shibden's name is the combination of *shib*, referring to sheep, and the old English suffix *denu*, meaning valley.

That's the takeaway from the first entry on the Shibden Hall timeline on PackedWithPotential.org, which documents the 600-year history of the home and grounds that meant so much to its most famous resident, and now, to her legions of admirers.

This information-packed resource is the result of painstaking research spearheaded by Jenna Beyer in collaboration with a cohort of like-minded peers. According to her, closely working with a team to ferret out these extensive historical details is proof of how far she's come since watching *Gentleman Jack* in the spring of 2019.

"I've lived with social anxiety since I was about 12 years old, to the point that some of the time I was barely functional," Jenna explains. "There have been many times when it was really hard for me to connect with people because I was so terrified, and that's had a really huge impact on my life and my well-being. Anxiety has affected my ability to interact with people and make friends, and it has left me in a state of turmoil on the inside, especially in the last few years."

For a young woman often overwhelmed in social situations, Jenna found comfort, oddly enough, in escape to foreign countries. Like Anne Lister, Jenna says her curiosity about the world and a compulsion to travel sustained her during some of her lowest periods. Over the past decade, she's logged thousands of miles for sightseeing, school, and jobs abroad, studying in South Africa, Australia, and the Galapagos Islands, volunteering and vacationing in South America, and taking on a variety of environmental projects throughout the United States and in Equatorial Guinea.

"I actually found that traveling helps me feel less anxious, especially traveling alone," she says. "When I'm just passing through a place, it takes the pressure off because I'm not expected to make close connections with people."

As she approached her mid-20s, Jenna noticed that her globetrotting days were taking an increasing toll on her mental health. While she reveled in exploring new places and experiencing different cultures, she says moving around to so many states and countries took her away from her handful of close friends and left her feeling alone and isolated.

"My anxiety was getting progressively worse," she recalls. "I found it very hard to meet people whenever I arrived in new places. Most of the time, an objective observer probably wouldn't have noticed anything much out of the ordinary unless they saw me plunked into a group of new people. Then it would be obvious as I would try to find a corner where nobody would notice me and wonder who the weird silent girl was. But even if I outwardly seemed fine during this time, on the inside I felt like I was spinning out of control."

In 2016, Jenna's precarious emotional state was further exacerbated by the realization that she is gay.

"That's probably when my anxiety was at its worst," she says. "I was coming to terms with my identity, and I was not in a good place. Even so, it didn't keep me from seeing the world."

It was during a solo trip that year to the Jane Austen Festival in Bath, England that Jenna got wind of a new 1830s period drama on the horizon. A fan of the Georgian and Regency eras in 18th and 19th century England, Jenna was excited to have something to look forward to.

"When I first heard about *Gentleman Jack*, I was like, 'Oh, this sounds like it will be interesting,' and side note, there's lesbians," she recalls. "I was back at home in Colorado living with my parents when the show came out. I started watching it, and I was instantly blown away by Anne Lister. As the series progressed, I could just feel things changing inside. It was like turning on a switch and what I had been struggling with off and on for 15 years suddenly was just gone, all from this amazing TV show."

Jenna says an especially pivotal moment occurred, for her, when Anne Lister breaks down in sobs the night before Ann Walker leaves for Scotland during the heart-wrenching "I rise above it" scene in Episode 6 of *Gentleman Jack's* first season.

"That scene broke my heart into pieces, but then put it all back together the right way," she says. "It was so powerful, and I cried for probably two solid hours. It was like the cathartic cry that needed to happen. So much of the way I felt about myself was wrapped up in internalized homophobia and fear of what people would think if they knew who I actually was. *Gentleman Jack* broke down walls and let me accept who I am, and it said to me, 'It's fine. You shouldn't be ashamed.'"

Having undergone an astonishing metamorphosis in only eight

weeks—transforming from someone who often could barely speak to a "new, smiling little human," she says—Jenna was eager to break away from the constraints of her pre-*Gentleman Jack* self. First, she found herself connecting to the growing Anne Lister community by becoming a codebreaker, immersing herself in the world of historical Anne Lister through transcribing hundreds of pages of Anne's diary.

Driven by fascination with both Anne Lister and Ann Walker, Jenna headed to Halifax, luckily timing her visit to shortly before the coronavirus pandemic struck and made international travel off-limits. As a memento of her visit, she got a tattoo above her heart, in Anne's handwriting, that says "The half will be for you." It's a phrase lifted from a letter that Ann Walker wrote to Anne Lister in 1834 saying that, as long as Ann had a cottage or room, half would be for Anne. Jenna says it's a nice companion to the inked "I will never fear" on her

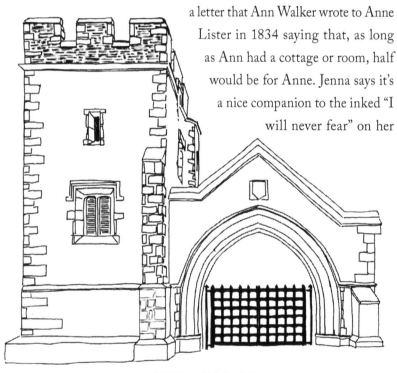

Gatehouse, Shibden Hall

right forearm in Anne's *crypthand* code from an 1821 journal entry.

"I could just feel Anne everywhere when I was at Shibden," Jenna says.

With that as her motivation following her trip into *Gentleman Jack* territory, Jenna began her deep dive into Shibden Hall's rich history, resulting in her creation of a timeline of the property's many owners, major events, modifications, and restorations. This at-a-glance chronology is enhanced with artwork, historical documents, and photographs that illuminate the heritage of this home-turned-museum from 1420 to the present day.

"I love old buildings, so the house has become my main focus to research because there is so much to look into. Among what I discovered is that Anne Lister and Ann Walker were living in a construction zone for most of their married life."

Lister enthusiasts will especially appreciate the details about the extensive renovations that Anne made to the Lister estate between 1834 and 1839, featuring the addition of her library tower and including a turret, gatehouse, coach house, and many other major improvements inside the house. Anne's desire to create an ideal English landscape was behind her dredging a lake on her property and planting the hundreds of trees that continue to delight Shibden's thousands of local and international visitors.

But codebreaking and historical research were only the beginning of the "new" Jenna.

"Now I'm doing all of these things that would have been the most terrifying things I could have imagined two years ago," she says.

No longer painfully timid and shy, Jenna has close friendships with fellow codebreakers and others in the *Gentleman Jack*/Anne Lister online communities. Regularly contributing to the Packed with Potential website also gave her the confidence to take on being a facilitator at the 2020 Anne Lister Research Summit, a role that would have been impossible for someone who previously shrank from even the thought of public speaking.

Fired up with Anne Lister-inspired courage, in 2020 Jenna moved 9,000 miles (14,500 km) from Colorado to Australia to enroll in a master's degree program in nursing, a person-centric field which she acknowledges would have been completely out the question before *Gentleman Jack*. In contrast to her past experiences as an undergraduate, she boasts she is one of the most participatory people in her classes.

Jenna says anyone meeting her now has no idea of the fearful and anxious person she was for more than half of her life.

"When you have a mental illness like anxiety, it is kind of always there, and I am very aware of the fact that it is something that can come back if I find myself in a stressful situation," she explains. "But now I have this thing I can always fall back on, like I have this buildup of support basically from Anne Lister when I start feeling that sort of fear creeping up. The way I think of myself now means I have a lot more resilience to any sort of stress going forward because I am much more comfortable with myself and who I am. I am so different from who I was before *Gentleman Jack* that I literally don't even recognize myself sometimes. The most important thing is that now I live a life that is true to me."

Perhaps the best of the many profound changes in Jenna's life because of *Gentleman Jack* is that she, at long last, is at peace with herself. Now, openly out, she says she also feels connected to the queer community in general for the first time, thanks to Anne Lister as her role model. Anne's refusal to conform to gender expectations in her day, along with her determination to live life on her own terms, has been an invaluable lesson in authentic living for Jenna.

"I identify as a nonbinary woman because neither gender feels quite right to me," Jenna explains, "and I don't feel that I fit exactly within the gender binary—I'm in between somewhere. I really have a lot of respect for Anne's ability to build her identity and find a way to understand herself. She was just fearless, though she had her moments of self-doubt like the rest of us, and she had vulnerable days too. Seeing that vulnerability in her journals definitely made me cry more than a few times, but having that kind of holistic image of her makes her even more courageous and attractive to me."

Jenna acknowledges how indebted she is to both Anne Lister of historical record and the fictionalized version of her in *Gentleman Jack*.

"Knowing she actually lived and I can claim that I am like her is very powerful, plus she is someone who is part of my queer history. This entire experience has changed the direction of my life, and I am a totally different person now. I am very, very grateful to Sally Wainwright and Suranne Jones and everyone involved in *Gentleman Jack*," Jenna says. "I owe them a lot."

∞

Walker Coat of Arms

IN SEARCH OF ANN WALKER

ELEVATING A HEROINE FROM A FOOTNOTE IN HISTORY

*A*nn Walker did what other women before her had been unable or unwilling to do: she married Anne Lister. Their self-styled version of a private wedding ceremony took place in York on Easter Sunday in 1834 at Holy Trinity Church, Goodramgate during a time when known same sex liaisons were a hanging offense for men and guaranteed social damnation for women. Exactly who was this brave soul who defied her family and risked her reputation to be with the woman she loved?

Viewed apart from the prism of Anne Lister, what was Ann Walker really like? She had never been of any particular interest to historians, and it seemed only a few letters were all she left behind. There were no portraits to show what she looked like, no known diaries to reveal her thoughts, no Wikipedia page to provide even the most basic facts about her life.

Gentleman Jack rescued her from obscurity and introduced Ann Walker to millions of viewers. Now, armchair sleuths around the world are filling in the blanks to fully document her remarkable life. Steve

Crabtree, Diane Halford, and Alexa Tansley are leading the charge to ensure that Ann Walker gets the recognition, respect, and rightful place she deserves among the ranks of historical lesbians. Together, they're advancing Ann Walker's position in history and cementing her legacy.

In Search of Ann Walker welcomes anyone interested in helping discover facts about Ann Walker and telling her story. Contact information is available at InSearchofAnnWalker.com.

STEVE CRABTREE

Sowerby Bridge, West Yorkshire, England, UK

A FANTASTICAL TALE

*M*any mornings he arrives early and has the old house on the hill all to himself. He lets himself in through the back door and disarms the security system. Room by room, he passes from the kitchen through the great hall to the study, dining room, and parlor, turning on the lights as he goes. His footsteps echo as he mounts the dark oak stairs to prepare the upstairs bedrooms. Until the curious and devoted begin arriving, it is dead-of-night quiet in the house, the spirits of centuries' old occupants long gone or not yet roused.

Steve Crabtree says working at Shibden Hall in visitor services is the best job he's ever had. Welcoming guests, handling administrative and light maintenance duties, and showing people around Shibden Hall is a perfect fit for this modest Halifax native who describes himself as an amateur local historian and also occasionally leads heritage walks in the area.

Since 2019, *Gentleman Jack* has drawn thousands of new visitors to Anne Lister's home.

"There is a kind of hush that falls over people when they make their way into the main part of the house," Steve observes. "They naturally kind of drop into this respectful whisper, particularly Anne Lister fans. I often hear them saying to each other, 'These are the floors where she walked. This is the bannister she would have held to climb the stairs.' It's clear they feel a personal connection to the Hall."

While much is known about Shibden Hall's most famous resident from her journals and the books that have been written about her, information about Anne Lister's wife has been sketchy, inaccurate, or both.

Red Room, Shibden Hall

"I personally felt quite bothered about the amount of ignorance there was about Ann Walker," Steve says. "Particularly in the 1980s and 1990s, when there wasn't a huge amount of attention given to the Annes, there was a kind of narrative flourish, rightly or wrongly, that was injected to the elements presented about them and passed down to volunteers and guides. The story I was told when I first started working at Shibden Hall—and one I admit I was partly responsible for spreading —was that after Anne Lister had died and Ann Walker was living in the Hall, she had locked herself in the Red Room with a brace of pistols prepared to go 'last stand at the Alamo,' and her evil brother-in-law swept in, broke down the door with help from others, and they wrestled her out of her home, bundled her off, and nobody knew what happened to her."

While it may have captured people's imagination, Steve long thought that this wild tale didn't seem right, especially since there was no historical record to back it up. With encouragement from author and historian Jill Liddington, who urged him to examine the local archives and read the primary source material himself, Steve set out to find the truth.

"I felt like I had an obligation to at least get it right for myself so that when visitors to the Hall asked me what happened to Ann Walker, I would be able to say a little bit more than she was dragged out of the Red Room," Steve explains.

"I had always seen the archives as a preserve of serious academics and very learned individuals scrolling through mountains of dusty paperwork, but I thought I'd give it a go," he continues. "The archives people were wonderfully helpful, and I began to examine the MAC 73 file that deals predominantly with Ann Walker in the post-Anne Lister world. The things I read kind of horrified me because obviously what happens to Ann is so sad and also because all of these narratives that had sprung up were completely wrong and particularly unfair to her."

Steve didn't expect to find that Ann Walker was such a stubborn and determined woman.

"She has an edge to her," he says. "One place you see it is in her approach to making the alterations to Shibden Hall that Anne Lister wanted."

He points out that multiple solicitors had warned Ann of dire consequences if she persisted with her intentions. Anne's will allowed Ann to live on the estate until her death, but since it didn't convey ownership of the property, making substantial changes to the house and grounds could have placed her in legal jeopardy with Lister descendants. Still, Ann continued to search, unsuccessfully, for a legal opinion that would grant her permission to fulfill Anne's dream of an expanded, grand home.

Steve says he was touched to run across a letter written by one of her attorneys that reflected Ann's determination to improve the Hall because it was the desire of her "lamented friend."

He also uncovered Ann's spirited challenge to a survey team working on behalf of Queen Victoria to create the first detailed topographical map of the United Kingdom. Ann was incensed about their coming onto the Shibden Hall estate (even though they had a legal right to do so without her permission), and she accused them of damaging the Hall's formal gardens.

He came across proof that Ann had stubbornly resisted paying a small debt she didn't believe she owed to one of her tenants, a defiance that ultimately led to sheriff's officers forcing their way into Shibden Hall, taking up residence in the kitchen, and preparing an auction to sell off property for payment of an amount less than 100 pounds, an insignificant sum for someone as wealthy as Ann Walker. At the last minute, Ann's sister stepped in and discharged the debt, but Ann's recalcitrance set off a chain of events that would alter the rest of her life.

Ann's repeated pattern of mishandling estate affairs raised growing concerns about her mental state. Steve's research was painstaking as he delved into the communications from attorneys and Ann's family leading up to the 1843 legal proceedings that declared Ann Walker to be a lunatic. He carefully transcribed letters he discovered that were written in 1843 by Ann's lawyers, her sister Elizabeth, and her brother-in-law Captain George Sutherland, and then arranged them in a timeline for closer examination.

Viewing the information in chronological order was an eye-opener.

"I came into it with certain preconceptions that were perhaps a bit unfair, but I don't think they were entirely unavoidable," Steve explains. "I was looking for a conspiracy that these people were terrible and out to get Ann, but the more I transcribed, the more I started to build the picture that dispels that sort of sinister edge I thought I would find. It's only when you start to put all you read and have at your disposal in the right order that the focus becomes sharper."

Based on historical records which had never been fully examined before, Steve came to the conclusion that the Sutherlands and others were, in fact, looking out for Ann Walker's best interests because they were convinced her "torments of the mind" required their intervention.

Because of what he found in the Calderdale archives, Steve has been able to debunk the Red Room myth once and for all. The documents reveal that, rather than being dragged kicking and screaming from the bedroom that she and Anne Lister had shared during their five years of living together, Ann Walker voluntarily left for mental health treatment in a private facility in York under the supervision of Dr. Stephen Belcombe.

Although after her release from treatment she would return for periods of time until 1847, Ann Walker never again lived alone at Shibden Hall. Steve has continued to sift through documents that deal with Ann's life after the death of Anne Lister.

"There were bits about Ann that surprised me in a good way," Steve says. "Ann Walker does make references to Anne Lister where she talks about following the example of her lamented friend, and obviously she can't use the language of lover or wife. It holds out that they have this relationship that you know has transcended the death of Anne Lister, and she wasn't gone from Ann's mind. She not only thinks about her, but thinks about her with such an intensity that she wants to expend quite a considerable amount of money on Shibden as a memorial of sorts."

Of course, any revelation of Ann's ardor for Anne comes as no surprise to passionate *Gentleman Jack* fans. After all, Ann had more than proved her love and legendary devotion by escorting Anne's body home on the months-long, arduous journey from Russia to England after Anne's passing in 1840.

Or had she?

Steve's discovery of a March 1841 letter to Ann Walker from one of the co-executors of Anne Lister's will expressing concern about the overdue ship *Levant Packet* would prove to be pivotal in answering the question once and for all. Using his online moniker Steve Halifax, Steve posted his find on Facebook. Just 16 miles (26 km) away in Leeds, genealogist Diane Halford took note.

∞

DIANE HALFORD

Leeds, West Yorkshire, England, UK

A HISTORICAL OVERSIGHT

On February 28, 2019, an enthusiastic crowd cheered the York Civic Trust's unveiling of a blue plaque at York's Holy Trinity Church, Goodramgate, marking the location as the site of a historic union between Anne Lister and Ann Walker in 1834. When Diane Halford saw the plaque some months later, an obvious mistake immediately caught her eye.

Had no one else noticed? Why was Anne Lister's name the prominent one on the plaque and Ann Walker's name half the size and buried in the text near the bottom of the historic marker? Doesn't a union of historic proportions involve two *equal* partners?

This seemed an egregious slight to Ann Walker. Ann's risks in symbolically marrying a woman in the 19th century certainly were no less than the other bride's. Since Diane had watched *Gentleman Jack* and been drawn to the Ann Walker character, she had noticed a disturbing pattern. Ann Walker appeared to be habitually treated as a historical afterthought. In place of scholarly research about her, there were only myths, rumors, and anecdotal stories without any historical basis.

Diane is no stranger to unlocking the secrets of the past. As an amateur family historian, she is adept at scrutinizing genealogical archives and sorting out labyrinthine paper trails of ancient family records, historical documents, and legal proceedings.

Now she had a new subject: Ann Walker.

Blue historic plaque unveiled at Holy Trinity Church, Goodramgate in York on 28 February 2019 to mark the location of Anne Lister's and Ann Walker's 1834 commitment ceremony

"I started doing Ann Walker's family tree," Diane says. "I also was reading all the Facebook fan groups when I saw a post by Steve Halifax (Steve Crabtree's online name for Facebook posts)."

What Steve had stumbled upon in his Ann Walker research at the Calderdale archives was a faded 1841 letter to Ann Walker from attorney William Gray, a co-executor of Anne Lister's will, expressing concern that there had been no news about a particular freight ship from his friend and fellow solicitor in London—a Mr. Brodrick—who was keeping an eye out for it.

Diane was intrigued.

Weeks later, while she was in London at the National Archives searching for her great grandparents' divorce papers, Diane decided to take a look at records pertaining to Ann Walker—the Walker v. Gray papers—also housed there.

That's where she discovered a critical piece to fill in the puzzle of Ann Walker's life. Diane was aware of a February 1841 letter to Ann

Walker's attorneys from a parish minister noting that "Ann Walker is recently returned." If this were true, it clearly contrasted with the popular assumption that Ann was on the boat with Anne's corpse, a boat that didn't dock in England until April 1841.

"While I was looking at some ginormous Chancery papers and getting really dusty fingers and sneezing, I saw the name Brodrick on one of the documents," she explains. Suddenly, it clicked—this Broderick was the same person on the lookout for a ship experiencing an "extraordinary delay" mentioned in the March 1841 letter that Steve had earlier posted about.

"I found an entry in an Ann Walker account that Mr. Brodrick had been paid £57.16.9 for freight," Diane says. "In the same account was another entry for 'freight of deceased from Trebizond to England' in the same amount."

What Diane had come across was confirmation of the true manner of Anne Lister's final journey back from Russia to home soil. Here was the proof that Brodrick had paid the freight charges for bringing Anne's body back from Trebizond (now known as Trabzon), situated on the Turkish coast, on the freight ship *Levant Packet*, and that Anne's remains were unaccompanied by her widow.

It was a critical finding, disproving the long-held and oft-repeated myth that Ann Walker had escorted her wife's body back from Kutaisi, Georgia (then part of the Russian Empire) where Anne had died.

"When I realized that Ann hadn't brought Anne's body back as was always told, it made me go, 'Well, what else isn't true?' Shortly after, I reached out to Steve, and we decided to start researching together."

However, before they could continue their collaboration, the coronavirus pandemic forced the closure of archives across England for months.

Nevertheless, this downtime was an opportunity for Steve, Diane, and the third member of the team, Alexa Tansley, to create the In Search of Ann Walker website. It is both a repository for the growing volume of new information about Ann and an invaluable resource for anyone interested in knowing more about her.

When the Calderdale archives finally reopened in the fall of 2020, the threesome was ready with their list of priority research projects. The hunt was on for a document to verify the date on which a Rawson relative of Ann's was given responsibility for overseeing her welfare and the management of her estates, a requirement resulting from her having been declared of unsound mind.

On Tuesday morning, October 20, 2020, Diane arrived at the archives and called for the folder containing a large parchment pertaining to the Rawson matter, short versions of the wills of Ann Walker and Anne Lister, and one of Anne Lister's travel diaries. She spread everything out on a table and took a photo, intending to post it on the InSearchofAnnWalker.com website. She picked up the small notebook with a blue and cream marble-patterned cover.

"I thought I would have a look at it because I've never really looked at an Anne Lister diary up close because I'm not a codebreaker," Diane says. "As soon as I opened it, I just randomly turned to a page, and the first thing I saw that caught my eye was 'Mr. Wilson.' I just went, 'That's the same 'W' that Ann Walker uses,' and I could tell it was her writing, but I couldn't believe it was her writing." But it was Ann Walker's writing.

She texted Alexa and Steve that she thought she had found Ann Walker's diary. There were expletives. There were exclamations. There were tears.

"I'm shaking. I'm crying," Diane recalls. "It's not hers. It is hers.

It's not hers. It is hers. Why would I have found it?"

Within three days, the diary had been authenticated by former Calderdale archivist Dan Sudron as having been written by Ann Walker. It is a monumental discovery. Here is the data that, for the first time, reveals Ann Walker's side of the Lister/Walker love story. It provides a glimpse into her personality, her relationship with Anne Lister, and a record of her activities and travels during their first months of married life from June 4, 1834 to February 19, 1835.

This extraordinary 78-page diary gives us many new details about Ann Walker in her own words and her own handwriting. Diane says Ann comes across as well-spoken and well-educated, and she clearly exults at beating "dearest," her pet name for Anne Lister, at backgammon. Shopping also seems to be a favorite pastime.

"We see that she isn't one to back down from her sister or aunt when they complain that she hasn't told them of her plans," Diane says. "She's also quite good at making pithy, sarcastic comments. I like that it shows she had a little bit of sass."

The discovery of Ann Walker's diary unleashed a tsunami of thrills in the *Gentleman Jack* fandom. "I might have been the one who found it," Diane says, "but it's really because of the research we've been doing as a team and everybody's support and work in searching for details about Ann's life."

During the months after the diary was found, the Ann Walker team could only dole out short excerpts from the diary on Twitter as they worked to resolve complicated copyright issues that prevented them from publishing the diary in full.

Gentleman Jack played a part in bringing Ann's fictional and real-life story to light. Diane says she was first drawn to the show because of its positive lesbian representation, and it quickly resulted in her wanting to satisfy her curiosity about Ann Walker. Learning more about Ann and correcting misinformation about her morphed into what she now calls 'a proper hobby.'

"*Gentleman Jack* led me to focus on something that's bigger than me," she says. "Searching for Ann has taken up an awful lot of my time, but it's really been time well spent. I've made friends from all over the world that will be my friends for life. It's got my creativity flowing again. And being part of our team has been hugely beneficial—the three of us feed off one another to come up with ideas and make things happen. It's hard to put into words how much this all means."

While Ann's silence finally has been broken, there is still more to do before her voice reaches a wider audience. Work continues to secure a vaunted place for her in the annals of LGBTQ+ history—and in the Old St. Matthew's Churchyard in Lightcliffe.

Alexa Tansley has made it her mission to deliver on both fronts.

∞

ALEXA TANSLEY

Leeds, West Yorkshire, England, UK

A ROCK IN A CEMETERY

The first season of *Gentleman Jack* hadn't yet completed its eight-episode run in the US and UK in the spring of 2019 when a disturbing photograph appeared on Alexa Tansley's Twitter feed. Pictured on straw-colored grass was a flat gray rock barely big enough to be a stepping stone. Ann Walker's name in capital letters had been scrawled on it with a black felt tip pen, along with the dates 1803–1854.

Surely this couldn't be the grave marker for the woman who had had the audacity to marry Anne Lister. Alexa was appalled at the very thought.

This would never do.

As Alexa soon learned, a volunteer at the Old St. Matthew's Churchyard where Ann Walker was laid to rest in the mid-1800s had placed the handmade marker in the Lightcliffe cemetery in the general vicinity of where Ann's grave is likely to be. It was a makeshift effort to identify a place for the increasing number of visitors to lay flowers and pay their respects to someone who had so touched their hearts.

"Ann Walker had to make a very brave, brave choice to do what she did without a supportive family," Alexa says. "To have that level of conviction is so impressive to me—to know the world around you isn't going to like it, but you're going to do it anyway. There are many of us who can relate to making a decision that isn't going to be well-received and doing it anyway because it matters so much to us."

Alexa was of a mind that Ann's bravery deserved recognition, not the least of which was a well-marked grave.

"My goal was to create a permanent memorial for Ann in the churchyard," Alexa says.

She had no idea what she was getting into.

To begin with, Ann Walker is no ordinary deceased Lightcliffe resident. The Walker family had been an integral part of the Lightcliffe community for generations, and Ann's grandfather had provided a great deal of the money to build St. Matthew's Church in 1775. Ann was baptized and worshipped there, and when she died at the age of 51, her social position and lifetime devotion to the church earned her a prominent burial location under the church's pulpit. But when the old 18th century building was torn down in the 1970s, the pulpit marking Ann's grave went with it, and no new grave marker was ever laid. All that remains of the old church is its distinctive bell tower where a deteriorating brass plaque honoring Ann Walker is locked inside.

Since St. Matthew's is still an active Anglican parish, the Church of England has the first and last say about

St. Matthew's Church Tower, Lightcliffe Cemetery

what goes on in the cemetery and old church grounds. No changes or additions are allowed, and that includes new tombstones. To further complicate matters, the oversight of the cemetery and old churchyard falls to two groups: the Friends of St. Matthew's, a local group of volunteers who maintains the centuries-old churchyard, and the Friends of Friendless Churches, a nondenominational charity that looks after the tower.

Given all the players who would have to agree on what and how to erect a suitable monument to honor Ann Walker, a weaker soul might have thrown up her hands in frustration. Not Alexa. In Anne Lister fashion, she took on task of building consensus.

"Honoring Ann is now a collaborative project between In Search of Ann Walker, the Friends of St. Matthew's, and the Friends of Friendless Churches," Alexa explains. "It's the three of us coming together to make it happen. We've agreed the first stage is to restore the original brass memorial plaque that hangs in the tower, and the subsequent plan is to restore the tower itself and actually open it up to the public. All of us want people to be able to go into the tower to pay their respects to Ann, so we hope the tower itself can be a permanent memorial to her."

Progress on the project was slowed by the coronavirus pandemic, but the first priority is the restoration of Ann's 19th century brass plaque if it can be saved. If it can't be salvaged, plans call for a replica to be produced.

"Our intention has always been to create a lasting legacy for Ann," Alexa says. "We're focused on getting things right and not rushing. These things take time."

Alexa knew from the beginning that creating a legacy in keeping with Ann's historical significance would require more than a permanent memorial at her final resting place. Joining up with Steve Crabtree and Diane Halford was a logical next step.

"In early 2020, I was aware of the research they were doing and I was working on the memorial piece, so I got in touch and said how about we collaborate together," Alexa says "It just felt right to work together to learn about Ann's past, get her voice and the truth about her out there, and create her lasting legacy. That's how the three of us came up with In Search of Ann Walker (ISAW). It's nice that we all come from three different backgrounds and we're doing our own thing, but actually the power of us coming together as a collaborative has made In Search of Ann Walker the success that it is."

The recent discovery of Ann Walker's diary was an unmitigated thrill for the team.

"After Diane found the diary, the most special time was the next three days before we were able to publicly announce the find," Alexa says. "There was only Steve, Diane, and I with the copy, and it really did feel like we were the first people to read Ann's words in nearly 200 years. As we went through and discovered some of her beautiful phrases, like her describing a view as 'an amphitheatre of mountains,' I couldn't help but feel close to her. I've always felt rather protective of Ann Walker, and this only increased with the find of the diary."

Besides remarkable research discoveries, the trio's combined efforts also have led to a robust website, a blog, and an online presence with Twitter and Facebook pages. They've created a Wikipedia page for Ann, and they've assembled a group of about 30 people working to find all of the references to Ann Walker and her homes in Anne Lister's journals. The plan is to create a searchable database so people can easily find Ann and other key words in Anne Lister's 23 years of diary entries.

"We strongly encourage people to get involved in research about Ann," Alexa says. "Truly it will change your life. Everyone is welcome to contribute whatever they can."

ISAW is also fulfilling Ann Walker's wishes to help the Lightcliffe community.

"In Ann's will, she left 10 pounds a year to the poor of Lightcliffe," Alexa explains. "We wanted to carry out her legacy, so for Christmas in 2020 we raised more than 1,300 pounds and donated the money to a local food bank. It's not a one-time thing, so doing something for charity is something we're planning doing year to year."

The team behind In Search of Ann Walker says they don't see their work coming to an end anytime soon.

"It's not like we found a diary, and now our job is done," Alexa says. "We have so many plans going forward. Ann Walker is part of LGBTQ+ history, and she deserves to have her story told. Lesbians aren't some glitch in the genetic code that will be gone in 50 years' time. Ann is someone we can all relate to. We've existed for many, many years, and we always will. Ann Walker's incredible courage is appealing, and she pushed through her mental health challenges to live the life she wanted. Her legacy will continue long after we're dust. It is our honor to honor her."

∞

ℐDVENTURE ℐEEKERS

ROAD TRIPPING & MOUNTAIN CLIMBING
IN ANNE LISTER'S FOOTSTEPS

Mount Vignemale, French Pyrenees

ADELINE LIM

Bonn, Germany

TWO LARGE CHICKENS

*I*t all started when her dog Ziggy died a month short of his 15th birthday and left Adeline Lim heartbroken. Anyone who's ever had a special bond with a pet knows the anguish that engulfs you when they're gone. Around the same time, *Gentleman Jack* was wrapping up its first season, and Adeline, newly fascinated with someone she'd never heard of, was able to find some solace in books about Anne Lister.

"After Ziggy died, I needed a distraction and a purpose to get up every morning," Adeline recounts. "So I decided I would follow in the footsteps of Anne Lister when she left Shibden in 1833 after suffering disappointment and heartbreak as a result of her failed courtship of Ann Walker."

No matter that they lived in different centuries—it turns out that Anne Lister and Adeline Lim shared far more than heartache. Same initials: A.L. Same height and approximate weight: 5′4½″ and 114 pounds (52 kg). Command of multiple languages. Indomitable sense of adventure and penchant for writing about their travels. Both women were 42 years old when they embarked on the trip that would take each of them through Germany and into Denmark, one by carriage, the other in a fast, 335-horsepower Audi A7.

Adeline says it was therapeutic to plan her town-by-town route based on Anne Lister's itinerary as reported in the books of Anne Choma and Angela Steidele. Since complete transcripts of Anne's diaries and travel journals from 1833 weren't readily available at the time, she didn't yet have the benefit of Anne's take on all the places she was about to encounter. (Months later, Adeline used her own transcriptions to backtrack and revisit some of the stops on Anne's first trip to Denmark to better see them from Anne's point of view.)

"I pledged to visit major landmarks built before the 20th century, ascend all cathedral towers, and walk everywhere in 25 minutes," Adeline says. "I was traveling with a purpose, a determination to discover what Anne had discovered."

On July 6, 2019, the day after Ziggy's ashes were delivered in a small, cream-colored urn, Adeline waved goodbye to her husband and set off on a solo 3,000-kilometer (1,800+ miles) journey that would forever change her perspective on travel.

Between Adeline's departure point in Trier in southwestern Germany and her destination in Copenhagen, there were plenty of memorable points of interest. Sticking to her plan to see what Anne saw and do what Anne did, in Kassel, Germany Adeline hiked uphill through the woods from the Devil's Bridge and up 530+ steep steps from Neptune's Grotto to the top of the Hercules monument, the equivalent of 66 flights of stairs. (*Gentleman Jack* fans will recall this landmark, with its cascading 800-foot waterfall, from the final episode of Season 1 when Anne stops there en route to Denmark.)

"I managed to climb to the top of the monument in 18 minutes," Adeline says. "It was hard work even in shorts and a t-shirt when it was 48°F (9°C). Anne did it on quite a warm day in August wearing all her layers and a corset."

In Bleikeller, Germany, Adeline made it a point to stop at St. Peter's Cathedral to view the same eight mummified bodies that Anne had seen in 1833. As Adeline was looking at the remains of the English countess, Swedish general, murdered student, and the rest displayed in glass-topped coffins, it dawned on her that she was seeing exactly what Anne Lister had seen 180 years ago.

"No matter how macabre it sounds," she says, "It was exhilarating to realize I was standing there and looking at the very same things that she saw. It was an indescribable feeling."

Once in Copenhagen, Adeline kept up the pace. Anne had noted in her journals that three times a week she walked seven miles (11 km) along the Danish capital city's Roskilde Road, so of course, Adeline matched her step for step. "It was exhausting," she says, and further proof of how physically fit Anne must have been.

Over the course of her 19-day road trip Adeline passed through dozens of the same villages, towns, and cities that Anne Lister had visited. She bounded through the same churches and museums and gazed at much of the same scenery Anne viewed from her narrow carriage window.

"Somehow, during my travels, the things I saw came to life and had more historical significance when described in Anne's words," Adeline says. "It put me on a quest to travel to as many of the places she had travelled to as I could."

Anne Lister didn't end her travels with that 1833 journey, and neither did Adeline. In the ensuing months, Adeline made more than 80 trips following in Anne's footsteps in Germany, France, Italy, England, the Netherlands, Belgium, Luxembourg, Sweden, Norway and Switzerland, with ambitious plans to eventually make her way through Russia to Kutaisi, Georgia, where Anne died.

When she wasn't traveling, Adeline worked independently and also collaborated with other Anne Lister travel enthusiasts on descriptive story maps of Anne's many trips. The story maps, which appear on the Packed with Potential website, include paintings, etchings, and modern-day photographs of the places Anne visited, along with her running commentary about where she stayed, what she saw, and of course, the weather.

Adeline's off-road endeavors picked up considerably when the unthinkable happened and the coronavirus pandemic made the world off limits for travel during most of 2020. Much to her dismay, Adeline was suddenly grounded, with time on her hands and a raging case of armchair wanderlust.

"That's when I started transcribing Anne Lister's travel journals and diaries," Adeline says. "After a shaky start, I began to familiarize myself with her style with help from other codebreakers. One of the reasons I started transcribing was because there was no material on Anne's travels in 1827, and I was interested in her journey through France, Italy, and Switzerland."

Through transcribing her diaries, the world of Anne's travels in the 1800s immediately came into sharper focus for Adeline in spite of the challenges of interpreting Anne's difficult handwriting which, occasionally, can lead one to a wild surmise. That was the case, Adeline recalls, in her first week of transcribing when she came across an 1827 travel journal entry where ever-observant Anne wrote about the attractions in a small French village.

"Everywhere Anne Lister goes, she's always talking about a church here, and then another church there," Adeline explains. "But it seemed unlikely to me that such a small place would have two churches, so I interpreted her entry to say '*two large chickens*.'" Fellow codebreakers, after a good laugh, helped Adeline sort out the correct interpretation. The French village of Châlons-sur-Marne (its present-day name is Châlon-en-Champagne) does indeed have two large *churches*, which Adeline has since visited.

During occasional breaks between European lockdowns, Adeline was back on the road every chance she got, tracking Anne's paths across the Continent. In Switzerland, she contended with sleet and pockets of ice and snow in July when she climbed the peaks in the Swiss Alps that Anne had climbed in 1827. She visited the same churchyard cemetery in Grindelwald where Anne paid her respects at the graves of the many climbers who perished on the surrounding treacherous mountains. Adeline climbed, through snow, to the source of the Garonne River high in the Spanish Pyrenees, where Anne had trekked under the watchful eyes of Spanish soldiers who suspected she might be a spy and, therefore, was "someone of interest" during the July Revolution in 1830.

Nothing is off limits when Adeline is on Anne's trail, wherever it may take her.

"It's been challenging for sure," Adeline explains. "But the upside is that I've learned that we shouldn't set parameters as to what we can or cannot do. We should just go for whatever we want."

Not only has Adeline traveled thousands of miles, crossed seas, hiked up and down mountains, and visited hundreds of places that attracted

Anne Lister's attention, but now she's heading for those places that Anne never had the chance to explore.

"Anne's bucket list is going to be my thing too," Adeline says.

Norway is a case in point. Bad weather prevented Anne from making it to the top of the Gausta (also called Gaustatoppen), the tallest mountain in southeast Norway, where on a clear day one-sixth of the rest of the country is visible. So Adeline did it for her.

"It was such hard climbing because it's just rocks, and you could easily break a leg," Adeline says. "It was so cold even in the summer when my husband and I climbed it, but the view was very good."

When the fall of 2020 brought another lockdown throughout continental Europe, Adeline wondered what to do with so much time on her hands again.

"I looked at all the transcriptions I had, and then I just decided I'm going to try my hand at writing," Adeline says. The result is *In the Footsteps of Anne Lister, Volume 1*, an engaging 250-page travelogue that combines Adeline's own observations with her transcriptions of Anne's 1833 diary entries and travel journal. She's provided rich context for the journey via her excellent, comprehensive overview of Anne's life and relationships, and she's included updates about historical sites, helpful map illustrations, and a list of the 70+ locations that she and Anne both visited.

"What I like about Anne Lister is that she was smart and bold and not constrained by what was acceptable behavior at the time," Adeline reflects. "Her sense of adventure is amazing. I don't know if I would be so brave or adventurous if I lived in her time. What really stands out about her is that she is this amazing force going to all of these places. When you're at the bottom of the huge mountains that she climbed and you see the clouds covering the tops, and then you're standing on the summits, you really wonder how she did it over and over. Now, I cannot travel without having her on my mind or by my side or trying to describe things in a candid or sardonic way as she does."

There's no letup in sight for Adeline's Anne Lister-related travels, journal transcriptions, and accounts of Anne's adventures. She's closing in on deciphering 1,000 journal pages, continuing to locate illustrations and transcribe Anne's commentaries for new story maps, and planning more trips to investigate destinations that piqued Anne's interest.

What compels a modern middle-aged woman to walk in the footsteps of a lesbian who chronicled her travel escapades a couple of centuries before Adeline was even born? One explanation is that it's the same thing that drove Anne Lister to explore her 19th century world in the first place: *ferocious curiosity*. Another reason is that, for both Adeline and Anne, adventure is the best healing balm for a weary soul and suffering heart.

Buffeted by wind as she stood on the Alte Liebe pier in Cuxhaven, Germany, where Anne Lister set sail for home across the North Sea in 1833, Adeline realized, there, at the end of her first trek in Anne's footsteps, that her life had changed.

"I know that an invisible yet definite line separates my life before I learned of this remarkable and fascinating woman, and my life after," Adeline says. "What I also know is that travel is enriched when accompanied by the spirit of an adventuress like Anne Lister."

In the Footsteps of Anne Lister, Volume 1: Travels of a remarkable English gentlewoman in France, Germany and Denmark *is available on Amazon. Adeline's story maps can be found on PackedwithPotential.org.*

∞

ALEX CHAPMAN & RUTH CROFTS

Yarm, North Yorkshire, England, UK

PATHS OF DISCOVERY

*A*nne Lister often roved around the countryside in a green and gold two-seater carriage whose wooden wheels and stiff suspension ensured a bone-rattling ride on the rutted dirt roads of early 19th century England. Two hundred years later, two of her staunchest fans are following her tracks—although in a considerably more comfortable fashion.

Enchanted by Anne Lister's bold spirit and sense of adventure evident in *Gentleman Jack*, Alex Chapman and Ruth Crofts have set out to replicate many of Anne's explorations in their gray Volkswagen camper van. You'll be able to recognize it—it's the one with the *Lister Sisters On Tour* and *)56p2n3* decals on the window. (Those familiar with Anne's *crypthand* code will recognize the word *courage*).

The couple, who've been together for ten years and married for six, have already toured Denmark, the site of Anne's consolation trip in 1833 when her relationship with Ann Walker was on the rocks. They've also made a sweep through Scotland, where Anne and her ex-lover Sibbella MacLean wandered for several months.

As teachers, Alex and Ruth have plenty of time off for travels in the summer, and they're also well-situated for frequent overnight trips near their home.

"We're lucky to be close to the North Yorkshire moors and the Yorkshire dales, and only a couple of hours from the Lake district," Alex says. "Our van has given us so much freedom, so at a moment's notice, we can just pick up and go."

And go they have—to York to visit where Anne studied at the manor school and where the Annes were married in the Holy Trinity Church, Goodramgate, along with repeat trips to Halifax where they frequently pop in at Shibden Hall.

But it was a chance encounter in a pub in Todmorden, a small former mill town near Halifax, that set their lives on an exciting new trajectory. That evening Alex and Ruth met up with two other Lister Sisters, known only through social media, to talk about *Gentleman Jack* and the Sally Wainwright lecture they'd all just attended. The conversation veered to Anne Lister and her many escapades. Alex mentioned that she and Ruth were thinking about climbing Grand Vignemale, the highest peak in the French Pyrenees that Anne had climbed in 1838 and made history as the first person in the world to reach its summit.

It didn't take more than a couple of beers and a glance at the Vignemale map on Alex's phone for the foursome to hatch a plan to organize a group mountaineering expedition.

"The main reason I want to climb Vignemale is that it's a challenge, a physical challenge that at my age and fitness level will be hard," Alex says. "But to do something like that in Anne Lister's footsteps . . . it will be so special. I am determined to get to the top, and nothing is going to stop me."

Ruth concurs.

"I've never been up a mountain apart from ski holidays before," she says. "I've always thought it was something difficult that you couldn't do, but it *is* doable."

With their growing friendship solidifying their resolve, the ringleaders of the Vignemale hike spread the word on social media that an all-female group was forming to climb Anne's mountain. By early

2020, 10 hardy souls from five countries committed to join them for the adventure.

Calling themselves the Blister Sisters, they began to make preparations for the ascent. One of the group located and contracted with a French guide service to lead them to the top, and another led online weekly High-Intensity Interval Training (HIIT) workouts and fitness challenges to kickstart the process of getting everyone in shape.

Then disaster, in the form of the global coronavirus pandemic, struck. The world went into lockdown, and plans for the looming Vignemale climb had to be put on hold. Twice.

What would Anne Lister do?

The group quickly reset its sights and selected an auspicious new date. On August 7, 2022, 184 years to the day that Anne took in the splendid view from atop *Pique-Longue* (the French name for Grand Vignemale), 14 American, British, Irish, Australian, and Belgian women ranging in age from 28 to 67 will be doing the same.

Ruth thinks it's remarkable that she and Alex are embarking on yet another Anne Lister experience.

"Two years ago I knew nothing about her and now suddenly, there are all of these places that we can go to where she's been," she says. "It's like magic, like a pilgrimage."

Alex and Ruth agree that their affinity for Anne Lister extends well beyond their following in her footsteps to nearby and distant destinations. Ruth marvels that the looming Lister-inspired climb has led to new and unexpected relationships.

"All my life people have talked about 'the gay community,'" Ruth says. "I thought, 'Who is this community? Who are they? Do they have meetings?' I've never had any gay friends, and now because of social media and our climb, I am part of a community I wasn't sure actually existed."

Alex has discovered another community in her own backyard and has become a member of the West Yorkshire Archive Service codebreakers, who are deciphering all of Anne's journals. She credits Ruth for finding out about the diary project and downloading the details.

"It was the best thing she's ever done for me," Alex says, noting that the transcription project is just one more enjoyable aspect of her Anne Lister obsession.

"I thought it would be something that would keep Alex occupied in the evenings and give her something to do so she's not working on homework from school until 11 o'clock every night and having no quality of life," Ruth explains.

She was right. Not only has working with Anne's journals been an absorbing diversion for Alex—she estimates she's transcribed more than 100 journal pages plus the detailed entries Anne recorded about her Vignemale experience—but it's also been a boon to improving her mental health.

"A couple of years ago I was diagnosed with depression and anxiety," Alex says. "I don't think it's just the transcribing that's helped me cope with that. It's everything about Anne Lister's and Ann Walker's story. It's been quite a positive thing, and it's really helped me. I feel as though I've come out on the other side."

And that's on top of a spontaneous revelation to her students.

"I accidentally came out to my geography class," Alex confesses. "They wanted to see photos of our trip to Denmark, and I had left in a picture of Ruth by mistake. One of the boys said, 'Who's that?' and I heard myself saying, 'My wife.' It was unintentional, but I just thought, 'God, it's about time.'"

Ruth sees it as a matter of bravery.

"*Gentleman Jack* has given people the courage to live their lives and admit who they are, and that will be one of the lasting benefits of this show," she observes.

"Obviously, Anne was a unique and outstanding person when she was alive, so it's not surprising that her life is now having such an effect on people because she was so strong and such a trailblazer," Alex adds.

Anne Lister was 47 years old when she reached the top of Vignemale on a cool summer day in 1838 and placed her name in a bottle left on the summit as proof of her achievement. Once again she rose above 19th century expectations for how a woman should act and what she should do. Nearly 200 years later, other women, middle-aged and otherwise, are now following her lead . . . up mountains, across barriers, and past their fears.

Alex sums it up best.

"Finally having the role model that we never had in our teens or 20s, 30s, or 40s, it's like, just wow!"

BEV ROWLEY

Todmorden, West Yorkshire, England, UK

ANNE LISTER AND I ARE KINDRED SPIRITS

*T*he irony of being a 67-year-old gay woman living true to her nature only 15 miles (24 km) from Shibden Hall, having never heard of the brave soul who lived so close by and did the same, hasn't escaped Bev Rowley. When *Gentleman Jack* introduced her to Anne Lister, it instantly awakened her interest in her and their comparable lives. Bev says she had the same reaction as many others: *Who the hell is she? Why do I not know about her?*

Born 164 years apart, Anne Lister and Bev Rowley are both Yorkshire women with similarities so obvious they could be Lister Sister poster girls. They share fearlessness, confidence, physical fitness, diverse interests, and a tenacious sense of adventure. Back down from a challenge? Never. Abiding love for standing on their land and no hesitation about working it? Check.

"There's so much of my life that is like Anne Lister's," Bev says. "I'm into everything, and she was into everything. My mother threw me out at 15 because she couldn't come to terms with who I am. Anne had issues with her parents too. People thought I was a boy. Same for Anne. I'm transgressive, and so was she."

Bev's discovery of Anne Lister coincided with a year-long sabbatical as she was considering when to retire from her position as a college lecturer and how her new life would unfold.

"The break from the stress I was under was really good for me," she says. "It's been good for my body, and it's been good for my mind. I think something we need to look at is why we are doing things, and what is our purpose. I had got to the point where I didn't want to continue what I was doing, so it's just new starts all way around."

One of her new starts is "climbing Vignemale with the girls." Bev had already planned a trip to France by herself to tackle Mont Perdu, the third highest peak in the Pyrenees range, one that Anne Lister also was the first to climb in 1830. When Bev found out about the pending group climb of the adjacent and taller Grand Vignemale, she decided she might as well climb it too.

"Then the plague hit," Bev says, "and everything was off."

What concerned Bev at first was whether as the oldest trekker she would be able to keep up with the 20- and 30-somethings as well as the middle-aged climbers. Considering she has maintained a high level of physical fitness throughout her life—as a swimmer and runner as a young woman and now someone who walks her dog 5 to 7 kilometers (3 to 4+ miles) every day rain or shine—she had no reason to worry.

"Besides," she says, "I'm as fit as a butcher's dog," a proper Yorkshire phrase that refers to a healthy pooch that's been well-fed on meat scraps.

"I've always done outdoor pursuits," Bev explains. "I'm very familiar with how my body works, and I know as the 67-year-old I'll be when I climb Vignemale that I cannot do what I did when I was 46, and definitely not what I could do when I was 26. For me, it's all about knowing what your body will do and knowing what it's capable of. And I've climbed a lot of mountains."

Trust in herself is part of Bev's DNA. It comes from a lifetime of tackling and succeeding at multiple careers.

"I've done and been everything," she says. "I was a boilermaker, and a motor vehicle mechanic. I've been a farmer. I did quite a lot of e-learning with disadvantaged kids. I've taught math, public services, outdoor pursuits, and business computing. I liked teaching in recovery centers and prisons. I like teaching the great unwashed that nobody else will work with and people whose lives have gone wayward. That brought me joy, and I will miss that."

Early experiences also shaped her resilience.

"I got used to being a disappointment very young," Bev says. "If you can get being a disappointment out of the way really young, you can move on with your life and not bother about what anybody thinks of you."

Bev has a can-do approach to anything she faces.

"I don't ever see anything and think I can't do it. I see a thing and think, 'How can I solve that?' Necessity is the mother of invention, and I guess you could say I've been very needy."

Now her joy comes from new sources. When she was frustrated by when and how to retire, Bev says she knew just what to do.

"When I get mad, I dig. I have an acre garden that needed a lot of work doing on it, so I just set to the pick and shovel and a wheelbarrow and cleared it," she says.

It's part of her plan to share her small piece of paradise—a small plot of forested and wildlife-protected land in a dark sky area in Calder Valley—with others who love the outdoors as much as she does.

"It will be a place where children and anybody can come and play, and I'll play too," Bev says.

Gentleman Jack widened Bev's horizons in significant and surprising ways, beginning with the new friends she has made. She admits she had doubts about whether she would fit in.

"Since my last relationship of 20 years ended six years ago, I'd become very insular," Bev says. "I'm somewhat eccentric and very reticent about trying to make new friends. I don't know if all the Vignemale girls are just nutters, but I can't tell you how welcome I've been made to feel and how wonderful it is for my mental health to have acceptance and know I'm part of a group all with a similar sort of mindset."

As much as Bev admires Anne Lister for being true to herself, she says it's Ann Walker who is serving as her inspiration to make the Vignemale climb and why the story of the Annes resonates so strongly with her. Bev was only 25 when her parents were killed in a traffic crash in Germany, and she and one of her four brothers had the task of bringing their bodies back to England.

"Even with modern technology, planes, and everything else that's in place, it took us nearly two weeks to get them back into the country," Bev recalls. "From my own personal experience, I can't tell you what labor of love it must have been for Ann Walker to do all she had to do to bring Anne Lister's body back home in 1840. She loved Anne, and she proved it."

Bev's retirement and the *Gentleman Jack* community have delivered the opportunity and incentive to do what's she's wanted to do for a long time.

"Life is too short for us not to be doing absolutely everything we possibly can with life. When I realized at the age of 60 that I wasn't, that was hugely disappointing to me. So now I'm back on track."

And she's not wasting any more time.

"I've always wanted to learn to sail, so I'm going to learn to navigate oceangoing vessels. I'm looking forward to having my older brother with me to help me fulfill my dream of sailing to somewhere exotic. I'm going to build an Airbnb cabin on my land by myself, and also a treehouse and a couple of hobbit pods. I'm going to pass my motorcycle test, and I want to ride my bike to explore some of the old coach roads that Anne Lister and Ann Walker traveled."

The prospect of new activities and new adventures at this stage of her life has prompted Bev to put her thoughts about aging into words.

"I'm in good health, and I shouldn't waste it. Life doesn't end when you turn 60. I've got lines now, and my skin started to get baggy, and I don't care. Women over 60 are not invisible, and we need to stop thinking of ourselves in that way. Life is for living as long as you've got it. It's like climbing Vignemale. Let's have a go."

JANNE MONBALLIU

Antwerp, Belgium

ADVENTURE IN ANY LANGUAGE

Montaña. Montagne. Montagna. Berg. Thanks to Janne Monballiu's command of six languages, the word for mountain in Spanish, French, Italian, Dutch, German, and English has become synonymous with adventure. At 28, she is the youngest of an international team of women who, in 2022, will repeat Anne Lister's feat of trekking to the top of the tallest peak in the French Pyrenees.

"Before I even knew a group was going to climb Mount Vignemale, it was something I wanted to do in remembrance of Anne Lister," Janne says. "Now just being able to do it with interesting people, hearing all of their different stories, and sharing this experience together will be very special."

Janne says she could never have imagined when she watched *Gentleman Jack* that it would lead to so many changes in her quiet life as a secondary school language teacher who hikes and rides horses in her spare time.

The show was something she'd been looking forward to since reading an article in 2017 about Sally Wainwright's involvement in a new miniseries about the formidable woman Janne had first encountered in *The Secret Diaries of Miss Anne Lister*, a 2010 film starring Maxine Peake.

"*Gentleman Jack* totally exceeded my expectations," Janne says. "I absolutely loved that it was filmed at Shibden Hall because that adds so much more authenticity to the story. It also made me want to go there and see it for myself."

She made her first of four visits to Halifax shortly after *Gentleman Jack* completed its run on BBC One.

"I was alone and actually didn't enter Shibden that first day because it was such an overwhelming experience to think I was actually going to walk in Anne's footsteps," Janne says. "That night I went to an event at the Halifax Minster and saw someone who recognized me from Twitter. She introduced me to a bunch of other people, and we all went to Shibden together the next day. We've been several times since, each time with a different guide who put emphasis on different parts of the house and its history, which made it all the more interesting. We've become good friends and stay in contact almost daily through social media."

Besides their mutual affection for Shibden Hall, Janne also shares with Anne Lister a wide-ranging curiosity and love of learning.

"Anne had so many different interests, like anatomy, and reading, and finding out about everything, which I also have," Janne explains. "That clicked with me, and so did her fascination with languages, which I have too. I liked that she wrote in code because I also did that when I was between 8 and 12 years old. A neighbor and I made up a code with letters and shapes, and we would put notes in each other's mailboxes about what we did during the weekend and other silly things."

It follows that Janne's childhood experiment with inventing and writing in code would lead her to becoming part of the West Yorkshire Archive Service diary transcription project.

"It comes back to language," she says. "Decoding is something I find very interesting, especially the passages that have quite a lot of French abbreviations. Just trying to figure out what Anne wrote is fun for me. I enjoyed transcribing about when she was in Paris, but what I like most are the coded bits because it's an extra challenge. It's like a mirror into Anne Lister's mind, and it's a gateway into how she thought and what she did."

But it's more than Anne's intellectual pursuits and her travels that have resonated with Janne.

"Before *Gentleman Jack*, I lacked a bit of confidence," Janne says. "What I like so much about Anne Lister is just the fact that she was intelligent, she wasn't ashamed of it, and she had the confidence to just do whatever she wanted. She stood up for herself when confronted by men, which was quite brave to do. That I now have more confidence is due to her and her example."

This has resulted in Janne's speaking her mind and opening up to fellow teachers and others.

"Whereas I used to hold my tongue when a colleague or an acquaintance said something I didn't quite agree with because it could potentially be construed as hurtful language," she says, "now I will now stand up for myself and others and call them out on their behavior. I join in conversations with male colleagues about their cars and motorcycles without being afraid of them looking at me funny because I'm a woman and those subjects are typically considered to be quite manly. I guess confidence also comes with age, but from admiring the confidence in women like Anne Lister, I discovered my own voice and proudly use it."

Along with more confidence has also come self-acceptance.

"I no longer feel that I have to hide myself or the fact that I prefer to be single because I've never been attracted to anyone of either gender," Janne says. "What I learned from Anne Lister is that it's ok to be who I am."

Besides inspiring a more positive view of herself, *Gentleman Jack* also has opened Janne's world to new friends.

"It's amazing that I've met so many different people from so many different backgrounds in so many countries that have all come together because of a genuine interest in someone who lived 200 years ago," Janne says. "We have a connection that you don't necessarily have with people you see every day because we talk about stuff that is more personal. We support each other when someone is going through a hard time or is excited about something like getting engaged or married. Also, those of us who are training for Vignemale share pictures and videos, and we're always encouraging each other to work out more and be healthy."

Janne acknowledges that *Gentleman Jack* has broadened her horizons.

"I get to go to places I've never visited before. I get to know things that maybe I otherwise wouldn't have," she says. "It's been enlightening to get access to Anne's diaries and just to read everything from a female's perspective in those days and not have it be censored by men. The series just opened my eyes to history, culture, and a wonderful group of people." Janne plans to continue to follow in Anne Lister's footsteps—traveling where she traveled, and living fearlessly. But she has drawn a line.

"I had this crazy idea of maybe climbing Vignemale in a skirt and an outfit similar to what Anne Lister wore," Janne says. "But then I came to my senses and decided I'll be glad if I survive in my own proper technical clothing."

That's good thinking—*buena pensamiento, bien pensé, pensare bene,* and *gute Idee*—and definitely merits a thumbs up in any language.

HEATHER McCLAIN

Atlanta, Georgia, USA

REACHING FOR NEW HEIGHTS

Keeping score isn't just for sports. We all count things. Maybe it's social media likes, comments, and followers, or how many pounds we need to lose to fit into a pair of skinny jeans, or how many more work days until the next holiday. Psychologists have even devised a scorecard to calculate the toll that life's ups and downs take on us. By their count, Heather McClain has racked up an excess of stress points.

She and her partner of 25+ years have recently gone their separate ways, 75 points. Downsized from her 30-year career, 47 points. Change in financial situation, 38 points. More exercise and more socialization, 37 points. Vacation to England, 13 points. Almost everything in Heather's life is up for grabs, but don't expect an invitation to a pity party at her house. Heather credits *Gentleman Jack* for her optimism and confidence to tackle whatever comes next.

"My partner and I are going through some interesting changes at the moment," Heather says. "We're the best of friends and we love each other to the ends of the earth, so we know we'll always be in each other's lives. But among the many things that have happened to me as a result of *Gentleman Jack*, I've found the courage to recognize and name the situation I'm in, and I know it has to be different."

Heather has three powerful forces on her side to help reinvent her future: motivation, determination, and the *Gentleman Jack* nation. First of all, she's got her sights set on mastering mountains. One would think that coping with so many personal changes happening all at once might be enough to test her mental toughness, but Heather looks past the daily challenges to Mount Vignemale looming on a distant horizon. The climb in the French Pyrenees will measure her grit and physical fitness when she heads for the summit with 13 other women on the 184th anniversary of Anne Lister's achievement as the first person in the world to get to the top.

"What's been going through my thoughts are the many regrets I have," she says. "I realize I haven't been living authentically for most of my life, and it has cost me. I hid in corporate America for decades, and finally I've woken up to the fact that by not being myself, I've robbed myself of so many experiences and harbored feelings that have harmed me physically and emotionally."

Heather is taking steps to prove to herself that she's got what it takes to achieve her new goal to live as her true self—about 5,400 steps, to be more precise. Hiking up a 10,820-foot peak (3,298 meters) is no small feat, but it's in keeping with her resolve to rise above life's challenges.

"When I first heard about the Vignemale climb, it just sparked something in me," Heather says. "It just sounded really, really cool. For me, doing something that is in alignment with Anne Lister's climb is just something that is so momentous that when I heard about it, I just wanted to jump on board."

Heather says it's the characters in *Gentleman Jack* who have inspired her and shaped her positive outlook. Anne Lister's sense of adventure and her dynamic personality are part of her appeal, she says, but Heather's heart belongs to Ann Walker.

"When you look at everything she had to overcome, I'll say it: she's head and shoulders above Anne Lister," she explains. "She had so much more to deal with, and she didn't have the level of comfort with herself that Anne did."

Exploring the lives of women in the past has been a welcome diversion during a difficult time. As an active participant in the West Yorkshire Archive Service's volunteer transcription project, Heather says decoding and recording the contents of Lister's journals is fascinating and challenging work.

"I enjoy it so much," Heather says. "It's a puzzle, and you're pulling back the curtain and looking at somebody's life who really, really lived. From actually reading her journals myself, my whole feeling about Anne Lister, God love her, is that she was so courageous, but she's certainly a bit of a drama queen too. When she's writing about what was going on with this woman or that one, and her day-to-day fits and threatening to just walk away, it makes me wonder if she truly understood what love is. I hope she did."

Heather says Anne's journals have connected her to scores of supportive women who share the same zeal for delving into the life of lesbians in the 19th century.

"Transcribing has been the one thing in my life that I can get a grip on," she says. "I can just go and look at something else in another era and a simpler time and see a woman who's like me from a sexuality perspective. It's been a great escape."

Training to climb Vignemale also has had its advantages and is proving to be the fast track to what's ahead for Heather. She is delighted that it includes a brand new set of what she expects to be lifelong friends. "I'm having a great time," Heather says. "I've never made friends with a group of people so fast. I'm part of a team of really nice folks. Every single day, we're encouraging each other. It is so much fun to be able to have this kind of camaraderie with people so far away. Plus I'm on the production team making a documentary of our adventure."

Their shared commitment to support each other includes group virtual training, and in Heather's case, plenty of online team cheerleading for her daily five-mile walks and endurance hikes up Stone Mountain near her hometown. She's also made several trips to England to train in person with her fellow climbers.

"What I am so looking forward to about this climb is just laughing and spending time with a fantastic group of women, so diverse and from all over the world," Heather says.

"I see myself standing on top of Vignemale and acknowledging the fact that Anne Lister climbed this very mountain on two hard-boiled eggs and in a skirt. I may just give her a little wave in heaven and say 'Great job, Anne!'

KATIE SPENCELEY & MARIE SCHULTZ

London, England, UK

HATS OFF TO CLIMBERS

hen you see someone putting on his Big Boots, you can be pretty sure an Adventure is going to happen. English author A.A. Milne's Winnie-the-Pooh got it right. Footwear and other accessories send signals.

Ever practical, Anne Lister laced up a pair of men's hobnail boots when she set out to climb Mount Vignemale. When Katie Spenceley and Marie Schultz make their way to the top of the same peak, Katie will be sporting something new on her feet. Her old and much-loved hiking boots were a casualty on the Indonesian island of Lombok. That's where she and Marie hiked to the summit of Mount Rinjani, an active volcano that rises to 3,726 meters (12,224 feet).

"It was an extremely steep climb, extremely hot and rocky and dusty," Katie says. "The soles actually fell off my boots when I got to the top of that one. Lucky for me the guides were very resourceful and took bits of twine from the tents and tied the soles back on my boots so I was able to get down the mountain."

Now they're preparing for something slightly tamer: a summer trek to the summit of Vignemale with a group of like-minded, adventure-seeking women who were complete strangers until just months ago.

Katie has had her heart set on climbing in the French Pyrenees ever since a family friend piqued her interest with tales of cycling in the breathtaking beauty of these jagged granite mountains hovering over crystal blue lakes and ancient glaciers. When she learned about Anne Lister's climb and the chance to repeat it with *Gentleman Jack* fans, Katie was quick off the mark.

A bit skeptical at first, Marie tapped into her inner Australian and came around so she wouldn't miss out on the fun.

"There is something really appealing about it, being out in nature, and I just think it will be exciting," Marie says. "What makes this climb interesting and so special is the story of Anne Lister doing it, all of us meeting on Facebook and having a common interest, and then doing the climb itself. When we tell people about it, it brings a smile to their faces."

Katie shares the same sentiments.

"I just like the idea of being in the middle of nowhere, somewhere up a hill with a bunch of people," she says. "And the getting to the top with our hats on."

It was, in fact, an intriguing picture of a top hat that is partly to blame for the chain of events that led to their upcoming adventure. It began one weekday morning when Katie was commuting to her civil service job, and in the Charing Cross Underground station in London she saw, plastered on the wall, a massive poster with a photo of Suranne Jones suited up as Anne Lister promoting *Gentleman Jack*.

There is no ignoring a giant poster of a beautiful woman in a top hat and a cravat.

"Of course we had to watch *Gentleman Jack*, and it is just so brilliant," Katie says. "It was lovely to see a butch woman as the hero of her own story. I've never seen a character like Anne Lister on prime time TV, ever. It was incredible."

As an art director, Marie was struck by the show's production quality as well as its storyline.

"It's like the stars have aligned, and everything is just perfect," she says. "You've got an amazing story with a larger-than-life character with a secret diary written in code, a beautiful Yorkshire setting, a very talented writer, and a very talented team of actors. I wonder whether we'll ever get a show again as good as it is."

Gentleman Jack's impact on both women was immediate and affirming.

"I learned how comfortable a figure in gay history was with her own sexuality, and I found that really moving and quite profound," Katie says. "It definitely gave me more confidence. I used to feel that I had to sometimes moderate myself or hide myself to be safe. I feel less like that now."

Marie observed that it is rare for lesbians to be so positively portrayed in books, film, or TV that are directed to a mainstream audience.

"I'd be talking to my colleagues about *Gentleman Jack*, and they'd be enjoying it as much as I was," she says. "For me, the show was just so validating and empowering."

Their first trip to Halifax for an Anne Lister weekend in the summer of 2019 reinforced their feelings of pride and self-acceptance.

"It had a kind of happy festival feel," Katie recalls. "There was a big queue to get into Shibden Hall, and there were all of these gay women and also families with kids. I really liked that there was this mix of gay people and straight people all interested in Anne Lister, and I wondered, 'What on earth would Anne Lister make of it?'"

When the opportunity to join the Vignemale climbing group presented itself a few weeks after their visit to Shibden Hall, it reignited their newfound connection to Anne Lister and added a welcome spark to their day-to-day routines.

"Completing the climb will be great," Marie says. "I do think it's going to be tough. A few in the group are very, very fit, but we're a bit more normal. Sometimes I do worry that something will go wrong."

Katie admits to being more gung-ho about most things.

"I remember once I said to Marie that I'm going to cycle from London to Paris, and she said, 'Katie, you don't even own a bike!'"

Between Katie's playing saxophone in London's 40-member Gay Symphonic Winds and Marie's penchant for tackling DIY renovations in their flat, they still find time for regular online meetings and exercise routines with their fellow climbers. As a result, Anne Lister's exemplary strength and courage is ever-present, and Katie believes that's what led to her unexpected revelations to colleagues at the office.

Katie found herself sharing, for the first time, what it's like to be a gay woman in a still-challenging and often disapproving world.

"Being gay is something that I deal with every single day," Katie explains. "Every time I meet someone new I have to decide whether I come out or not. Even though I look feminine, people see my short hair and suits and think I'm a man. I get shouted at sometimes, or people will look me up and down. It's tiring, and it takes constant effort to be myself. When I'm out with Marie, I always think about where it's safe for us to be a couple. It's just something other people don't have to live with."

Marie hopes *Gentleman Jack* and the story of Anne Lister will change that.

"*Gentleman Jack* is a wonderful introduction about being a lesbian for many people," she says. "It's such a fun story too. It gives you a chance to say, 'Have you seen this show? Maybe you'd like it. It's really great.' That can bring people together on both sides."

Katie and Marie are delighted that being Blister Sisters has brought them into a tight community of women who understand and can relate to the same challenges that Anne Lister faced 200 years ago. They're grateful that Anne's example of indomitable self-esteem has ushered confidence and validation into their lives.

And it's all thanks to a serendipitous sighting of picture of a woman in a top hat at a London tube station.

While Katie and Marie have recently embarked on a new adventure—new jobs and a new life in Sydney, Australia—they're adamant it won't keep them from joining the other Blister Sisters for the Vignemale climb in 2022.

∞

LISA CUTLER

Lympne, Kent, England, UK

AN IRRESISTIBLE CHALLENGE

First it was a grueling hike down the steep and almost mile-long rocky trail to the bottom of the magnificent Grand Canyon in the US, and back. Then came skydiving. Next was scrambling around the ancient Inca ruins at Machu Picchu. Trudging through a dense rain forest in Uganda to see mountain gorillas followed.

No one can accuse Lisa Cutler of not having a sense of adventure. "I thought these things were challenging, and I find it difficult to say no to a challenge," she says. "If someone challenges me, I do tend to take it up whether it's wise or not."

Naturally Lisa couldn't refuse an invitation to join the trekkers headed to the top of Mount Vignemale.

"I'm excited we're going to go and climb Anne Lister's mountain," she says. "Also, because my dad has Alzheimer's, it was a given for me as soon as I knew we'd be climbing to raise money for the Alzheimer's Society in the UK and the US."

Preparing to climb a mountain is a welcome change of pace from Lisa's job as a part-time legal secretary for a British law firm based in Paris. As a part-time Parisian, Lisa knows from exploring the streets that it's a city with many Anne Lister associations: from the places Anne visited with her aunt on their extended visit in 1819 to the site of her encounters with Maria Barlow, and the pied-à-terre where she studied anatomy after having attended lectures by Monsieur Georges Cuvier.

What started as a six-month assignment in 1999 has morphed into a 22-year career that had Lisa commuting to the City of Light every other week—until the coronavirus pandemic kept her in lockdown on the English side of the Channel.

However, her former strolls down the Champs-Élysées or walking in the predominantly flat countryside near her village in Kent isn't going to prepare her for the mountaineering that's ahead, Lisa says. That's why she upped her training regimen in 2021 by co-founding Wednesday Walkers, a lively social media group of 75+ women from more than a dozen countries who support each other to get out and get moving.

"We all walk whenever we can and are having the best time getting fit and posting pictures of what we see on our hikes and strolls all over the world," she says. "We have friendly competitions and lots of challenges, like posting pictures of anything from sunsets and wildlife to Pride ideas and street art that we see when we're out and about."

When it comes to racking up fitness mileage, Lisa and co-founder Lesley Brown lead by example. Though they live in different parts of England, they often walk at the same time and keep each other company with cheerful banter using a free app on their cell phones. Between January and March 2021, the pair logged an impressive 500 miles *each*. Next, they challenged other Wednesday Walkers to help raise money for the Alzheimer's Society, and within two days, the group exceeded its goal of £1,000, then £2,000, then £3,000.

"As much as I enjoy walking near my home, if you want the exercise of climbing proper hills, you have to look beyond Kent," she explains. "In Yorkshire, there are hills everywhere, so I like to go there."

Lisa's regular trips to Halifax are more than just part of her training routine, they're also keeping her connected to her fellow climbers and to Anne Lister, whom she acknowledges is a driving force behind her taking on the latest test of her capabilities.

"What makes Anne Lister fascinating to me is the complexity of her character," Lisa explains. "She makes no apology for how she does business nor for who she is, and that's quite surprising in a positive way. It's inspiring to see someone who knows her worth in the world. It's incredible what she did."

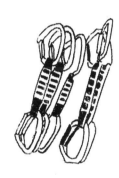

Lisa's Halifax trips invariably include a stop at Shibden Hall.

"It's hard to explain what keeps drawing me back," Lisa says. "I want to picture the woman who lived there and what her life was like. It's quite powerful when you go there. It's a very odd feeling because you shouldn't have a particular connection to it, but so many of us do. Shibden has character, it's beautiful, and it's something much more than a just a house."

It's because of *Gentleman Jack* that Lisa's life has taken on so many new dimensions.

"I've never seen anything like it," Lisa says. "I've never joined a fan page before, and if you talk to a lot of people, they would say exactly the same thing. And yet here we all are. Our reaction to *Gentleman Jack* is huge, and you don't question it or understand it. You don't know why you feel this visceral connection to somebody you've never met, you've never known, and in most cases you've never even heard of before. It's a strange thing to try to analyze, and I'm happy that so many people besides me have found the same thing."

Lisa's own connection to *Gentleman Jack* delighted members of the official HBO/BBC *Gentleman Jack* Facebook fan group. Her clever and highly entertaining recap of all eight episodes of the series, which she posted within weeks of the conclusion of Season 1, gave her a reaction she never expected.

"I've never done anything like that before, and I don't even know where it came from," she admits. "I only did it for a bit of fun after being challenged to try it. I would go off on lots of tangents, and then bring myself back to the story. Some people said I should get them printed, but it was all just for fun and it was nice to get positive feedback."

Whether it's taking on what she sees as the smaller challenge of writing about *Gentleman Jack* or the much bigger challenge of climbing the tallest peak in the French Pyrenees, Lisa says we all need something in our lives to drive us forward.

"Instead of staying where you are, challenges are a lovely way to keep you invested in what is going on around you," she says. "Because of Anne Lister, people who've been stationary for such a long time are moving forward and supporting each other to do the same."

Besides putting in the time and effort to become physically fit, it's the encouragement of the other climbers that Lisa knows will help her reach the top of Mount Vignemale.

"I'm very lucky to be part of a group that is so welcoming and supportive," she says. "What's going to help us reach our goal and get us up that mountain is the combination of physical strength, mental toughness, and helping each other."

Romance is adding a spring to her step, too.

"Something unexpected and delightful developed between me and fellow Blister Sister Heather McClain," Lisa explains. "We met in person in Halifax and travelled together to a group training exercise between lockdowns in 2020—eleven of us hiked for miles on an incredibly soggy and cold day in the Lake District, which is a couple of hours from Halifax—and Heather and I had such a joyous and fun time together. We stayed in touch when she returned to the US, and things just grew and grew from there. I am blessed to have been so lucky to find such a wonderful woman!"

Lisa is approaching the 2022 Vignemale climb with anticipation and *Gentleman Jack*-inspired confidence. Recalling when she and a friend were on their Uganda adventure, Lisa says her friend could easily climb the short, steep trail to the gorillas' habitat while Lisa struggled. But when the next trail was a long and gradual uphill climb, her friend faltered while Lisa had no trouble with the slow and steady pace.

"One of the best challenges is pushing yourself beyond what you think you can do," Lisa says. "That's the idea of it. We all have different skills. Sometimes you are the mountain goat which can bound up the trail, and sometimes you are the rhinoceros which just keeps moving steadily ahead. All of us have a mountain of one sort or another to climb. We just have to do it in our own way. And when you have a supportive environment, it helps and pushes you to do even more."

Lisa's summaries of each episode of the first season of Gentleman Jack are posted under her username Lisa Joa on the Gentleman Jack Fans (HBO and BBC One TV Show) private Facebook group.

ARDRA MORSE

McKinney, Texas, USA

I PICTURE WHAT THE STARS LOOK LIKE

*I*t wouldn't be an exaggeration to say Ardra Morse is obsessed with *Gentleman Jack*. Most days, she performs editing magic on her Mac and posts at least one photo or video clip from *Gentleman Jack* on Instagram, Facebook, and Twitter. She meticulously adjusts light levels and color saturations on close-ups of Suranne Jones or Sophie Rundle to present their Anne Lister and Ann Walker characters at their very best. Her video clips might zoom in on a kiss, a conversation in a coach, a swagger.

Ardra knows a thing or two about cinema, having spent more than 20 years working as a booth engineer, a quality control expert who has made sure movie projectors at theater complexes from California to Florida deliver a perfect picture to the wide screen. She's seen thousands of films, observed countless performances, and developed a keen eye.

Ardra's love affair with *Gentleman Jack* began with its first episode on HBO in April 2019. Within four weeks, she was creating the first of more than 1,000 edited photos and video clips that she has posted online so far. "I see a picture, and I think I just want to make it more awesome. I want to put it out and show it to everybody because I think they're going to enjoy it too," she explains. "Everybody" has grown to more than 9,000 Instagram followers (#gentlemanjackedits).

What Ardra wasn't expecting when she first tuned in to *Gentleman Jack* was such high quality in a television period drama about a woman she'd never heard of.

"I love period dramas and I never miss a chance to watch them," she says. "*Gentleman Jack* is one of the best productions I've ever seen on film or TV, and it hits the mark on every single measure. Story line, casting, location, directing, amazing actresses, editing—everything about it is fantastic."

Many of Ardra's social media fans who share her love of *Gentleman Jack* have become new friends.

"I love each and every person I've met online," she reports. "It feels so natural to have made so many new connections, and it's like we've always known each other. The people I've met in this fandom have genuine kind hearts. I feel so close to some of my new friends that I'd even be willing to move to the UK if I could."

Ardra says it has become her mission to stoke and keep interest high in *Gentleman Jack* during the long drought between Seasons 1 and 2.

"I see Suranne's and Sophie's faces every day," she says. "I don't want people to forget how wonderful the show is. When they watch a clip or see a photo, I want them to say 'Oh my gosh, I remember that scene.' I'm always thinking how can I post something else that's new and refreshing. For me it's never been about how many followers I have. It's that I am so passionate about Anne Lister and her story and the show and I just want to share that passion with everyone else."

Ardra says it's been a joy to tap into her creative side by focusing on *Gentleman Jack* photo and video edits, which has given her the motivation to say goodbye to her engineering career to become a full-time portrait photographer.

"Anne Lister has inspired me to close one chapter of my life and start something new," she says. "The reason I love pictures is that they capture emotion so well and can say so much. People make me happy, and that's what makes pictures of people so rewarding to shoot and work on."

The biggest coup in Ardra's new line of work is her selection as the official photographer for the 2022 Anne Lister Birthday Week in Halifax.

Besides a new career, another adventure also is on Ardra's horizon.

 In August 2022, she will join 13 of her new friends to follow in Anne Lister's footsteps on a two-day climb of Mount Vignemale in the French Pyrenees. She's been tapped to join the production team that will be making a documentary of the climb and will serve as the film's director of photography and assist with post-production.

"*Gentleman Jack* has changed my life in so many different ways," Ardra says. "I've gained a lot of new friends and people who are interacting with my Instagram page. I've definitely improved my editing skills. I'm not afraid to leave a job I've had for 24 years to do something different. I've discovered Anne Lister, and I have so much respect for her. And now I'm going to climb a mountain just like she did."

∞

MICHELLE TUCKER

Halifax, West Yorkshire, England, UK

ANNE LISTER IS MY NEXT DOOR NEIGHBOR

*E*very hour on the hour, the church bells at Halifax Minster strike the time with the same even-paced trio of sounds. Bong. Bong. Bong. It's one of the things that Miche Tucker loves about her new home, along with its stunning view overlooking the 12th century church and its tall clock tower from which the peals emanate.

"I feel very lucky to finally have found such a wonderful place since I decided I wanted to live in Halifax," Miche says. "I can't think of a better place to be, so close to Anne Lister, the streets where she walked, and everything that was so special to her."

This geographical relocation is just one of the ways that Miche's life has been completely reoriented, courtesy of *Gentleman Jack*.

It all started as Miche approached her 50th birthday and found herself questioning everything, including her relationship of 14 years.

"I had a quite comfortable life," she says, "but I was feeling a bit lost. I was always helping everybody else and not really thinking about what I wanted to do. I was just plodding on with life, and then *Gentleman Jack* came on."

Miche says finding out about Anne Lister was like a bolt of lightning. Here was a strong and brave woman who did everything on her own terms and lived life fully. Through social media, Miche suddenly found herself meeting dozens of like-minded women from around the world, and she could no longer ignore that something big was missing in her life.

The reality of her situation coincided with growing excitement about her volunteer involvement in the 2020 Anne Lister Birthday Weekend. Miche's helpful nature and strong organizational and research skills were a perfect fit for the job of overseeing activities for women traveling solo and for tracking down information on hotels and transportation options for the hundreds expected to attend.

"For the first time in a long time, I was really enjoying what I was doing," Miche recalls. "I'm the one that likes to please everybody, so it was a bit of a shock to me to be blocking out everything else and just focusing on what I wanted to do."

Anne Lister's example and Miche's recognition of the importance of being true to herself was the harbinger of major changes to come. With 2020 on the horizon, Miche made the monumental decision to walk away from everything—home, relationship, job—and start fresh.

"Learning about this amazing woman gave me courage to step out of the box I was in and take a different path," Miche says. "I knew I could no longer stay with my partner, and I felt a draw to Halifax that I couldn't really describe. I thought this is the first time I've been a little bit selfish because I want to do something for myself."

Miche says she had always played by the rules, usually someone else's. After she graduated from university with a degree in textile design, she set up an art studio and small business in Nottingham with support from the Prince's Fund and kept at it for eight years. Yielding to her mother's suggestion that she get "a proper job," she turned to recruiting for the National Health Service for five years before she took up property management.

"Life is too short to be unhappy," Miche says. "I've turned 50, and I thought I didn't want to be waking up in my 80s and thinking, 'What

I have done with my life? What have I *not* done that I wanted to do?' Sometimes you just have to have the balls to do something different, no matter how old you are."

For Miche, something different meant embracing something extraordinary.

"The problem was that for the longest time the people around me weren't up for it," she says.

But three of Miche's new *Gentleman Jack* friends also were interested in a challenge, and they all began bouncing around the idea of replicating one of Anne Lister's many remarkable achievements. Why not climb Mount Vignemale on the 182nd anniversary of her being the first person, male or female, to reach the top?

It wasn't long before they spread the word on social media that an all-female team was forming to climb Anne's mountain in the French Pyrenees, and 11 other hardy souls were quick to join the three ringleaders. Miche took on the task of coordinating arrangements and schedules, looking for sponsors, and keeping all the climbers informed and encouraged.

She's also part of the film production crew making a documentary of the climb.

"So many of us have been dramatically affected by *Gentleman Jack* and Anne Lister," she says. "It feels like we are part of one big family, and we've all got each other's back."

When the coronavirus pandemic forced the cancellation of the 2020 Vignemale climb, the group, in true Anne Lister fashion, naturally rescheduled for the following year. And when the pandemic dragged on, of course they reset 2022 as the new summit date.

Miche's playful artistic side has also recently re-emerged. Using photographs from the series, she has created more than 100 *Gentleman Jack* memes by adding amusing thought and conversation bubbles to keep the mood light among the fandom.

"I love doing the memes, and I hope my quirky humor and observations make people smile," she says. "I just pick a shot and think about what I can add to the scenario. It's just a silly sense of humor kind of thing."

As she settles into a new life in a new community, Miche marvels at where she finds herself. She's exploring her surroundings and considering what kind of work she wants to do next. Most days she trains for the Vignemale climb on the same steep cobblestone path that Anne Lister used for walking between Shibden Hall and Halifax Minster. She revels in the same panoramic Halifax views that Anne saw more than 200 years ago. She lives just steps away from Anne's final resting place.

"There is such a draw to Halifax that I still don't fully understand. I just know I feel very much at home here. I think it's all the lovely people I've met and am going to meet. I could count what I thought of as good friends on one hand, but now that one hand is turning into two. It is fascinating that Anne Lister has got such an impact on us all. I feel her all around. I like to think she is always watching us and would be pleased with what she sees."

∞

MARY GAVAGHAN

Knocknacarra, Galway, Ireland

YOU ONLY LIVE ONCE

She's been to the top of Mount Pilatus, a 7,000-foot peak in the Swiss Emmental Alps that loom over Lake Lucerne. She's hiked across a glacier in the Southern Alps on the South Island of New Zealand. She's been hill-walking in the rugged Connemara National Park in western Ireland.

So it's no surprise that Mary Gavaghan jumped at the chance to join the group that will hike up to the summit of Mount Vignemale (elevation 3,298 meters/10,820 feet) in the summer of 2022.

"As soon as I heard about the climb, I knew I wanted to be part of this collective of women," Mary says. "I so want to do that hill, even if I had to do it by myself. It's probably going to kick my ass now for calling it a hill, but it's really important to me to get to the top."

Mary says it's not only that she's been inspired by Anne Lister's conquest of the tallest peak in the French Pyrenees. Her motivation is more personal.

"I want to be part of this group climb because it's one of those things where I don't like the idea of having regrets," she explains. "In 10 or 20 years, I want to look back and say I was a part of that first group that got to the top of Vignemale. I know all of those women. I was one of them."

Mary doesn't expect it to be easy.

"Without doubt, this is going to be the hardest physical challenge I think I've ever attempted," Mary says. "This area in the Pyrenees gives

me the heebie-jeebies. At first I wondered if all of us know what we're getting into. It's a technical climb that involves ropes and helmets on the upper part, and it's a proper expedition even though we're not following Anne's exact route. But this is just something I want to do, something I need to do for myself."

Mary knows her physical limitations are a consideration, so she is carefully training on her own and with the group.

"From playing soccer I have dodgy knees that required surgery several years ago," she reports. "I have to be careful with my legs, too. I do a lot of preventive rehab, and I try to do yoga every day. I run three times a week and do long distance walks. There's a whole process to getting my body ready."

Mary isn't one to back off a challenge that tests her limits. At 18, she volunteered for the Reserve Defence Forces (*na hÓglaigh Cúltaca*) and trained to support the Irish army in crisis situations.

"As a teenager I had a strong sense of national duty," former Corporal Gavaghan explains. "But after 10 years, I learned through experience there are many ways to serve my country. I have some fantastic memories, and some of my dearest friends are from my 10 years with the RDF."

Mary's national service now takes the civilian form of sharing information as a tour guide at Aughnanure Castle, one of Ireland's many heritage sites. It's a 16th century, six-story tower house once occupied by the O'Flaherty family, whose motto *"Fortune favors the brave"* seems particularly applicable to a young woman intent on following in the footsteps of Anne Lister.

"Even if I didn't identify as a lesbian, I would still really like Anne Lister for the woman she was," Mary says. "I admire this individual who did her own thing, even when it wasn't the done thing for somebody of her class to do. She didn't conform to the notions of gender at the time, even though she got a lot of grief for it. I find that extremely inspirational. Even now, in the 21st century, I've had the same experience of being told I can't do something because I'm a girl. I think it's really a fitting tribute that more than 180 years later a group of women are doing what Anne did by climbing the same mountain she climbed."

Since her first viewing of *Gentleman Jack*, Mary says Anne Lister has become a regular presence in her life. She jokes that her friends gauge her mood by whether or not Mary has mentioned Anne Lister at some point during the day. Mention of Anne, good day. No mention of Anne, could be better.

"With help from other people, I've gotten through some mental health issues in the past, " Mary says. "Sally Wainwright showed us in *Gentleman Jack* that Anne Lister was very, very healthy when it came to her mental health. Writing in her diaries was therapeutic for Anne, and we are so lucky to have her diaries and the legacy she left us."

Mary says she's "old school" and prefers to engage with people face-to-face, but she is quick to give kudos to the online community that has sprung up as a result of *Gentleman Jack*.

"Without social media, I'd have never known about the Vignemale climb, and I'd have never met so many people that have become my friends."

Mary believes *Gentleman Jack* has come at the right time in her life when she has the time, money, and motivation to take on the challenge of climbing Vignemale.

"I am extremely privileged to get the opportunity to do this when there are so many others who would like to do the same thing, but can't for whatever reason," Mary says. "I get to enjoy this experience on behalf of those who can't, and that makes it all the more worthwhile."

Mary says that, as an Irish woman, she can't help but feel a connection to two Irish mountaineers who relished the adventure of scaling the highest peaks in Europe. She thinks about Dublin-born Lizzie Le Blond, who created the Ladies' Alpine Club in 1907 to support female climbers, herself having made more than 100 ascents. Mary also admires the achievements of Count Henry Russell, who considered Vignemale his favorite mountain in the world, scaled it many times, and even erected a two-meter tower on the top to make it an even 3,300 meters tall.

"I see climbing Vignemale as a tortoise-and-hare kind of thing," Mary explains. "I see myself starting off slow so I can be a strong finisher and I don't spend everything in the tank straightaway. It's so impressive that our group is doing this together. We're going to have a bit of banter, and the girls are recording it as a documentary, and all of that's going to be quite fun. I think everyone will have a challenging moment, whether it be physical or mental or emotional. We'll have a cauldron of stuff going on, and I think that's what will make it quite special actually."

Mary says what she's looking forward to about getting to the top of Vignemale—and safely getting down—is the aftermath.

"It will be a big achievement mentally, and I'll be able to say 'I did that' and know I've gotten my body to do it and accomplished something that's very visible," she says. "I like that Anne Lister is a role model for getting the most out of life. I remember hearing an actress say, 'You only live once, but if you do it right, once is enough.' I feel the same way."

The American actress whom Mary quotes is Mae West (1892-1990), who also was a vaudeville performer and screenwriter.

∽

FANEAL GODBOLD & DANI PALFREEMAN

Fayetteville, North Carolina, USA &
Hebden Bridge, West Yorkshire, England, UK

LOVE IN THE TIME OF CORONAVIRUS

Once upon a time there was a television show about a brave and bold woman named Anne Lister. It was as brave and bold as she, but there was something else that set it apart from other TV shows. *Gentleman Jack* had magical powers.

It caught viewers off guard, and they didn't know what to think when their lives suddenly began to change. Without warning, *Gentleman Jack* transformed couch potatoes into world travelers. It cracked open tightly shuttered closets where secrets had been carefully hidden for a lifetime. Women began reporting unexpected bursts of self-confidence. Many claimed they stood taller and walked faster. Overnight, untold numbers became enchanted by life in the 19th century and the comings and goings of two lesbians who died almost two centuries ago.

But perhaps the most astounding thing was that viewers throughout the world became fast friends, and complete strangers became lovers.

Consider what happened when American Faneal Godbold fell under Anne Lister's spell. It wasn't long before social media introduced her to scores of women similarly afflicted, and she made two key decisions. First, she would use her background as a filmmaker to produce a documentary about how *Gentleman Jack* was drawing women together from around the world. Second, she would join 13 other women to follow in Anne's footsteps up to the summit of Vignemale, a peak in the French Pyrenees, and film that too.

That's how she came to cross paths with Dani Palfreeman, one of the co-captains coordinating the Vignemale group climb. Dani was meeting with the two other captains in early March 2019—pre-coronavirus lockdown—and commented on a profile picture of blonde and blue-eyed Faneal, who had recently signed up for the climb. She remarked that Faneal was an attractive woman. "Beer talk," she said, and thought nothing of it. But Dani's throwaway observation unleashed a chain of events that soon turned her quiet life upside down.

First, it unleashed her fairy godmothers. Her new "friends," she said, decided to set her up with Faneal.

"I'm English," she recounts. "I don't do things like that."

Still, the godmothers dispatched a flurry of "she likes you" messages, and Faneal's reaction was what Dani expected: "I don't care. I don't know anyone named Dani."

Dani, recently out of a seven-year relationship, had no interest in pursuing any romantic partnerships. But the matchmakers, emboldened by mischief and good intentions, were a persistent and relentless lot. One sent Dani a detailed list of Faneal's obvious attributes as a "match." The others chided her for being a coward and goaded her to take a risk.

Finally, Dani gave in.

"I decided to take an Anne Lister-kind of approach," she recalls. "I just sent a short message to this woman I didn't even know. I said our mutual friends were being tinkers, and I made a joke about it. As I hit 'send,' I just put my head on my desk and thought, 'What am I doing? This is crazy.'"

The last thing either wanted was a new girlfriend.

"What you have to understand is that I was out of a relationship and I didn't want another one," Faneal explains. "I was done. I certainly wasn't looking for anyone."

But the fairy godmothers had sprinkled just enough fairy dust that she couldn't help but be slightly intrigued. Faneal responded to Dani's short message, though she says doesn't remember what she wrote.

"You were cheeky," Dani reminds her.

It was early April 2020. The world was under a coronavirus quarantine. The Anne Lister Birthday Weekend in Halifax where many of the Vignemale climbers, including Dani and Faneal, would have met for the first time had to be postponed.

To everyone's surprise, Dani and Faneal began exchanging casual messages through Facebook. Every day. Then came WhatsApp and Zoom and their first actual phone conversation. It lasted six hours. Was it magic, or destiny, or serendipity that prompted Faneal to ask Dani out on a virtual movie date in May? Ever the romantic, Faneal sent Dani virtual flowers and a virtual teddy bear.

"We got all dressed up, and watched one of my movies on Zoom," she says. "And then we had dates two or three times a week."

"It was all so weird," Dani says. "Before Covid hit, I had never been on Zoom. I'd never had a video call of any kind, and now I found myself living online with Faneal in the little virtual world we created."

Separate time zones kept them five hours apart, so Dani, who had been furloughed from her job as a graphic designer, converted her life to run on Eastern time in the United States so she and Faneal would be on the same schedule. They got up at the same time, worked out together at the same time, went their separate ways throughout the day, ate their meals together, spent evenings together, and went to bed at the same time.

With help from technology, love blossomed—on laptop screens, across an ocean, 4,000 miles (6,400 km) apart. Less than two months after their whirlwind online courtship began, Faneal and Dani met in person in Manchester, England.

"When I picked her up at the airport, it really felt as if she'd just been away for awhile, like she was coming back from a business trip," Dani says. "It was a really strange thing, but it wasn't at all like I was meeting her in person for the first time."

Faneal agrees.

"The moment I stepped off the plane and Dani was waiting for me at the gate, it was like we had been together for years," Faneal says. "I tell her all the time that we had to have been together in another life. We just clicked from the very beginning. I know I keep saying it, but the universe definitely has its hand in the middle of this."

What Faneal was expecting to be a three-week visit in England stretched to six weeks, then three months, then five months. She bought a car and learned to drive on the left side of the road. She applied to and was accepted into the law school at the University of York. She and Dani moved into their new house in Hebden Bridge. Summer took them on jaunts throughout the UK so Faneal could explore her newly adopted country. They continued to train for the Vignemale climb. And anticipating a future together, they began the process of collecting the required information for Faneal to apply for British citizenship in two years.

They made plans to visit Faneal's family in North Carolina for the Christmas holidays in 2020, even under threat of mayhem.

"I was looking forward to my first visit to the United States," Dani jokes, "until Faneal's grandmother threatened to kill me and bury me in the back yard. Which makes me not want to go as much."

In all fairness, it should be said that it is only the thought of her grandchild making a new life so far away in England that brings out the wicked witch in Grandma. The sense of humor that Dani and Faneal share makes Grandma's threat a good laugh, though having to cancel the trip due to the pandemic did provide at least temporary protection for Dani.

The couple credits *Gentleman Jack* for its role in bringing them together. Dani notes that the television show spawned a new and welcoming community that included historians, romantics, artists, and friend groups like the ones where she and Faneal eventually found each other.

"Definitely *Gentleman Jack* and Anne Lister and certainly the various groups that we were involved in were very much crucial to us getting together," Dani says. "There were a lot of serendipitous moments as well where if we hadn't met *here*, we would have met *there*. Out of all the thousands of people in groups thousands of miles apart, we were put together in lots of different scenarios."

Faneal takes the cosmic view.

"It was set up as if we had no choice but for it to happen," she believes. "I can't help but think the universe played its cards and had absolutely everything lined up that we were going to meet."

Anne Lister had a hand in this romance, too.

"Anne Lister and everything she achieved and everything she did, including educating herself and climbing a mountain—and how bold she was—was really inspirational to me," Dani explains. "I think Anne Lister reminded me of myself 10 years ago. When I finally decided to message Faneal, I was thinking I should be the person I used to be: bolder, more free-spirited, and just let the chips fall where they may."

In a year that will go down in history as incredibly difficult, dangerous, and disruptive, most people will place 2020 among the worst on record.

"But for us, 2020 has been an amazing year, and we have been so fortunate that there has been so much positive within the negative," Faneal concludes.

Faneal and Dani recently announced their engagement to close family and friends and are hoping for an intimate mountaintop wedding ceremony in the French Pyrenees after their Vignemale ascent in 2022. Thanks to *Gentleman Jack*, two distinctly different women on separate continents managed to find each other and are on their way to living happily ever after.

Cinderella moments when the slipper fits perfectly are rare.

It's magic.

Dani is the designer behind Listerwick Press and creates beautiful things inspired by strong women (listerwickpress.com). Due to Covid restrictions and postponement of the climb until August 2022, the documentary Vignemale—A Walk in Anne Lister's Footsteps *also has been delayed and is not expected to be released until 2023.*

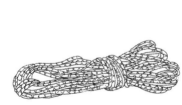

CREATIVE EXPRESSIONS
ANNE LISTER IN WORDS AND DEEDS

AMANDA WALGROVE

Nashville, Tennessee, USA

MRS. BEAN, MARIANA SAUCETON, AND FRIENDS

During the earliest days of the 2020 coronavirus global lockdown, 31-year-old writer, actress, and comedienne Amanda Walgrove stepped before the largest audience of her budding career. She had been tapped to entertain at the 2020 Anne Lister Birthday Weekend scheduled in Halifax, West Yorkshire to celebrate Lister's 229th birthday, but her show was moved online when coronavirus pandemic fears forced the original event to be cancelled.

Amanda took a deep breath, adjusted her Anne Lister-like fur hat, looked straight into the laptop camera perched on a TV stand in the guest bedroom of her Nashville home, and launched into the first of six live comedy sketches interspersed among a handful of prerecorded vignettes.

She was playing to an empty room—and 2,000 invisible faces. Lesbians on their laptops, tablets, and smart phones in the United States, United Kingdom, the Netherlands, France, Australia, Canada, and other countries began to laugh. Amanda couldn't hear a single one of them.

"It was my first ever livestream gig," she says. "It was fun doing it, but I was very, very nervous. I couldn't see the audience, and I couldn't get their reaction. But the feedback later was great, and I think people enjoyed it."

She needn't have worried. For months, Amanda had been posting videos on social media that spoofed the characters in *Gentleman Jack*. Her clever inside jokes, parodying and subverting lines and catch phrases from the TV series, had endeared her to the worldwide Anne Lister and *Gentleman Jack* fandom.

She was ready for this moment. She'd been performing in one way or another since she was a kid growing up in suburban New York, appearing in dozens of productions and musicals during middle school and high school. After college, she honed her acting and writing skills as a cast member at the Upright Citizens Brigade, a popular comedy club in Hollywood. Living in Los Angeles, Amanda also had tried her hand at commercials, joking that her index finger played a starring role in a GrubHub spot by ringing a doorbell, and her entire body appeared for five seconds in a commercial promoting entertainer Kelly Clarkson's talk show.

Though comedy and acting is often an ensemble activity, Amanda says she especially enjoys working solo.

"I left LA to focus on writing and performing my own material," she says. "When I have complete control over what I do, I can give myself permission to just be weird and have fun."

Amanda's zany side definitely shows in her original sketches, and she shines in her online parodies of the cast of characters in *Gentleman Jack*.

"I watched the first four episodes of *Gentleman Jack,* and one day I was coming home from a rehearsal and I just decided I needed to order a top hat and a pocket watch and make a video of Anne Lister," Amanda says.

That video, posted on Facebook, Instagram, and Twitter, was the first of more than 20 takeoffs of Miss Lister, Ann Walker, Marinara Sauceton (aka Mariana Lawton) and others in the TV series, earning her a devoted fan base and thousands of social media followers.

Fans can't help but laugh at the sharp writing, homemade costumes, and unleashed wackiness that Amanda brings to the growing collection of *Gentleman Jack* online videos on her YouTube channel. Curly wigs are always askance. Props are clever lifts from the TV series—a wall thermometer ("it's not illegal!"), a finger-stroked teacup, a pocket watch on a chain. Ann Walker's ridiculous and exaggerated blue puffy-sleeved dress—lampooned by Amanda as a silly construction engineered from a giant cardboard box with duct tape, a long metal rod, and a cheap bed sheet—stretches across the video screen from one side to the other.

Amanda's Mrs. Bean, clad in a school-bus yellow rain slicker and floppy hat, is a dead ringer for the slapstick persona of Mr. Bean of British comedy fame. She's mastered the same goofy Bean facial expressions, too.

"I'd been creating Mrs. Bean videos for a couple of years before *Gentleman Jack* just because I love Mr. Bean and we share a resemblance," Amanda explains. "When I saw real-life umbrella saleswoman Mrs.

Bean mentioned in the Anne Choma book that's a companion to the TV show, it felt like kismet and an invitation from roughly 200 years ago to place my Mrs. Bean in Anne Lister's world. It let me give her more of a purpose—selling umbrellas—and of course a new audience. I think Mrs. Bean is my favorite character to do because I helped bring her to life, plus that video got a response from Sally Wainwright (*Gentleman Jack* creator, writer, and director), and that meant a lot to me."

While she makes comedy look easy, it's a hard and time-consuming process to put together the *Gentleman Jack* vignettes, Amanda says.

"I could just dress up as the characters and do the accents and that might be funny, but as a writer I need to take it a step further and write my own version of a scene—like take one line and go crazy with it. There are two parts to it: nailing my version of the impression and then writing my own version of the content. Writing, filming, and editing a two-minute video clip can take many hours stretched over a couple of days."

Amanda credits the *Gentleman Jack* series for inspiring her personally and professionally.

"It's amazing that Anne Lister has reached out a hand from 200 years ago and has affected all of us so strongly," she says. "Just to have the kind of representation lesbians have in the show means a lot to me. When I watched the hilltop scene in the last episode of Season 1, I remember thinking this is one of the most important shows—if not the single most important show—I've ever seen, and I felt I just needed to be a part of it somehow."

Gentleman Jack motivated her to tap into something different for her comedy that she could never have anticipated.

"It helped me give myself permission to go into all of these new characters and do more of the silent comedy that really appeals to me professionally and makes me stand out among others doing online comedy," Amanda says. "Plus I built a fan base, and I haven't had anything like that before."

Among her fans are two people Amanda especially admires.

"Attracting the attention of Sally Wainwright and Anne Choma has been a huge and welcome surprise," Amanda admits.

And because of their enthusiastic support of her self-made videos, Amanda is expecting to make her television acting debut on the BBC, appearing in a future episode of *Gentleman Jack*.

That's sure to bring a smile to everyone's face.

Amanda's skits can be viewed on her YouTube channel at youtube.com/user/ amandawalgrove.

ANNA JAXE

Liverpool, Merseyside, England, UK

TAKING ART TO THE STREETS

On a warm July day in 2019, passersby in east London's hip Shoreditch neighborhood might have chanced upon a young street artist blasting assorted colors of Belton Molotow graffiti paint onto a wall near the neighborhood's tube station.

Inspired by *Gentleman Jack*, and taking advantage of a legal place to paint assigned to her by local arts organization Global Street Art, Anna Jaxe was creating a large street mural with spray paint and stacks of hand-cut stencils. In its background was a sea of Anne Lister's secret code, and in the foreground, a larger-than-life portrait of Suranne Jones as Anne Lister in her top hat, black military-style jacket, and full-length black skirt, posing with her trademark silver-tipped walking cane.

"I decided to paint something that just felt natural to me," Anna recalls. "I didn't speak to anyone about it. The show was still running on BBC One and no one in my life was watching it, not even my girlfriend. I just did it, and then the reaction went crazy."

"Crazy" is an understatement. The mushrooming online fan community began posting links on social media to Anna's creation. The mural became an instant must-see attraction for locals and tourists. It even sparked a phone call that Anna thought was a prank.

"Basically this guy said something about Suranne Jones seeing my mural and showing it to Sally Wainwright and Sally saying 'Let's hire her' and me not believing any of it," Anna says. "It took me awhile to work out it was a real thing."

The "real thing" was a commission to paint a nearly three-stories-tall giraffe wearing red high heels for Wainwright's *Last Tango in Halifax* television production.

Anna says it was quite an arduous operation to bring the giraffe named Percy to life in an episode in which one of the main characters is distressed to find a gigantic, Banksy-like illustration suddenly appear on the side of her barn. (Banksy is a famous anonymous graffiti artist who's been plastering walls and buildings in England with stencil art for 25 years.) After months of going back and forth on the design and logistics, it took Anna two long days to create Percy on a fake wall affixed to the barn, starting at the bottom and working her way 20 feet (6+ meters) up to the top.

Like her original Anne Lister mural, Percy also was short-lived.

"Percy was taken down not long after I painted him," Anna says. "Street art gets removed or painted over all the time. I know a lot of people are really upset that my Anne Lister mural isn't there anymore either, but unfortunately that's just what happens."

Having her work featured in a high-profile TV show was Anna's payoff for four years of refining her skills as a street artist, a stark departure from the traditional paintings she had focused on after she earned her art degree.

"I started out with oil and acrylic paintings that I intended to sell at art fairs, but it just didn't feel that great," Anna explains. "I was attracted to stenciling because of the accessibility factor—people are automatically drawn to street art. Then I did Upfest in Bristol, which is the biggest street art and graffiti festival in Europe. It was incredible the amount of people who were walking around and interested in your work. That's when

I decided I should be doing this all of the time instead of pretentious art fairs."

Anna relishes seeing people engage with her work on the streets. The overwhelmingly positive response to her Anne Lister mural prompted her to undertake the Queer Visibility Project, her series of street portraits depicting LGBTQ+ individuals, including Australian comedian Hannah Gadsby, Canadian indie pop band Tegan and Sara, and American drag queen RuPaul.

Percy, Last Tango in Halifax

"As a queer artist myself, I'm devoted to creating work that celebrates our community," Anna says. "I use the word 'queer' as a positive thing, reclaiming something that people have often used against us. In my work, I value incorporating people with followings who are coming out and saying things about queer issues and human rights and other social matters that are so important."

Anna says it was *Gentleman Jack* that ignited her passion for using her art to give voice to LGBTQ+ issues and individuals. It also affected her attitude toward herself. "I definitely feel a deeper sense of validation," she says. "Some people seem to assume being gay is a phase or something you grow out of or you haven't found the right man. No one chooses this, so I like the fact that Anne Lister wasn't struggling with her sexuality. She's just like, 'yeah, this is who I am.' *Gentleman Jack* made it easier for me to talk to my family too. They saw me do the Anne Lister mural, and they watched the show, so now it's like they're more on board and understand me better."

Since her original Anne Lister mural in London had such a dramatic impact on the direction of her work, Anna is excited that she was selected to paint another *Gentleman Jack*-themed mural, this time in Halifax, West Yorkshire at Westgate Arcade.

"It's a dream to be able to paint someone like Anne Lister in her own hometown," Anna says. "This one will be protected so it will be there for awhile."

Anna intends to modify her Shoreditch piece, this time placing Suranne's Anne Lister in front of a stenciled version of Shibden Hall while again using Anne's secret code in the background. But the coronavirus pandemic put plans for the mural on hold, and it also put a stop to street art projects for local businesses that she envisioned in Liverpool, where she now lives.

"There is no one on the streets, which is a problem for a street artist," she says. "Tell me the point of street art when there is no one taking pictures and being part of the experience."

Until she can once again return to painting on the sides of buildings and designated places for public art, Anna splits her time between working as a freelance social media advisor and creating smaller originals and limited-edition prints that reflect her goals as an issues-based visual artist.

Anna's work is what makes her stand out in the white male-dominated art world.

"Often people compare me to Banksy if they catch me on the street when I'm painting, and I like to joke that I'm better than Banksy," Anna says. "We're both street artists, but I'm a woman, and I'm queer. That makes what I do very different from Banksy, and it allows me to make a different kind of statement that I want people to see and relate to. Queer visibility and representation are very important to me. I give *Gentleman Jack* a lot of credit for giving me more confidence and motivating me to use my art in a way that focuses on diversity. The best thing ever is just seeing someone engage with my work, and it's even more rewarding when people appreciate it."

For originals, prints, free downloadable coloring pages, and access to Patreons-only content, visit AnnaJaxe.com.

∞

JOHANNE PELLETIER

Montreal, Québec, Canada

A VERY FINE DAY INDEED

*A*rchives are the special places where history lives and breathes. Their treasures reveal our past and connect us to those who came before us. Minus the letters, diaries, and other day-to-day ephemera of lives lived long ago, how would we ever discover the secrets of departed souls without the written evidence they left behind?

It's no wonder, as a former archivist, historian, and now communications expert and storyteller, Johanne Pelletier was among the first to volunteer to transcribe Anne Lister's diaries.

"After I did a master's in history, I had a chance to do some archival work, and that led to a 15-year career in archives and museums," Johanne says. "I was very much an advocate for local history, and I had a reputation for being a strong advocate for old stuff and making it new."

Having left the field in the late 1990s for university communications work, Johanne recalls what it was that drew her to archives in the first place.

"I loved the quietness of the work, and the intimacy that brought me close to someone else's life, where I could find things that were inspirational," she says.

After she watched *Gentleman Jack* in the spring of 2019, Johanne immediately called the West Yorkshire Archive Service. "I think I can help," she offered, and as soon as she completed the test pages qualification process, she was transported back to her archival roots for the first time in 20 years.

"It was so unexpected to find myself doing what I had loved so much, and something that also gave me so much joy in my early career," Johanne says. "I found Anne Lister to be an inspiration in many ways, but she was also a woman of her time. In some parts of her diaries, as we all can be, she could be judgmental, and difficult, and a terrible snob. She was very human, and in some ways, that is what I actually like most about her."

Other than appealing to her intellectual curiosity, Johanne could never have predicted the pivotal role that Anne Lister would play in the months that followed.

It all began when Johanne became dehydrated while running on a hot summer day, passed out and fell to the ground, and sustained a concussion. It wasn't as if she hadn't suffered a blow to her head before. As a former boxer, she's taken her fair share of punches.

But this time, it was different. This time, the effects of her head injury made her very sensitive to sound, and it was Anne Lister's diaries that paved the way to her recovery.

"The symptoms of my concussion were sound-related," Johanne explains. "I could read and look at screens, but noise really bothered me. I bought some massive noise-cancelling headphones and started transcribing. It was a kind of cocoon, quiet, with just me and these crazy diary pages, and there was something very healing and soothing about it."

Johanne says she came to the conclusion that we aren't truly aware of how fast-paced our lives are until we're forced to slow down.

"You often have to go slow when you're transcribing Anne's handwriting and code," she says. "You also may have to stop and look up places that she visited or find translations for the languages she used.

Oddly enough, even that helped me improve. I blew through pages and pages of her diaries because I was able to focus and shut out the noise. In a strange way, I associate my getting better with Anne Lister. There was something very healing about just sinking into something from the 19th century."

Anne Lister also provided content for Johanne's favorite pastime. Five years ago, she became involved in the Moth style of live storytelling, which originated in the United States in 1997. Named after the insects that flit around porch lights on summer evenings when people used to gather to share tales, Moth stories—always true and delivered without notes—are featured on National Public Radio's *The Moth Radio Hour* in the US, the global Public Radio Exchange (PRX), and *The Moth* podcasts. They're also the basis of storytelling competitions held all over the world in which Johanne participates.

"I was working with an academic colleague to help him prepare for an event where people tell a seven-minute story about their work," Joanne says. "It's not easy to get your life's complex stuff down to seven minutes, so I decided I should try to do this myself and figure out what's going to matter to an audience. I did it, and I thought it was super fun. So now I tell true stories about my childhood, my dad and his roofing business, my love of boxing, Anne Lister, and various other topics—virtually—since we can't appear at in-person events until the pandemic gets under control."

Her transcriptions of dozens of diary pages give Johanne plenty of Lister material to present to her audiences.

"Anne is an extraordinary character," Johanne says. "I'm interested in the daily things she does. She is constantly on the move, and always searching, always in motion. Her confident voice, strength of spirit, and persistence come through in her diaries, as well as her courage to declare who she is. Friends will ask me what exciting things I am learning about Anne when I'm decoding. Some days all I have to report is that she went for a stroll and came back and the weather was great and it was 'a very fine day, indeed,' or it was really a shitty day and she'll still write 'a very fine day, indeed.'"

Johanne's storytelling audiences are invariably interested in what Anne writes about in her secret code, and Johanne admits there usually isn't anything sexy to recount. Still, there's something about a woman from the early 1800s who stood up to the men she encountered, managed her own estate, and wanted a wife that grabs people's attention.

"I always get a big laugh when I tell something simple from a diary page I transcribed," she says. "In one of my stories, for example, I include that Anne wrote, 'I washed and scaled my teeth with a pen knife. Dinner at 6:07. Roasted chicken piece, potatoes and a very bad gooseberry tart.' It's not exactly stuff of a lesbian Rosetta Stone, and if someone is expecting something really provocative, the pen knife and bad tart is as far as it goes. But I love the ordinary things she writes about because she probably ends it with 'a very fine day.'"

Johanne says what she also likes about the diaries is seeing how things change in Anne's life and how history unfolds.

"What appears in Anne's 19th century journals can also resonate with our current lives," Johanne says. "I read Anne's diaries and sometimes I can't help but think about the solitary life she had. These many months of my working from home and living alone and restricting myself from social gatherings give me a taste of Anne's solitary life, and I really appreciate that the diary project has given me a bit of pandemic relief. I admire Anne's willfulness that there will be a woman somewhere for her, and I believe that for myself too."

As she reflects on the impact of *Gentleman Jack*, Johanne says she was glad to see the positive representation of lesbians that we so seldom see.

"There are a lot of layers about what has attracted so many to this program, and what fascinates me is how it continues to evolve," Johanne says. "In her diaries, as in the television series, Anne refers to 'my partiality to the ladies.' That's delicious, isn't it? She didn't have any role models in the way that we might, but she found her voice anyway. Let us never forget the courage that Anne Lister and Ann Walker showed. While they may have had the protection of their class, their relationship represented a powerful threat to the world around them in the same ways that our lives today can present a threat to others. *Gentleman Jack* got me thinking about representation and identity, and that our stories, then and now, are important wherever we are in our political advance as queer people."

Johanne has a soft spot for Anne's diaries because they reconnected her to a piece of her career that she felt very far away from.

"To be able to go back to archival work was very sweet, and still is," Johanne says. "As much as I've resisted over the months, I've become very connected to Anne Lister's spirit. I now also have new friends and the many connections I've made with other transcribers. It's a testament that if you have something that brings you together, then something good can come with it."

A collection of Johanne's stories and writing can be found at jpelletier.ca. Moth stories and a schedule of virtual storytelling events are available at TheMoth.org.

∞

BILJANA POPOVIĆ

Užice, Serbia

THE DRAW OF ANNE AND ANN

The forerunners of the cartoons we enjoy today date back to the 16th century, when artists like Leonardo da Vinci began drawing caricatures as guides for reproducing the facial details of the people in their paintings.

The English word *cartoon* comes from the Italian *cartone* or Dutch *karton*, both referring to the thick paper that artists used centuries ago for their preliminary sketches. Over time, cartoons evolved to ink drawings and colorful illustrations that quickly communicate with little to no explanation, proving the adage "A picture is worth a thousand words."

Artist, illustrator, and graphic designer Biljana Popović (Bica Pop) is an expert in the medium. She's been entertaining *Gentleman Jack* fans with her Big Anne and Little Ann cartoons since Season 1 began airing in 2019. So far, she's drawn more than 130 delightful stories-at-a glance that feature her humorous renderings of Anne Lister, Ann Walker, and others from the series.

"I love British shows, such as *Pride and Prejudice* and all in that style—everything BBC," Biljana says. "I was mesmerized by the fact that *Gentleman Jack* is actually about lesbians, so I jumped at the chance to watch it. I quickly became obsessed and got completely wrapped up the fandom and various Facebook groups."

Photos, social media posts, and details about the lives of the real Annes generally deliver a steady stream of ideas for Biljana's artwork.

"All of those things helped me because I didn't just focus on accuracy and illustrations based on Anne Lister's diary entries," Biljana explains. "I created the cartoon characters in my own way. They aren't Suranne Jones or Sophie Rundle or historical Anne Lister or Ann Walker. They are cartoon characters on their own."

Biljana says ideas came easy in the beginning.

"In the first year, I felt such need to draw that I just had to," she says. "I was lucky that I had enough inspiration for it, such as the chemistry between Anne and Ann and the various things they did together."

Biljana says it's especially important to have an abundance of ideas when participating in the annual Inktober challenge, as she's done using *Gentleman Jack* as her theme. It's a worldwide endeavor for artists and illustrators to create a new ink drawing every day for 31 straight days in October—hence the name Inktober—and post their creations online. As a result, Biljana has treated followers to an eclectic assortment of imaginative portrayals of Anne and Ann on their travels and enjoying evenings at home, along with many cartoons that feature inside jokes especially geared to die-hard fans.

Though Biljana had heard of Anne Lister before she watched *Gentleman Jack*, learning the details of Anne's life has resulted in more than subjects for her artwork.

"Just the mere existence of such a person in the time that she lived in got my attention," Biljana says. "She didn't really care about being accepted by society, and sometimes she is explaining how people look at her and what they say. I went through something similar, so I could relate to her experience."

Attitudes in Užice, Biljana's hometown along the banks of the Djetinja River and southwest of Belgrade, affect how open she is willing to be as a gay woman. While Serbia, as of 2017, has its first female and first openly gay prime minister (a first for Europe as a whole), Biljana says it remains a largely conservative nation.

"I'm out to my family, but not to the rest of the world," Biljana says. "The only reason I'm not out to everyone else is because my family will be ostracized. I don't care for myself, but I don't want my parents to be known as the family that has that 'strange daughter.' Maybe, in time, people here will accept the fact that gay people exist and they should accept them because their gayness doesn't change their personality, and they are the same people they were before anyone found out they are gay."

As many other fans have experienced, Biljana says Suranne Jones's performance as Anne Lister was addictive.

"I guess you could say I went through a Suranne obsession phase," Biljana explains. "I wanted to see everything she was in, but eventually I came to my senses and remembered she is just a woman like any of us. She's a wonderful actress, but she isn't her characters, and I respect her very much."

Biljana especially appreciates the way Suranne Jones portrayed Anne Lister's boldness.

"I like the way Anne Lister doesn't take stuff from anyone," she says. "I have had a bit of that attitude my whole life. We—women—start with that boldness when we're born, and we're sure of ourselves. But as we grow up, that boldness slowly goes away as a result of social norms that are still geared toward elevating men and putting women 'in their place.' *Gentleman Jack* and the fandom around it brought boldness back to me and made me much more aware and appreciative of myself."

The fandom has had its influence on Biljana in other ways too.

"I think one of the rare positive things about the internet is that it's broadened our connections with people and helped us realize that there are other people and other cultures that have the same problems in different social backgrounds," she says. "Now I communicate through social media and other ways, so I regularly chat with 10 or 15 people that I never knew before, and I've also made a couple of really close friends. I have a feeling that if any of you were to decide to come to Serbia, you could just call me up and I would arrange everything for you—you know, just come."

Gentleman Jack fans are looking forward to when Biljana's cartoons and other creations become widely available.

"People keep asking me about it, and I do want to put them somewhere to be accessible to the fans," Biljana says. "I didn't want to do it at first because I felt like the cartoons were not just my creation, but more the creation of the whole fandom. But since *Gentleman Jack* has made me become a go-getter and encouraged me to stop procrastinating, I've decided to make it happen. So in true Anne Lister spirit: Seize the day!"

Her fans hope Biljana's *carpe diem* moment comes soon.

Visit redbubble.com for t-shirts, stickers, and an assortment of other Bica Pop products.

∞

CHRISTINE SANTOS

Brasília, Brazil

THE ART OF WORDS AND PICTURES

*S*he is a young woman of twos. Christine Santos is a 23-year-old who speaks two languages: Portuguese and English. She lives with two families in Brazil's unique capital city renowned worldwide for its modernist iconic architecture, sharing a home with her parents and younger sister, as well as her aunt and uncle.

Two countries vie for her affection; Chris loves her hometown in South America's largest nation, but she dreams of living in England. She is both a writer and an artist who is wrapping up her second college degree.

Chris Santos and *Gentleman Jack* make quite the pair too.

Chris says both female characters featured in the TV series tug at her heartstrings, even though she and the Annes are separated by two centuries.

"I loved the show from the very first time I watched it with a friend at the university," Chris says. "I always watch everything that has a lesbian character in it, but I've never seen anything as good as this. When I saw it, all I could think of is that I have to know more about these amazing women."

Gentleman Jack appeared at a fortuitous time.

"I had been struggling with the way I felt about myself," Chris says. "After I came out to my parents, we had problems. My mother said I would bring disgrace and shame on my family, and I felt guilty about it. Therefore helped, but I still wasn't all that sure of myself. Then Anne Lister and Ann Walker showed up, and everything was different for me after that."

When she set out to discover all she could about them, Chris had no idea where her search would take her and how it would transform her life. Eager to find out as much as possible about this unconventional 19th century couple, Chris began looking for more information, only to be shocked and disappointed that there was absolutely nothing about them in her native Portuguese. How could non-English-speaking women in Brazil learn about these important lesbian historical figures in the absence of material they could read themselves?

That's when it dawned on Chris that the story of *Gentleman Jack*—illustrated and written in Portuguese—would make a perfect subject for her master's thesis in social communications (what many would describe as advertising and public relations). Her professors at the University of Brasília agreed.

"Anne Lister's intensity, complexity, and confidence inspired me," Chris says, "and so did Ann Walker's courage and passion. Their story deserves to be told, so other lesbians like me in Brazil can learn about them and know our history has existed for a long time.

Ann Walker's blue dress appears in multiple scenes in *Gentleman Jack*, including the hilltop reunion in S1Ep8

It's important for anyone in search of her identity and sexuality and self-acceptance to know about these women, and I decided an artbook would be a good way to introduce people to them."

So began the arduous six-month task of not only researching how the television period drama was conceived and produced, but also creating 40 watercolor drawings to bring the story of *Gentleman Jack*, Anne Lister, and Ann Walker to life on the page.

"I've always liked to draw and paint," Chris says. "But this was a different kind of project than I've ever done because I was telling the story about women that I admire so much as they are portrayed in *Gentleman Jack*. I researched their history, and I illustrated how their costumes were designed, the scenery in the show, and then I created descriptions and paintings that reflected what was happening in the various episodes."

The result is a charming 25-page artbook that Chris calls *Um diáro para Anne Lister e Ann Walker* (*A Diary of Anne Lister and Ann Walker*), as well as an accompanying 121-page thesis that fulfills her master's degree requirements, details her academic research, and discusses her narrative and artistic approaches. Fans of *Gentleman Jack* will be delighted to see the artbook's depictions of the show's cast of characters—including Shibden Hall—as well as Chris's interpretations of the kissing scenes in the series, Anne's escape by ship to Copenhagen after her breakup with Ann Walker, the couple's hilltop reunion, and their wedding at Holy Trinity Church, Goodramgate, among dozens of other elements Chris has depicted from episodes in the show's first season.

"This is a project I could never have completed without the many friends I've made in the *Gentleman Jack* fandom," Chris acknowledges. "The codebreakers helped me understand what Anne Lister wrote in her diary so I could include some of her journal entries in my artbook, too.

Everyone helped me so much, and I am so grateful to Anne Choma, who even wrote a short introduction to my artbook. Next I plan to translate it from Portuguese into English."

Spending so much time in Anne's and Ann's company as a result of detailing their relationship and drawing multiple portraits of them only increased Chris's respect and admiration for these historical figures whom she credits for her new self-acceptance, pride, and confidence.

"Anne Lister inspired me," Chris says. "She lived according to her own nature. Courage is such an impressive virtue. I've never seen heroines like Anne Lister and Ann Walker, and their strength to make the choices they did makes you wonder if love is the key to everything. They've showed me we can all be the protagonists of our own queer history. What a legacy they've left us! I know I'll never be the same."

Chris's substantial social media following clamored for access to some of her artbook's illustrations, so she's made a selection of products available at redbubble.com/people/alligatortearsq/shop?asc=u. She expects an English version of her artbook to be available in the future. Follow her on Twitter @alligatortearsq for information.

∞

QINGWEN HUANG

Brisbane, Queensland, Australia

OUT AND PROUDER THAN EVER

*A*s a landowner and hands-on manager of her estate, of course Anne Lister knew how to wheel and deal and collect her own rents. Thanks to Qingwen Huang, *Gentleman Jack* fans can now take a turn at being a West Yorkshire real estate mogul too. Qing has created a delightful and entertaining Anne Lister version of Monopoly, the classic board game played by millions in 103 countries and available in 37 languages.

Billed as "The Fast-Walking Property Trading Game," Qing's adaptation gives players a chance to snatch up familiar properties like Shibden Hall, Crow Nest, Anne's coal pits, railroad stations, and many other places of local Halifax interest, all while avoiding a "Playing with Fiyah" tax or landing in Wakefield gaol.

"I just jumped on the whole parody bandwagon and had so much fun making the game," Qing says. "I'm a huge fan of *Gentleman Jack* so I made it for myself. When a few people found out about it, they said they wanted to buy it, but it's not for sale—anyone can download it for free from my Instagram or Tumblr account and make their own full-sized board and game pieces. It's great fun for anyone who likes Monopoly and has a sense of humor since it does have a few naughty aspects."

Finding ways of connecting with other fans in a playful way is just one of the many outcomes Qing has experienced as a result of *Gentleman Jack*. She's grateful, she says, for it wouldn't have happened if a friend hadn't recommended the show to her.

"The poster I saw with a woman in a top hat, and just a little bit of another woman's face, looked a bit weird, but 'OK, I'll check it out,' I thought," Qing says. "I started watching it on my lunch break. Big mistake—there are some scenes that should not be watched at work. I was instantly hooked."

Qing found herself binge-watching the show, with certain scenes in heavy rotation, and she convinced her wife to view it too. Qing admits she's hopelessly addicted to *Gentleman Jack*; her very tolerant wife, not so much.

"Gay women have grown up in a world where everything is a portrayal of straight relationships," she says. "Finally we see a positive relationship between two women portrayed in *Gentleman Jack*. It represents so many things we've been craving for so long. It's like a drop of water in the desert, and you realize you need more, you need more, you need more. The show just fills an emptiness I never knew I had."

Positive representation has universal appeal, but it especially resonates with Qing, who's a native of the island city-state of Singapore, where homophobic laws and anti-LGBTQ+ sentiments still prevail. It's no wonder that Qing prefers to live in a country that recognizes her marriage to the woman she loves and has lived with for 17 years and their right to parent their precocious 5-year-old daughter.

Qing said that, from Episode 1, she was overcome by a strong urge to be immersed in the world of *Gentleman* Jack. She upped her social media presence and began following a variety of Instagram, Twitter, Pinterest, and Tumblr accounts.

"I didn't feel like it scratched my itch," she says. "I started my own *Gentleman Jack* Instagram account linked to a Tumblr account to make and share my silly fan stuff. I found the Shibden After Dark (SAfD) podcast and SAfD Facebook page and that led to discovering a group of 13 other Aussies I talk to every day now."

She marvels at the ability of a television show to bring so many people together.

"The reach of *Gentleman Jack* is amazing and so far-reaching," Qing observes. "The global fan base is fantastic. I think one of the reasons is that we understand gay pain and gay trauma. It's such a diverse group that is generous and always supportive."

Besides new friends, *Gentleman Jack* has brought other changes to Qing's life. She says she has always maintained a low profile, taking particular care to keep her work as a photographer/videographer separate from her personal life. Not anymore.

"I'm really out and proud, and I'm not hiding anything," she says. "Now, I'm like, 'Guess what queer stuff I'm going to do this weekend?' Where I work is a lovely, accepting place and someone asked me if I wanted to be included in the rainbow families' inclusion thing on the agency website. So now I'm not only out and open, I'm actually on the website for anyone to see."

Working at a cultural institution gives Qing the opportunity to explore Australian history, and she's recently run across some Down Under ties to Anne Lister.

"I was blown away to discover mentions of the Rawsons in Queensland that link to the Halifax Rawsons that Anne encountered. I also found ties from the Hobarts in Australia to Vere Hobart. Connections are everywhere!"

Of course, there's no overlooking the appeal of Anne Lister's journals.

"I love Anne's diary entries, and I am fascinated by them. All the things she puts on paper, and the vulnerability involved with putting her real thoughts on paper is just so intriguing to me. It makes me wish I could meet Anne Lister to have a chat with her and get to know her."

Qing has a couple of big reasons for looking forward to the day when travel and social gatherings are once again possible.

"As soon as the coronavirus gets under control, our Aussie group would like to do a boozy Anne Lister meetup so we can finally meet one another in person," she says. "But that's not all. I've got Shibden Hall on my bucket list, and I'd like to see Anne's diaries in the flesh, and maybe even introduce myself to the conservators since I do some work in that field too. I'll be like, 'Here's my life savings, make it happen.' I definitely want to go to England and take the whole family."

She gives *Gentleman Jack* the credit for her boost in confidence and the inspiration to fully embrace who she is.

"I'm gay. So what?" Qing says. "I dress the way I like. You can't mistake me for a straight woman, not that you ever could before. I am conscious of where I can be more open and louder. I'm Asian. I have short hair. I behave in a certain way. With my family sometimes it's like, 'Oh, there's two women and a kid; what's that about?' Sure, sometimes we notice stares, but in terms of general well-being, I don't feel threatened."

Being able to be her true self has been life-changing.

"I'm out and gayer than I ever was," Qing says. "I think the biggest change for me is my pride. I'm no longer incognito in public, and I don't care what others might think. There is also something really small and silly. Sometimes I'll be looking at Instagram and I'll see a really hot picture of somebody and before, I wouldn't have said anything. Now I think shouldn't I have to conceal something like this, and it's ok to say 'Check her out!' I'm not worried about being too much in people's faces with my posting of queer content because our visibility is so important.

Gentleman Jack and Anne Lister have done so much for me, and I'm forever grateful."

Qing's free Anne Lister Monopoly game template is available on Instagram @bagga_coal or bagga-coal.tumblr.com.

BETHANY DRYSDALE

Columbia, South Carolina, USA

SHIBDEN HALL FOREVER

Without Rhodry, it's anyone's guess how life would have unfolded for an ex-Army missile specialist with a husband and two towheaded kids. The handsome canine's sizable social media presence caught the eye of Bethany Drysdale, who's always had a soft spot for dogs. When she discovered the shaggy deerhound had a starring role in *Gentleman Jack* as Argus, the Lister family pet, Bethany was intrigued and tuned in to the TV series.

She hasn't been the same since.

"I didn't discover *Gentleman Jack* until about 18 months after it had first aired, and that's when I was introduced to Anne Lister for the first time," Bethany says. "I just kept thinking I have a degree in British history, so why have I never known about this amazing woman until now? One of the reasons Anne Lister resonates with me is because I also have felt the expectation from many men that I wasn't good enough or

I wasn't equal to them. When I saw her, it's was like she was telling my story too."

Bethany has never hesitated to go after whatever she's set her sights on. Straight out of college, at 22 she became the youngest person in Ohio to become a director of one of the state's 88 Boards of Elections that oversee local, congressional, and presidential voting. Next came a stint as a volunteer firefighter and emergency medical technician, and two years as a high school teacher and softball coach.

But something was missing. Bethany longed to be making history instead of teaching it.

"I joined the U.S. Army when I was 28 years old," she says. "My family has a proud history of military service going back to the American Revolution, when 17 of my ancestors served. I've always felt a patriotic calling, but it wasn't until I went back to college for a second bachelor's degree that I decided to join ROTC (Reserve Officer Training Corps)."

An Army recruiter told Bethany she was very athletic, smart, would make an excellent officer, and the Army could help pay for her education. So she signed up.

"No one thought I could keep up with the guys marching 10 miles in three hours with a 65-pound pack on my back and carrying a rifle," Bethany says. "But I did, and I proved to myself I'm not weak and never have been, and I can do anything I set out to do."

Determined to succeed at any challenge the military offered, Bethany became the only woman in her prestigious Air Defense Artillery unit to operate mobile Avenger surface-to-air anti-aircraft missiles.

Bethany says she has never been a feminine girl, and in fact, one of the first and rare times she has ever worn a dress was when she married her high school sweetheart shortly after she graduated with honors from an officer leadership course. She was on track to be an Army captain when she became pregnant.

"I had to make a choice," Bethany explains. "I would have been deployed when my baby was only three months old, so I chose to be a full-time mother."

Bethany still gives orders, but now her unit is composed of energetic 5-year-old and 8-year-old boys who play hockey and share her fascination with LEGO bricks. During the pandemic, when she added home-school teacher to her resume, Bethany's history lessons involved making historic buildings from the favorite building materials of children around the world.

Like other obsessed *Gentleman Jack* fans, Bethany soon learned that once Anne Lister gets into your head she's there to stay. It was during a sleepless night in early 2021 that Bethany got the idea to honor her new heroine and test her hobby skills: she would recreate Anne's home and *Gentleman Jack* characters from LEGO components.

Inspired and single-minded, the next day she ordered the original blueprint of Shibden Hall from the West Yorkshire Archive Service and set about to assemble the materials to build it. She estimated that reproducing the 600-year-old Tudor style home with its tower, chimneys, scores of windows, and stone and wood features would take at least 4,000 LEGO bricks, which she scavenges from yard sales, eBay, and special LEGO sets.

Once the construction project began in earnest—scaled to match Anne's home in Halifax—Bethany estimates she spent 30 straight 8-hour days to design and build it.

"Shibden Hall means so much to so many people," Bethany says. "It's a lasting piece of Anne that we can all touch and experience. I believe we all have a human need for physical connection, and it's something we've all really missed during the pandemic. The LEGO house I made is how I can connect to Shibden in my mind until I can go there in person one day, and it's how I can connect with Anne Lister every time I see it. To me, she's a rock star."

Shibden Hall was just the beginning of *Gentleman Jack Land* at the Drysdale house. Bethany has also constructed a LEGO *chaumière*, a LEGO carriage, LEGO replicas of various *Gentleman Jack* scenes and rooms, and LEGO versions of Anne, Ann, and other *Gentleman Jack* characters, including Argus, a particular favorite. Bethany's boys have added their special touches to their mother's creation by placing a LEGO dragon and LEGO Batman on Shibden's roof as its ever-vigilant guards.

Bethany has no plans to dismantle her architectural masterpiece, which has been featured on #fanartfriday by @gentlemanjackofficial, the Instagram account for *Gentleman Jack* series producer Lookout Point.

"These thousands of LEGO blocks are going to stay Shibden Hall forever, until I die, or this place burns down," she jokes.

Bethany's husband is in the Air Force and was deployed to Saudi Arabia when she discovered *Gentleman Jack*.

"It's fair to say I quickly became obsessed with Anne Lister, and I had the luxury of being able do research, read all the books about her, and watch the TV show as much as I want, like every day."

Besides the representation she feels from an historic figure who successfully maneuvered in a male-dominated world, Bethany says Anne's strength and courage to live life on her own terms has been especially inspiring.

"I may not have dated women or loved another woman the way Anne and Ann loved each other, but I believe we're all sisters, and love is love.

It's what I teach my children," she says.

Acceptance also is personal, Bethany adds. Seeing firsthand the abuse and discrimination her gay brother and his husband have endured has cemented Bethany's staunch position as an LGBTQ+ ally.

"When I sum up Anne Lister's life and what she means to me, she reminds us to embrace our nature, be ourselves, and live out loud," Bethany says. "We get one chance at life, so we must embrace each day, fully, head-on, as Anne did. Life can be cut short by the smallest of things. I feel I live a life of wonder, adventure, curiosity, and love just as Anne did. This is why I admire this woman and feel so connected to her."

Many others share Bethany's view.

"I've often felt that sometimes I'm on my own little island," she says, "so being part of the community of *Gentleman Jack* fans has been such a wonderful feeling for me too."

Bethany has volunteered at a local elementary school to teach kids from kindergarten to 5th grade how to create their own LEGO building, figures, and robotic vehicles.

∽

CATALYST FOR CHANGE

LIVE LIKE THE ANNES

*J*n a perfect mash-up of entertainment and history, *Gentleman Jack* dramatized how Anne Lister defied social expectations and challenged the boundaries of propriety 200 years ago, all while gallivanting in fashionable men's accessories, from top hat to low heeled boots.

Anne Lister reveled in who she was, followed her heart, and made no apologies for what she wanted. In an era when the word *lesbian* hadn't even been invented and women's rights in general were severely restricted, Anne Lister had the wherewithal to overcome the limits that society imposed upon her not only as a woman, but also as someone who, as she observed of herself, loved and only loved the fairer sex.

Anne Lister shows us the way to self-actualization on two fronts—whether as a woman in a man's world, or as a lesbian on a path different from the straight and narrow.

Gentleman Jack 1.0 is an 8-hour "how-to" seminar in self-acceptance, risk-taking, and living out loud. The stories told by the people in this book alone are proof of the show's power as a catalyst for change by awakening the self-awareness, passions, and hidden strengths of women around the world. They're taking chances and no longer playing it safe—claiming their power to live authentically, speaking up, doing things they've never done before.

"Courage" tattooed on her foot, a middle-aged dentist walks away from job security and all its trappings for a new beginning to live her truth as a lesbian. An anxiety-ridden young woman breaks free from her fears, sets her sights on a people-centric career, and takes up public speaking for the first time. A shy animal lover unable to swim dons a life vest for the adventure of paddling alongside whale sharks 400 times her size.

Transcontinental strangers, both podcast rookies, launch a lesbian-focused weekly talk show and a 24/7 cyber clubhouse that becomes a lifeline for their global following. Lifelong introverts and technophobes turn into social media mavens on Facebook to dish about *Gentleman Jack*, lesbian life, and every conceivable topic, taboo or otherwise.

Homebodies are making pilgrimages to Halifax to experience for themselves the places where Anne Lister lived and loved, mountaineering neophytes are climbing the two-mile-high peak she conquered, and her impassioned acolytes are literally following in her footsteps by using her foreign travel itineraries as a 19th century version of Trip Advisor. A volunteer army of novice-turned-crackerjack transcribers has mastered Anne's *crypthand* code and *plainhand* scrawl to accomplish the mission of ensuring that Anne's life story, in her own five million words, is accessible to all.

That's the *how* of the *Gentleman Jack* effect.

To explain the *why* of it, we need only to look to viewers' parallel experiences to understand their reactions to Anne Lister (and, not incidentally, to Ann Walker as well).

Just as Anne Lister—female and homosexual—was born with two strikes against her in 19th century England, gay women today still confront the same type of repressive social and cultural expectations for how women should act or be.

Our fervent, emotional identification with Anne and her defiance of the hetero- and patriarchal norms of her day—a transgressive woman who welcomed her nature and rose above her circumstances to find lasting happiness—is life-affirming to all who have been misunderstood, shamed, rejected, punished, criticized, ridiculed, abused, maligned, misgendered, or relegated to living half lives in the shadows, simply for how they look and/or whom they love.

For gay women, Anne Lister is the mentor we've never had, an indomitable pathfinder to help us navigate and celebrate being "like that." The enduring impact of the *Gentleman Jack* effect is, ultimately, about the connections generated—to ourselves, to one another, and to the past. The show emboldened women, regardless of their sexual identity, to throw off self-imposed restraints and fully be themselves—capable, strong, assertive, resilient, proud.

It mobilized an alliance of activists and academics to update the historical narrative about Anne Lister and Ann Walker and make sure that they both have a prominent place in lesbian and women's history. It gave rise to *Gentleman Jack* Nation, a global community whose shared experiences and interests have burgeoned into a worldwide support system for lesbians and their allies, creating new relationships, mounting a defense against isolation and loneliness, and triggering a vital sense of belonging that will long outlast the memory of what appeared on a television screen.

Our reinvigorated *Gentleman Jack*-inspired sense of purpose—to live authentically—comes with opportunity and responsibility to pay Anne Lister's example forward. Just as she challenged the constraints of her day, each of us can be a change agent too.

It has always taken the persistence of a few to change the minds of the many. As we each draw on our inner Anne/Ann to live fearlessly, we are part of the collective still pushing for equality and social change—for all the little girls who will follow in *our* footsteps, just as we have been the beneficiaries of the achievements of those who paved the way for *us*.

There is more motivation and support to come—new *Gentleman Jack* episodes in production, new revelations about Anne Lister and Ann Walker on the horizon, new friends to welcome to the circle.

Just look at the impact of *Gentleman Jack* since 2019 and imagine where we're headed—all thanks to a television show about a 230-year-old lesbian in a snazzy top hat.

AFTERWORD

*I*n spite of puffy red eyes from an afternoon of pre-wedding sobs over the huge mistake I knew I was about to make, I was a lovely June bride in my exquisite candlelight gown and full-length Alençon lace veil. At 20, I married a genuinely nice guy and I stuck it out for five years, keeping my true feelings to myself until I couldn't.

So there I was, newly settled back in the conservative Texas Panhandle, freshly divorced, reinventing myself as a gay woman, and licking my wounds from my first failed love affair with a woman. (She swore we'd be together forever. I assumed forever would be longer than three weeks.)

Starting over in a new city, I poured myself into my new job.

On a Friday in mid-November in 1974, I was summoned to the office of the director of the agency where I was a social worker with a caseload of welfare mothers and their children. As for a face-to-face with the head honcho, I hadn't counted on a pat on the back so soon for pushing the bounds of my job description when I'd mobilized local businesses for free materials and labor for a disabled grandmother who was taking care of her three grandsons. The grandmother didn't have extra money for home repairs and the roof over the kids' bedroom had a hole in it so big you could drive a Volkswagen through it, so with winter snows on the horizon, the community, when I asked, was willing to pitch in to help.

How nice of the big boss to give me a high five, I thought, and what a perfect gift for my 26th birthday that day.

"I assume you know why I called you in today," he said when I popped into his office and he barked for me to take a seat.

"I want to know if you have ever been to a gay bar."

I had been out for less than six months. I was so naïve and new at being gay that it didn't occur to me to lie.

"Yes, I have."

"Why were you there?"

"Because I enjoy dancing with women."

"We absolutely can't have that. You work with children, you know. This is not acceptable."

I don't even remember the man's name, only the mass of dandruff flakes on the shoulders of his cheap brown suit. I was astonished that my social life was any of his business and outraged at the implication that the children I was working so hard to help were at risk because of some preposterous and misguided view that lesbians prey on kids.

And then came the fury as he droned on about giving me a new assignment to work with "our older clients," and that this had all been cleared by the highest authorities in the state capital, and how it was all for the protection of the community blah blah blah. What did I have to say for myself?

"I need a job so I'll take your transfer to the senior citizens unit for now," I said, and I could sense his relief. "But I have something else to say."

What came out of my mouth next surprises me to this day.

"You are the fucking pervert in this room, sir. Not me."

With that, I stood up, turned on my heels, and stormed out to my car, assuming I had just torpedoed any chance of a future paycheck. Luckily, I hadn't, and within only few months I found my dream job in a far more progressive city.

But that day in 1974 was my first baby step toward publicly claiming who I am, and I promised myself I would never again put up with working for any organization where I couldn't be myself. Over the span of the next 40+ years, I never did.

That early brush with job discrimination introduced me to lesbian survival skills. I learned when and with whom I could actually be myself. Most of the time it was simply safer, easier, and more expedient to stay under the radar, a matter of mastering the skill of accommodating the comfort levels of others rather than being outspoken or standing up for myself. I'm not the only one, for example, who tolerated introducing the woman I love as "my best friend" or "the person I live with." By the 1990s, we could refer to each other as "partners."

The possibility of ever being allowed to marry? Are you kidding? Over the years, things changed and so did I. I've been with my "partner" and now-wife for more than 40 years. For longer than I can remember, I've been completely comfortable in my own skin. It's been a very long time since I felt the need to explain myself or be anyone other than who I am.

To be honest, it simply never occurred to me that lesbian representation in the media was even missing from my life. That is, until it appeared in the form of a thoroughly entertaining and engaging TV show with a storyline that mirrored so many of my own experiences and emotions. So *this* is what it feels like to see yourself and your history presented in the person of a dashing, daring, and delicious lesbian who, by the way, looks awesome in a top hat.

I went nuts. You know the rest.

Two years on, the raging wildfire that *Gentleman Jack* stoked in me has burned down to glowing embers. My tolerant and supportive wife doesn't miss her former status as a *Gentleman Jack* widow, and our conversations only occasionally touch on Anne Lister or the 19th century. I haven't indulged myself with a *Gentleman Jack* marathon for months, though I admit that regularly re-watching the hilltop scene is still a guiltless pleasure.

In the course of writing this book I've come to the conclusion that the effects of both *Gentleman Jack* and a global pandemic were an invitation for all of us to hit life's reset button. Like the people you've just read about, I'm refreshed and different now too—more curious, more social, more appreciative, more everything.

I recognize I am just one in a long line of women across time who've challenged norms and broken society's rules to be themselves. I discovered my voice to tell the inspiring stories of lesbians and other women living their truth. I now live in a world that is enriched by the new friends I made because of what a television show stirred up.

Thank you, *Gentleman Jack*.

∽

ACKNOWLEDGEMENTS

Writing a book isn't a solo activity. Mine only happened because of Team Janet.

Mary Lou Mitchell – If it weren't for my wife, there's no way you'd be holding this book. She's worn many hats during the two years it took for me to complete it: grammarian, attentive listener, keen observer, BS detector, gentle critic. I'm forever grateful for her love and support for this endeavor and all the many others that bear her fingerprints over the past 40 years. If I ever got a tattoo, her name would be inked with flourishes inside a heart over my heart.

Vivian Swift – I won the writers' Sparkle Sweepstakes when Vivian took on my passion project. Illustrator and editor extraordinaire, she has an artist's eye, a writer's flair for description, and a reader's penchant for a well-told story. I'm the lucky beneficiary of her prolific talents as a high caliber wordsmith, skilled machete wielder, and sprinkler of golden fairy dust. Do yourself a favor and read her three terrific traveler's journals—on staying put, love and France, and the meaning of life and gardening—all with lovely watercolor illustrations.

Marilyn Carter – Proofing and fact checking are what keep every writer from seeming like a third-grade dropout. Marilyn's a stickler for accuracy, and her attention to detail catches fractured spelling, misplaced modifiers, and an assortment of other grammar faux pas. Add her burn-the-candle-at-both-ends work ethic to get the job done right and right now, and you've got just the kind of woman you want in your corner.

Rex Peteet – Yes, you *can* judge a book by its cover. Hats off to the best designer I know for a brilliant idea and perfect execution.

Klaudia Marino – You can't get the right answers if you don't ask the right questions. Thanks to a stellar researcher for our ride together on the *Gentleman Jack* information highway.

Sarah Muyskens – The world's best Excelmeister, Sarah is the reigning Queen of Spreadsheets and Formulas. Without her, I most certainly would have drowned in a churning sea of *Gentleman Jack* data. Thanks for the life buoy.

Roxanne Panero – There's a reason "artist" follows "production" in her job title. Kudos for the crisp interior design and layout of my book. Who knew fonts, margin widths, and text wraps could be so engaging?

The Halifax Contingent – These lovely people in Anne Lister's hometown opened their hearts to welcome a curious American on her Halifax pilgrimage. Thank you to Jane Finn, David Glover, Richard Macfarlane, Kirsty Davies, Sarah Hardcastle, Helena Whitbread, Rachel Whitbread, Jill Liddington, and Rachel Lappin for your gracious hospitality.

The Cheerleaders – Who couldn't use a gaggle of boosters to keep her spirits and confidence high when the going got tough? Thanks to Karen Purcell, Ruthellen Gruber, Sarah Muyskens, Adrienne Dealy, Melissa Wiley, Kiran Pereira, Kelley Amrein, Kristen Hotopp, and Karen Hotopp for your encouragement from the sidelines.

The Helpers – Thank you, Pat Esgate, for the push to travel to Halifax for the trip that launched 90,000 words. Thank you, Anna Jaxe for Percy, and Jane Kendall for Kindred Spirits, for permission to include your wonderful art in my book. Thank you to Helena Whitbread, Jill Liddington, Diane Miller, Kate Brown, Amanda L. Aikman, Jane Kendall, Rachel Lappin, and Pat Esgate for feedback on the initial manuscript.

It was an honor for me to tell the stories of the many people who shared their reactions and thoughts about *Gentleman Jack*. Special thanks to each and every one of you for your candor and your willingness to talk to a probing stranger about your personal and professional experiences. The Annes may have the lock on inspiration in the 19th century, but all of you are at the front of the 21st century inspiration pack. I salute you.

INDEX

ILLUSTRATIONS

ABOUT THE AUTHOR & ILLUSTRATOR

Janet Lea (janetlea.com)

Janet Lea has sold hula hoops, organized armadillo races, and been suspected of being a CIA spy. She's lived in a VW van with a beagle puppy, dodged military checkpoints in Tibet, and camped out on the Great Wall of China. There's a rumor that Misadventure is her middle name, but it's actually Marie.

A native Texan and a fan of big, as an ex-advertising executive she once brought the world's largest seat belt to stretch around the Alamo, and her inspirational stories for public service causes were featured on *The Oprah Winfrey Show*...twice. Having done her bit to make the world a better place, Janet now writes full time. *The Gentleman Jack Effect: Breaking Rules and Living Out Loud* is her first book. She and her wife live in Santa Fe, New Mexico near a dry stream bed inhabited by a coyote they call Sneak.

Vivian Swift (vivianswiftblog.com)

Vivian Swift is the author and illustrator of *When Wanderers Cease to Roam: A Traveler's Journal of Staying Put; Le Road Trip: A Traveler's Journal of Love and France; and Gardens of Awe and Folly: A Traveler's Journal on the Meaning of Life and Gardening.* When not traveling, she lives with a husband in Too Many Cats Manor, a 100-year old house on the Long Island Sound in New York.

Printed in Great Britain
by Amazon